THE TRAVELER'S ATLAS
NORTH AMERICA

THE TRAVELER'S ATLAS
NORTH AMERICA

DONNA DAILEY

BARRON'S

A QUARTO BOOK

First edition for North America published in
2009 by Barron's Educational Series, Inc.

All inquiries should be addressed to:
Barron's Educational Series, Inc.
250 Wireless Boulevard
Hauppauge, New York 11788
www.barronseduc.com

ISBN-13: 978-0-7641-6177-3
ISBN-10: 0-7641-6177-6

Library of Congress Control No.: 2007943950

QUAR.TANA

Conceived, designed, and produced by
Quarto Publishing plc
The Old Brewery
6 Blundell Street
London
N7 9BH

Senior editor: **Katie Hallam**
Co-editor: **Ruth Patrick**
Copy editor: **Clare Hubbard**
Designers: **Jatin Mehta, Rizwin Burji**
Cartographer: **Malcolm Swanston**
Art director: **Caroline Guest**
Design assistant: **Saffron Stocker**
Picture research: **Sarah Bell**

Creative director: **Moira Clinch**
Publisher: **Paul Carslake**

Color separation by **PICA Digital Pte Ltd.,**
 Singapore
Printed in Singapore by **Star Standard Pte Ltd.**

9 8 7 6 5 4 3 2 1

CONTENTS

MEXICO

"THE WORLD IS A BOOK AND THOSE WHO DO NOT TRAVEL READ ONLY ONE PAGE."
ST. AUGUSTINE

When the philosopher monk wrote these words in the fourth century, the world was a much smaller place. North America had not yet been discovered by Europeans, but native peoples had long been traveling across this land, north and west from Central America, south and east from the Bering Strait. It would be fascinating to know what they thought and felt as they read the pages of this vast, untamed continent.

I often think true travelers are born, not made. For all the joys and excitement of travel, there are stresses and challenges, too, and it takes a certain nature to continually propel yourself out of your comfort zone into the unknown. In my case, I've always been driven by an innate curiosity about the wider world, and a compelling desire to see it for myself.

Travel is easier today than it ever was, and in some ways less necessary, when television puts the world boldly at your fingertips. Or is it? To me it seems more vital than ever to experience firsthand this fascinating world that is rapidly changing. Only by being in a place and absorbing it with all your senses can you begin to understand it, whether it's a forest wilderness or a foreign city. The impressions made last long beyond the immediate thrill of travel.

I was lucky to be born into a family that traveled, and some of my earliest, best memories are of that quintessential thing: the great American road trip. Every summer we piled into the car and set off to explore a new part of the country. We seldom booked ahead. We stopped when something caught our interest and drove until we got tired, at which point we started looking for those two crucial road signs: "Vacancy" and "Pool." Those childhood trips left an indelible impression of the freedom of the road.

Our travels took us from New England byways to California's Pacific Coast Highway, and they were a far better teacher than

The author, Donna Dailey, landing on the Ruth Glacier during an exhilarating flightseeing trip in Alaska's Denali National Park.

any geography book. Through the salty taste of the Atlantic seashore, the prick of a cactus spine in the Sonoran Desert, the roar of Big Sur, the sulfur smell of a Yellowstone mudpot, the many contrasts of this great continent became real. The cliff dwellings of Mesa Verde left me forever intrigued by ancient cultures. The skyscrapers of Manhattan still lure me back to urban streets. In Boston, New Orleans, and Santa Fe, history became tangible.

Though I now travel the world for a living, I return each year to North America to find a new adventure. For me, that usually involves wildlife and wilderness: hiking the Rocky Mountains and Utah's canyons, canoeing in the Everglades, sailing among icebergs as ancient glaciers crash into the sea, driving the remote Alaska Highway my grandfather helped to build. In the national parks of the United States and Canada, the last large mammals of the continent still roam free. There you can hear the growl of a grizzly, or simply listen to the silence. One of the best things about traveling in North America is its accessibility. Yet, climbing a Mayan pyramid or landing on a glacier beneath Denali's peak, you feel you're at the ends of the Earth.

The Traveler's Atlas North America is but a sampler of the many adventures this continent holds. I hope this book inspires you to close the cover and go off to read for yourself the pages outside.

Donna Dailey

1 BANFF AND JASPER NATIONAL PARKS
PAGES 12-15

2 VANCOUVER
PAGES 16-19

3 QUÉBEC
PAGES 20-23

4 PRINCE EDWARD ISLAND
PAGES 24-27

5 NEWFOUNDLAND AND LABRADOR
PAGES 28-31

6 CHURCHILL
PAGES 32-35

7 THE GRAND CANYON
PAGES 38-41

8 MONUMENT VALLEY
PAGES 42-45

9 THE ADIRONDACKS
PAGES 46-49

10 PACIFIC COAST HIGHWAY
PAGES 50-55

AT A GLANCE: NORTH AMERICA

Get your bearings: all the places visited in this book are plotted on the map, so you can find where to go next.

11 NAPA VALLEY
PAGES 56-59

12 LAS VEGAS
PAGES 60-63

13 MANHATTAN
PAGES 64-67

14 ALASKA MOUNTAINS
PAGES 68-71

15 ALASKA HIGHWAY
PAGES 72-75

16 ALASKA GLACIERS
PAGES 76-79

17 NIAGARA FALLS
PAGES 80-83

18 YOSEMITE NATIONAL PARK
PAGES 84-87

19 YELLOWSTONE NATIONAL PARK
PAGES 88-91

20 CALIFORNIA DESERTS
PAGES 92-95

21 NA PALI COAST OF KAUAI
PAGES 96-99

22 HAWAII VOLCANOES NATIONAL PARK
PAGES 100-103

23 CHARLESTON
PAGES 104-107

24 SAVANNAH
PAGES 108-111

CANADA

"In wildness is the preservation of the world."

Henry David Thoreau, American writer and philosopher, 1817-1862

BANFF AND JASPER NATIONAL PARKS

This glorious landscape encompasses majestic mountain ranges with snowcapped peaks, glacier-carved valleys, moraine lakes, ice fields, waterfalls, and endless miles of coniferous forest.

Lake Louise (1) is Banff's most famous beauty spot, reflecting the surrounding Rocky Mountains in its crystal clear waters.

STRADDLING THE CONTINENTAL DIVIDE, the Canadian Rockies stretch north from the U.S. border for some 1,000 miles (1,609 km), forming much of the border between Alberta and British Columbia. Although they link up with the American Rockies, they are older and geologically distinct. Some of the most accessible scenery lies in a group of contiguous national parks that begins about 70 miles (112 km) west of Calgary. Banff, Jasper, Kootenay, and Yoho, together with adjoining provincial parks, form the Canadian Rocky Mountain Parks World Heritage Site.

The parks harbor a variety of wildlife, including many rare and endangered large animals. The gray wolf has been slowly reestablished in Banff and Jasper, as have mountain lions. The rocky cliffs and ridges are home to bighorn sheep and white mountain goats, while elk, deer, and moose roam the valleys along with North America's only protected herd of caribou. The forests shelter black bears and the much rarer grizzlies. Soaring above them all are magnificent osprey, golden eagles, and other birds of prey.

For humans, the Rocky Mountains Parks are a vast year-round playground. They contain six of Canada's best ski resorts: two at Banff, one at Lake Louise, another in Jasper, and two more in Kananaskis County. There are numerous day hiking

trails leading to one awesome viewpoint after another, and remote backcountry routes. Cycling, white-water rafting, canoeing, glacier walking trips, and other activities offer more "ways in" to the stupendous mountain scenery.

Banff National Park

Banff is Canada's oldest national park. In 1883, three construction workers on the Canadian Pacific Railway discovered the Cave and Basin hot springs here. Four years later an enlarged area was designated as Rocky Mountains Park, the second national park on the continent after Yellowstone. Today it encompasses 2,564 square miles (6,641 sq km). Luxury hotels were built around the springs in order to entice passengers onto the new railroad, and the town of Banff has been the bustling main base for the region ever since.

As Canada's most popular national park, Banff sees more than three million visitors each year, and the busy tourist town is a jarring contrast to the grandeur and solitude most people hope to find. For that you will have to travel beyond the park's southern section where the majority of visitors congregate. When in town, you'll find a number of museums, which focus on native culture and the development of the Canadian Rockies.

While the hot springs at the Cave and Basin National Historic Site are no longer open for bathing, you can test the mineral waters at the Upper Hot Springs Pool. The Banff Gondola takes you to the top of Sulphur Mountain for spectacular views of the surrounding peaks.

The main Trans-Canada Highway 1 runs through the park, but a more rewarding route is the parallel Bow Valley Parkway, Highway 1A. This smaller, slower road offers a better chance of spotting wildlife on your way up to Lake Louise. This is the park's second center, a famous beauty spot, Canada's largest ski area, and one of the best powder skiing resorts in North America.

Lake Louise itself is stunning, a deep, brilliant blue stretch of water 1 1/2 miles (2.5 km) long, ringed by mountains and backed by the sparkling Victoria Glacier. Get there early to avoid the worst of the crowds ambling around the lake path. Fit hikers can find more awesome views on an 8-mile (13-km) trek from the far end of the lake to the Plain of Six Glaciers.

The Lake Louise Gondola takes you up the side of Whitehorn Mountain for incredible aerial views. As impressive as it is, many visitors prefer the quieter and equally spectacular Moraine Lake, 8 miles (13 km) away via a winding road. This, too, is a glacial lake of the most pristine turquoise blue, backed by ten mountain peaks over 10,000 feet (3,048 m) high, a vista so stunning it once adorned Canada's $20 bill.

Along the Icefields Parkway

Highway 93, better known as the Icefields Parkway, runs 143 miles (230 km) from Lake Louise to Jasper. It is one of the truly spectacular drives in the world, a wilderness road through a remote landscape of towering peaks and mountain passes, alpine meadows, lakes, glaciers, and ice fields. It follows a route once used by natives and fur traders. Among its highlights are Crowfoot Glacier, Bow Lake, and

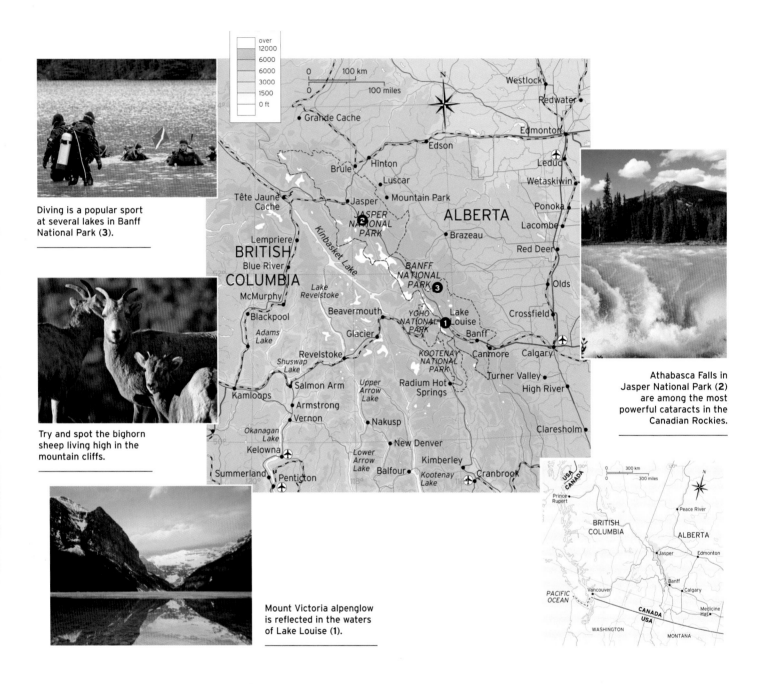

Diving is a popular sport at several lakes in Banff National Park (3).

Try and spot the bighorn sheep living high in the mountain cliffs.

Mount Victoria alpenglow is reflected in the waters of Lake Louise (1).

Athabasca Falls in Jasper National Park (2) are among the most powerful cataracts in the Canadian Rockies.

the lookout at Peyto Lake. It then parallels ice fields, culminating in the Columbia Icefield, the largest glacial region below the Arctic Circle. With many trails and beauty spots to enjoy, take your time on the four-hour journey.

Jasper National Park

Covering 4,200 square miles (10,878 sq km), Jasper is the largest national park in the Rockies. It is wilder, with more backcountry than the southern parks and its only town, Jasper, is smaller and less touristy. Here the mountains are capped by a patchwork of ice fields, which flow into rivers and glacier-fed lakes. The park is a backpacker's delight, its northern third reachable only by boat or hiking.

The Jasper Tramway is a 1 ½-mile (2.5-km) cable-car ride up Whistlers Mountain. Other favorite viewpoints are at Patricia, Pyramid, and Medicine Lakes. Beautiful Maligne Lake is the second-largest glacier-fed lake in the world, its tranquility a contrast to rugged Maligne Canyon, one of the deepest in the Rockies. Further east are the natural mineral waters of Miette Hot Springs. Within Jasper's southern bounds, the vast Columbia Icefield is overlooked by the striking peak of Mount Edith Cavell. Trips to the Athabasca Glacier and the dramatic Athabasca Falls are highlights here.

Explore the wilderness of Banff National Park (**3**) by paddling a canoe or kayak along the pristine lakes and rivers.

–> FACT FILE

CLIMATE Weather is variable throughout the year, with rainfall in summer and high snowfall in winter. Winter is bitterly cold, with January highs averaging 16ºF (-9ºC). July is the warmest month with average highs 72ºF (22ºC). In every season, altitude and local conditions bring great variations in temperature.

WHAT TO TAKE Outdoor clothing and gear, including rainwear for hiking. Warm clothing in winter.

BEST TIME The parks are open year-round, though some facilities are closed in winter. A variety of winter sports are centered on the ski areas. July-August is the most crowded time to visit. September and early October are quieter. November sees the start of winter snowfall. Spring comes late, with snow and muddy conditions possible in late May and early June.

NEAREST AIRPORT Calgary International Airport is 80 miles (129 km) east of the town of Banff.

ACCOMMODATIONS Ranges from upscale hotels at Banff and Lake Louise to comfortable lodges and campsites. Make reservations well in advance as the parks get very busy in peak season.

PARK PASSES Each visitor must purchase a pass to enter the national parks. Family and group passes are available. Annual passes are the best value if you are visiting for a week or longer, or visiting more than one park. Passes can be purchased in advance or at any park entrance gate.

VANCOUVER: MODERN METROPOLIS

With its stunning surroundings and its high-quality, laid-back lifestyle, Canada's third-largest city is one of the most livable cities in the world.

Totem poles set against the background of mountains and sea celebrate Vancouver's native heritage and natural beauty.

STANDING ON THE SHORES of the Pacific Ocean, backed by forested slopes and beautiful snow-capped mountains, Vancouver enjoys one of the finest urban settings in North America. Its vibrant downtown, packed with shining skyscrapers, rises like a mini Manhattan from a narrow peninsula surrounded by the Burrard Inlet, False Creek, and English Bay. With a vast outdoor playground on their doorstep, its residents can go from their city offices to the ski slopes, hiking trails, boats, and beaches in a matter of minutes. The coastline is dotted with gulf islands that shelter dolphins, sea lions, and killer whales among its splendid array of marine life. No wonder it is consistently rated as one of the best places on the continent to live—and to visit.

Long home to Native Canadians who fished for salmon along its rivers and inlets, this northwest paradise was claimed for Britain in 1792 by Captain George Vancouver. But settlers only began to arrive in the 1860s following the Cariboo and Fraser Canyon Gold Rushes. A rough settlement called Gastown, named for a talkative barkeeper called Gassy Jack Leighton, grew up around a sawmill on the site of the present city. After it became the western terminus for the transcontinental Canadian Pacific Railway, the city was renamed Vancouver, growing rapidly from a small lumber town in 1887 to a prosperous metropolitan center.

Vancouver's natural deepwater harbor became an important western port in the 1920s, after the completion of the Panama Canal made it a viable shipping point for grain and other natural resources from Canada's vast interior. Today it is the country's busiest seaport and one of the largest on the west coast of North America. As a gateway to the burgeoning markets of the Pacific Rim and a stopover for more than a million cruise passengers a year, the port is a dynamic part of the economy.

The Asian connection has brought a wave of new Chinese immigrants in recent years, swelling the ranks of Vancouver's colorful Chinatown and adding to its multicultural mix of Indian, Japanese, Italian, Greek, and other ethnic groups. Its residents are cosmopolitan and forward-thinking, yet refreshingly laid-back and environmentally conscious. This is, after all, the birthplace of Greenpeace. For visitors, the city's galleries, stores, bars, and entertainment

–> FACT FILE

POPULATION City 600,000, metro area 2.25 million.

CLIMATE Vancouver has a temperate climate with relatively mild winters by Canadian standards and warm, sunny summers tempered by sea breezes. Average highs in July–August are 72ºF (22ºC), while January averages 37ºF (3ºC) with only a few days of snowfall. Average annual precipitation is 48 inches (122 cm), with most rain falling between October and March.

WHAT TO TAKE Casual clothes for enjoying outdoor activities; umbrella and good walking shoes.

BEST TIME Summer is usually dry and pleasantly warm. Whale watching is best May through October.

NEAREST AIRPORT Vancouver International Airport is on Sea Island, about 9 miles (14 km) southwest of downtown.

ACCOMMODATIONS Not a problem in Vancouver, which has plenty of every kind of accommodation, from 5-star to budget, with lots of choices downtown.

WHAT TO EAT At least one meal in Chinatown.

The geodesic dome of **Science World (1)**, with exhibits and an Omnimax Theater, is a short ferry ride from downtown Vancouver.

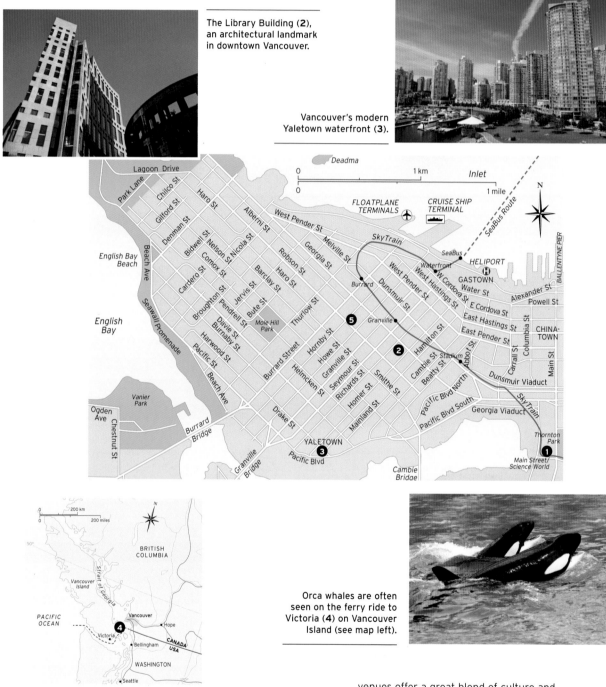

The Library Building (**2**), an architectural landmark in downtown Vancouver.

Vancouver's modern Yaletown waterfront (**3**).

Orca whales are often seen on the ferry ride to Victoria (**4**) on Vancouver Island (see map left).

venues offer a great blend of culture and counterculture. All eyes will be on Vancouver in 2010 when, with nearby Whistler, it hosts the Winter Olympics.

Exploring Vancouver

If you come to Vancouver by cruise ship, you are likely to arrive at the terminal at Canada Place, a perfect starting point for any visitor. Built as a pavilion for Expo '86, it juts into the harbor and provides fabulous views of the bustling port against the backdrop of the mountains. Signboards around the perimeter highlight important features and history. The best overview—literally—of the city is from the tower of the nearby Harbour Centre, one of the city's tallest buildings. It is 581 feet (177 m) to the tip of the spire above its circular observation deck, which affords a 360-degree view of the city and beyond.

The smart heart of downtown Vancouver lies with the stores, bars, restaurants, and cafés along Robson and Burrard Streets, in the vicinity of the Vancouver Art Gallery, which is housed in the old city courthouse. A short walk east of Canada Place is Gastown. The site of the city's humble beginnings has been spruced up with cobblestones, faux gas lamps, and a curious steam clock.

Vancouver's Chinatown is one of the largest in North America, and one of the most colorful, with bilingual street signs, markets, alleyways, and ornamental roofs sheltering small stores, and residents from many regions of China, who make up the city's largest ethnic group. Apart from the vibrant atmosphere, the main attraction is Dr. Sun Yat-Sen Garden, the first authentic Ming Dynasty-style garden built outside of China.

Take a water taxi to Granville Island, a favorite spot for many, with a fantastic public market piled high with fresh produce, gourmet foods, and ready-made treats. The old industrial warehouses have been converted into trendy spots to eat, drink, and shop. To the west, Vanier Park contains the Vancouver Museum, Maritime Museum, and the MacMillan Space Centre observatory and planetarium. Much further out, on the University of British Columbia campus, is the city's most impressive institution, the Museum of Anthropology. Crowning the fascinating totem poles and displays on Canada's native peoples is The Raven and the Beast sculpture by Bill Reid, which has become a city icon.

More totem poles grace the skyline in Stanley Park. Covering close to 1,000 acres (405 ha) at the northern tip of downtown, it is North America's largest urban park. The Seawall Promenade runs all the way around, providing wonderful vistas for walkers, cyclists, and skaters. Below the south side are a string of popular beaches. The park contains a world-class aquarium and other attractions.

With stunning scenery beckoning in all directions, Vancouver is an ideal base for several excursions. The famous ski resort of Whistler is only a two-hour drive away, while Vancouver Island, and its quaint capital Victoria, is even closer by ferry or float plane. The Gulf Islands lie between it and the mainland, and this waterway is undoubtedly one of the best places in the world to see orca whales as well as gray whales, humpbacks, and other marine mammals.

-> Hollywood of the North

Vancouver is the biggest center for film production in Canada; only Los Angeles and New York City make more movies. *Santa Claus*, *Fantastic Four*, and *Scooby-Doo*, as well as remakes of *The Pink Panther* and *The Wicker Man*, have all been made here. At any one time there are usually several films and TV series in production. There is even a special "BackLot" section in the Vancouver Sun to tell people who is in town and where they are shooting. See a crowd on a street as you travel around, and chances are it is a film crew.

The old city courthouse is a central landmark in downtown and now houses the Vancouver Art Gallery (**5**).

PICTURESQUE QUÉBEC

From its language, food, and architecture to its joie de vivre, this walled city on the banks of the St. Lawrence is delightfully French through and through.

"THE IMPRESSION MADE UPON THE VISITOR by this Gibraltar of America: its giddy heights; its citadel suspended as it were in the air; its picturesque steep streets and frowning gateways; and the splendid views which burst upon the eye at every turn: is at once unique and lasting."

Charles Dickens wrote these words after a visit to Québec City in 1842, and his description is as enduring as the ramparts that surround its historic heart. Situated on the Cap Diamant promontory, the Haute-Ville stands 195 feet (59 m) above the St. Lawrence River, with sweeping views over the fertile river valley and the Laurentian Mountains to the north. This is the only walled city in North America and is a UNESCO World Heritage Site.

Here, you could easily forget which side of the Atlantic you are on. Narrow cobbled streets wind between stone houses that date back to the seventeenth century, leading to quaint churches, old convents, grand cathedrals, and pretty squares. Public buildings tower above with pompous Second Empire roofs. The ambience and language are

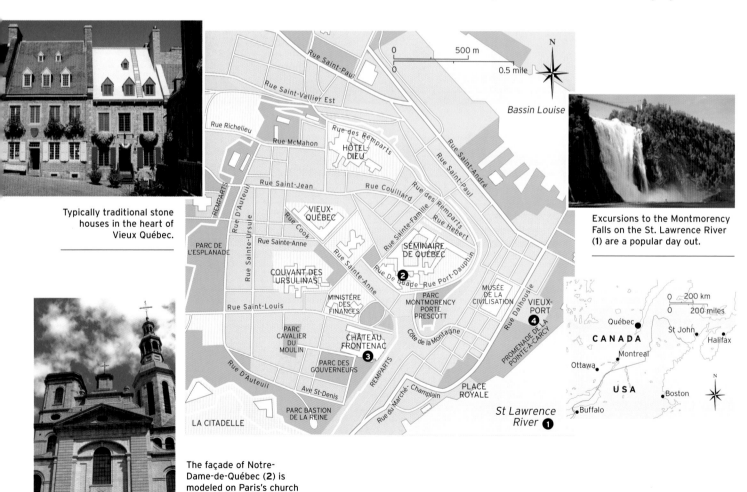

Typically traditional stone houses in the heart of Vieux Québec.

Excursions to the Montmorency Falls on the St. Lawrence River (1) are a popular day out.

The façade of Notre-Dame-de-Québec (2) is modeled on Paris's church of Sainte-Geneviève.

–> FACT FILE

POPULATION City 491,100, metro area 715,500.

CLIMATE Temperate with four seasons. Summers are sunny with daytime highs ranging from 68-77ºF (20-25ºC). Winters are very cold and snowy, with average January daytime highs of 18ºF (-8ºC) dropping to 1ºF (-17ºC) at night, though it can get much colder especially with the windchill factor. Québec receives nearly 14 feet (4 m) of snow annually, and occasionally sees snowfall in early May.

WHAT TO TAKE Jacket or sweater for cool summer nights. Warm clothing, hats, gloves, and snowboots if visiting in winter.

BEST TIME Summer is the warmest and sunniest time to visit, and there are several outdoor festivals. Mid-September to early October brings beautiful fall color. Québec's famous Winter Carnival in early February is hugely popular and attracts up to one million visitors.

NEAREST AIRPORTS Québec City Airport is 12 miles (20 km) west of the city and handles domestic flights. Most international carriers use Montreal Airport, about 145 miles (233 km) southwest.

ACCOMMODATIONS There are plenty of reasonably priced accommodations in the old town, often in renovated town houses. There are also many motels and bed and breakfasts in the suburbs. It is wise to book ahead for the Winter Carnival or the Summer Festival.

Towering above the ramparts of Vieux Québec, Château Frontenac (**3**) is a city icon and affords spectacular views over the St. Lawrence River and beyond.

Québec started in the Basse-Ville, now a pleasant shopping district, which adjoins the renovated Vieux Port (4) along the bustling riverfront.

resoundingly French—95 percent of the population speak it as their first language.

Québec was the first permanent settlement in Canada, founded in 1608 by the explorer Samuel de Champlain, who gave it its Algonquin name Kebec, meaning "narrowing of the river." The river made it an important trading post in frontier times, carrying the rich bounty of beaver pelts back to Europe. In 1620 Champlain built a fort where the Château Frontenac now stands, and the settlers moved to the clifftop.

Around 1690 Québec's governor, the Comte de Frontenac, began fortifying the city with its massive ramparts as the British and French struggled for dominance in the New World. But in 1759, during the Seven Years' War, British forces triumphed on the Plains of Abraham. They took the city, and

in 1763 all of Canada was ceded to Britain. The Québecois, however, did not easily acquiesce to British rule and they were formally allowed to keep their language, culture, and Catholic religion.

Québec's fortunes as a thriving seaport declined when railroads and steamships made Montreal the region's economic hub. But it remained the capital of the province of Québec, proudly upholding its French language and traditions.

Haute-Ville (Upper Town)

The Upper Town inside the ramparts is a good place to begin exploring Vieux Québec (Old Québec). Québec's most famous landmark, Château Frontenac, was built in the 1890s as a luxury hotel for the Canadian Pacific Railway. Its copper-topped main tower, which dominates the skyline, was added

in the 1920s. You can take a guided tour of the sumptuous interior.

Terrasse Dufferin, a popular hangout, runs alongside and affords magnificent views over the river. It continues past the Jardin des Gouverneurs (Governers' Garden), where handsome eighteenth-century merchants' houses line the streets surrounding the garden. The promenade runs all the way to the Citadelle, stronghold of the city's fortifications. Largely built by the British, the star-shaped bastion stands on the summit of Cape Diamond and now houses Canada's only French-speaking regiment. There are guided tours and a changing of the guard ceremony.

Place d'Armes, a former parade ground, is the Upper Town's main square, set around a fountain. Cathédrale St. Trinité, built in 1800–1804, was the first Anglican cathedral outside the British Isles and is modeled after St. Martin-in-the Fields church in London. Running between them is Rue du Trésor, lined with paintings and sketches by local artists.

Since its beginnings, Basilique Notre-Dame-de-Québec has been the site of the city's main church. The current edifice and its awesome interior have been rebuilt to its original 1647 appearance. Next door is the Séminaire, whose sprawling buildings once housed a Jesuit university founded in 1663. You can see its highlights on a guided tour, and visit the Musée de l'Amérique Française (Museum of French America), with fine collections ranging from an Egyptian mummy to Renaissance art. Some of Québec's oldest artworks are displayed in the Musée des Augustines, in the former Hôtel Dieu hospital. At another convent, the Musée des Ursulines displays fine lacework and embroidery.

Basse-Ville (Lower Town)

Peaceful Parc Montmorency has splendid views over the port. From here Côte de la Montagne follows the ravine once climbed by early settlers to the Lower Town. Just beyond the Porte Prescott gate, the steep L'Escalier Casse-Cou (Breakneck Stairway) leads to Rue du Petit-Champlain. This narrow street lined with craft stores is the city's oldest.

Alternatively, a funicular runs between Terrasse Dufferin and the Lower Town; the lower station was once the house of Louis Jolliet, explorer of the Mississippi River. The city's first settlement was built nearby on Place Royale, today a lively spot for outdoor entertainment in summer. Église Notre-Dame-des-Victoires, erected in 1688 and much restored, was named for two military victories, their stories depicted inside.

To the north is the outstanding Musée de la Civilisation, much lauded for its impressive architecture and its diverse exhibits on Canadian life and history. Despite its name, the Vieux Port (Old Port) is a striking contemporary complex of renovated buildings, which include an amphitheater, marina, and market.

Stretching along the cliffs west of the Citadelle, the Plains of Abraham where the fateful battle for Québec was fought are part of the Parc des Champs-de-Bataille (National Battlefields Park). On the park's western edge, the Museé du Québec has the city's most impressive collection of traditional and contemporary Québecois art.

In 1874, the Basilique Notre-Dame-de-Québec (**2**) became the first church in North America to be designated as a basilica.

PRINCE EDWARD ISLAND

Prince Edward Island is the smallest of Canada's provinces, but it contains within it an unusual and hauntingly beautiful national park.

Look out for great blue heron, one of the island's many bird species.

THANKS TO IMMENSE NATURAL LANDSCAPES like the Grand Canyon, Yosemite, and Yellowstone, the words "national park" usually conjure up an image of the natural world in all its grandness and greatness: an awe-inspiring vista of forests, mountains, waterfalls, canyons, or dramatic deserts. Canada's Prince Edward Island National Park is very different from these pictures, but equally beautiful and equally important in the role it plays in nature's fragile balancing act.

Prince Edward Island itself is rather unusual and special. One of the eastern Maritime Provinces—and the nation's smallest—it lies in the Gulf of St. Lawrence, east of New Brunswick and north of Nova Scotia. It was known to the native Mikmaq people as Epikwetk, or the "land cradled in the waves."

It has other less poetic nicknames thanks to its agricultural reputation, such as Million Acre Farm or just Spud Island.

The island is also the setting for the popular novel *Anne of Green Gables*, in which a farming brother and sister decide to adopt an orphan boy from Novia Scotia, but the precocious Anne of the title turns up instead. The island still trades on its Green Gables connection, as this is where the author Lucy Maud Montgomery grew up. Because of the book and the Million Acre Farm tag (that is no longer accurate anyway) most people have misconceived ideas about the place. They see it as a rural backwater, unaware that it harbors some of Canada's best beaches, and a special wildlife habitat that is protected in its national park.

People do not usually visit a national park to go swimming or sunbathing, but Prince Edward Island's park on its northern coast is blessed with about 25 miles (40 km) of glorious sandy beaches. These are backed by dunes and some woodland and wetlands. The park is unusual in that it runs in all for about 37 miles (60 km) along the coast but for much of that distance it is rarely more than a few hundred yards wide.

The Piping Plover

This narrow stretch of national parkland nevertheless shelters an impressive variety of wildlife—there are over 300 bird species alone—as well as some of the most relaxing coastal scenery in Canada. One of its most important visitors is the endangered piping plover, which is usually easier to hear than to see as it is scarcely bigger than a sparrow, and is so well camouflaged that you could walk right by it without noticing it unless it moved. The piping sound that gives it its name, though, is readily recognizable, as clear as a hammer tapping on a bell or the pinging note of a finger flicking a wineglass. If you hear the sound, stand still and search the shoreline for a tiny, sandy-colored bird with orange legs that runs in short, fast bursts.

When birds are common in one place, it is hard to imagine that they are endangered worldwide, but there are thought to be no more than 6,000

A Charlottetown (**2**) monument honoring veterans of both World Wars.

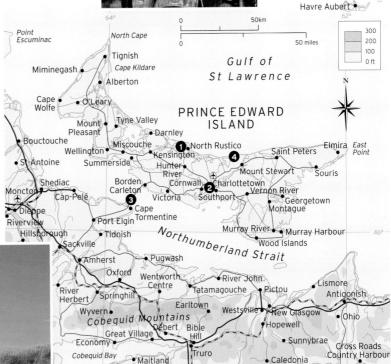

Covehead Light Station near Dalvay is one of many picturesque lighthouses dotted around the island (**4**).

Now a National Historic Site, the original house and farm of Green Gables (**1**) at Cavendish is one of the island's most popular attractions.

The Confederation Bridge (**3**) spans the Northumberland Strait between Prince Edward Island and New Brunswick.

of these pretty little piped plovers left around the world. Prince Edward Island is a welcome breeding refuge for them, along with other species that nest here in this idyllic coastal landscape of sugar-soft sand, whispering breezes, and the sunlight turning the water's surface to diamonds.

Other birds to look out for are the common tern, and the great blue herons that patrol the shorelines and ponds in a regal manner, moving slowly and carefully until they see a fish in the water or frog in a reed bed, whereupon they pounce, thrusting their beak like a sword. There are, for the moment at least, plenty of fish for them to feed on, as several rivers drain into the Gulf of St. Lawrence here, bringing freshwater and saltwater fish for the herons' supper, including salmon, perch, and trout. Less welcome are some of the mammals, like red foxes and coyotes, which must feed in their turn on the smaller creatures, but so far nature has kept its balance here.

Endangered Park

More worrying is that this refuge itself, which was established as a national park back in 1937, is now considered endangered, too—the most vulnerable in the whole Canadian national park system in fact. Some of it is quite simply disappearing. Changes in the weather patterns bring about fiercer storms than the area has been used to, leading to increased coastal erosion; the park slips beneath the waves.

Human activity is also to blame, where numbers of visitors leave the carefully planned tracks and walkways and clump their own way over the fragile earth. What may seem like just another patch of sand can be a complex little ecosystem of land, plants, bugs, and birds, all dependent on each other and capable of collapsing like a house of cards if the balance is disturbed. It is for this reason we must respect and protect the grains of sand on our planet, every bit as much as the grand canyons.

–> What's in a Name?

Prince Edward Island was previously the Île Saint-Jean, named by the French Acadians who settled here. When they were forced out by the British, the island briefly became New Ireland, until in 1798 it was named after Prince Edward, father of Queen Victoria, who was in charge of the British forces in Canada.

–> FACT FILE

POPULATION Prince Edward Island 140,000.

CLIMATE The climate here could be described as unpredictable. The winters can be harsh, with storms and blizzards, or they can be cold (around freezing) but fairly benign. Spring and early summer can see temperatures soar into the 80s–90s°F (about 26–35ºC), or they can equally plunge back down to 0°F (-18ºC). By midsummer it will be warm and mostly dry, but there is plenty of rain throughout the rest of the year, and snow in winter.

WHAT TO TAKE Clothing for all weather possibilities, including swimwear. Binoculars, and a camera to capture the park's natural beauty.

BEST TIME Late summer can be a lovely time, but each season brings its own pleasures.

NEAREST AIRPORT Charlottetown, the island capital, has its own airport.

ACCOMMODATIONS There are campsites within the park; cottages and inns at Stanhope and Dalvay, right by the park, with more options in Charlottetown, a 15-mile (24-km) drive away.

Behind its rocky coastline, fertile farmland and rolling hills cover the interior of Prince Edward Island.

NEWFOUNDLAND AND LABRADOR

Often described as desolate and bleak, these places on the northeast edge of the American continent have a dramatic beauty and a long history.

WELL BEFORE CHRISTOPHER COLUMBUS and other southern European explorers reached the Americas, brave Norsemen had crossed the bleak North Atlantic Ocean and settled at L'Anse aux Meadows, on the very northern tip of the island of Newfoundland. L'Anse aux Meadows is an interesting name, partly because its French origins indicate the numerous other nations who came here after the Norse, but also because of its meaning. It is an Anglicization and, in the process, a prettification of the French name of L'Anse-aux-Méduses, which means Jellyfish Cove. "Jellyfish" became "meadows."

For centuries, people migrated to the province of Newfoundland and Labrador and settled here, feeding at first on the rich haul from the sea, then by farming the land. Ports like St. Anthony on Newfoundland were used by French and Basque fishermen as safe harbors when they sailed out across the Atlantic in the early sixteenth century, but later they decided to stay despite the often harsh climate. It was also about then, in 1497, that the Italian explorer John Cabot sailed from England and named this island Terra Nova, or New Land.

The name Labrador comes from the Portuguese explorer João Fernandes Lavrador, showing yet another of the many nations who make up this patchwork quilt of a people. Some here speak a particular dialect of English called Newfoundland English, and there is also a Newfoundland French language. In the past there was Newfoundland Irish too, and before them the Native American Beothuk people were living here.

It is this history, as much as the rugged and unusual scenery, that makes this part of Canada quite special, and the language and topography combine in the striking and descriptive place names—Foxtrap, Heart's Content, Cape Spear, Bonavista, Bait Cove, Ragged Islands. They evoke a place where humans are close to the land, and where little of the modern world intrudes.

Icebergs float in the harbor at Hart's Cove (1) in northern Newfoundland, a common sight in these waters.

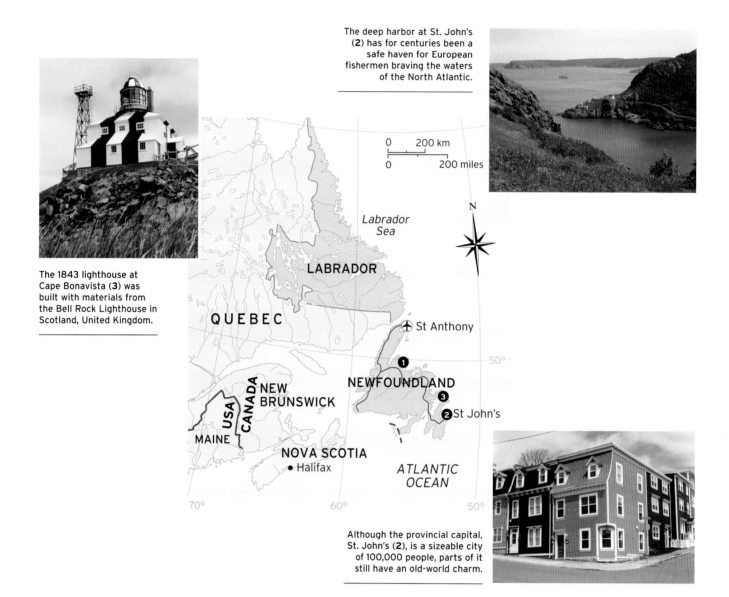

The 1843 lighthouse at Cape Bonavista (**3**) was built with materials from the Bell Rock Lighthouse in Scotland, United Kingdom.

The deep harbor at St. John's (**2**) has for centuries been a safe haven for European fishermen braving the waters of the North Atlantic.

Although the provincial capital, St. John's (**2**), is a sizeable city of 100,000 people, parts of it still have an old-world charm.

Labrador

The Strait of Belle Isle separates the island of Newfoundland from the Canadian mainland of Labrador. Labrador is one of the most remote and least developed parts of Canada, a region that is roughly the size of New Zealand but with a population of less than 30,000. There are fewer than 8,000 people in its largest settlement, the twin towns of Happy Valley-Goose Bay. It is a land still populated by Mother Nature.

There are caribou herds numbered in the hundreds of thousands, the largest in North America. Not for nothing do the Labrador people call their home the "Big Land." They have the largest of everything—whales, the largest mammal; polar bears, the largest carnivore on the planet; and moose, the largest land-based mammal in North America. But here, too, is one of the smallest birds in the world, the ruby-throated hummingbird, and

there are animals of graceful northern beauty, like the Arctic fox and the snowshoe hare.

Newfoundland

There are extremes in nature, too. Labrador's highest point is Mount Caubvick, which at 4,485 feet (1,367 m) is the highest peak east of Alberta. In fact, it is the highest peak in Québec too, as it straddles the border between Québec and the province of Newfoundland and Labrador, but its summit has been measured as being about 33 feet (10 m) inside the Newfoundland and Labrador border. These are not high mountains by the standards of the Rockies, but they attain a power all their own in the dramatic way they thrust up out of the land.

Along the coast there are mountains that seem to plunge straight down into the sea. Also here are some of the most breathtakingly beautiful fjords in the world, such as the Nachvak Fjord in the Torngat Mountains, or the Saglak Fjord, which is 50 miles (80 km) long.

Not to be outdone, Newfoundland includes North America's oldest English-founded settlement—St. John's. It possibly goes back to the 1497 arrival of John Cabot, although no one knows for sure, but it certainly predates the 1607 founding of Jamestown in the United States. Situated on the eastern end of the island, it is a setting-off point for whale-watching expeditions, although if there are no whales to watch you can observe the icebergs passing by in winter, and occasionally breaking up with a thundercrack of snapping ice.

Newfoundland is also rich in wildlife and, being an island, some are unique species. The native lynx is bigger than the mainland lynx, and the island's black bear is also a distinct subspecies. There are caribou here too, and the delightful white Arctic hare, though the unique white Newfoundland wolf was hunted to extinction in the nineteenth century.

Perhaps because there is no one single spectacular natural feature here—no Grand Canyon, no Mount McKinley, no Niagara Falls—the province of Labrador and Newfoundland is often overlooked when it comes to handing out superlatives for North America. And that is exactly what keeps it special, for those lucky enough to find it.

Fishing has always been a vital part of life in Newfoundland: some of the rivers have annual runs of up to 30,000 fish, and over 60 percent of North America's Atlantic salmon rivers are here.

-> FACT FILE

POPULATION 510,000, with 485,000 on Newfoundland.

CLIMATE Labrador's temperature can soar to 60ºF (15ºC) in summer, while dropping to 5ºF (-15ºC) in winter. Newfoundland is milder, with summer into the low 70sºF (low 20sºC); it is still below freezing in winter but not as severe as Labrador. Both places can experience strong winds, storms, and heavy rains.

WHAT TO TAKE Warm clothing, good hiking boots, binoculars for the wildlife, a sense of wonder.

BEST TIME Summer for the climate, with spring and summer good times for whale watching.

NEAREST AIRPORT St. John's International Airport is on Newfoundland.

ACCOMMODATIONS Newfoundland naturally has the better choice, but there are places in the main settlements on Labrador too, with comfort rather than luxury being the norm.

POLAR BEAR MIGRATION AT CHURCHILL

The tiny community of Churchill on Hudson Bay in Manitoba is transformed every fall into the "Polar Bear Capital of the World."

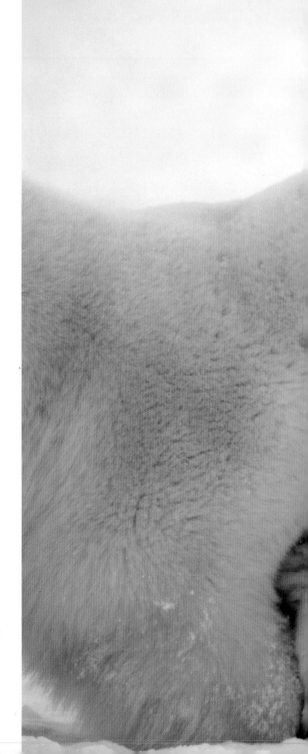

ABOUT ONE THOUSAND PEOPLE live year-round in Churchill, on Hudson Bay in northern Manitoba, but for a few weeks each October and into November they are joined by another thousand or so guests—polar bears. Churchill calls itself the "Polar Bear Capital of the World," and the bears turn up every fall, waiting around for the ice to freeze on Hudson Bay so they can head out in search of their favorite winter diet of ringed seals. Polar bears are the world's largest land carnivore, and an adult male can weigh up to 1,300 pounds (590 kg). A few hundred of these hanging around not far from town makes for quite an experience, especially when they are joined by about 15,000 tourists, who have come for the best close-ups of polar bears you can find anywhere.

It can be an uneasy mix, though. The polar bears are hungry, and impatient to get out to that rich source of food they know awaits them and will fatten them up for the freezing winter. The locals and the wildlife authorities know how to deal with the occasional rogue hungry bears, which might come sniffing around kitchens and trying to get into garbage cans. The main denning area for the bears is about 25 miles (40 km) outside of town, but individuals do go wandering sometimes. The organized tours keep away from the denning areas.

Arctic Safari

For most visitors, this is one of the most thrilling experiences of their lives, like an Arctic version of an African safari. Besides polar bears, there are many other creatures to be seen nearby, too, as Churchill stands at the junction of three different types of terrain. First there is the water, of course, a natural magnet for wildlife. Come here in summer and you may well see white beluga whales and their calves in the breaking ice of the Churchill River. But as well as the marine habitat there is also the coniferous forest that spreads across Canada, Alaska, through Siberia, and around the globe into Scandinavia in northern Europe. Finally there is the tundra, where the trees give way to bushes, shrubs, and the moss and lichens that many animals find so tasty.

Organized excursions take visitors out in tundra buggies, which are school buses specially adapted for crossing the terrain while providing panoramic

These playful polar bears may be cold but they're a hot political topic, with the World Wildlife Fund critical of the Canadian government's slowness in offering them any protected status.

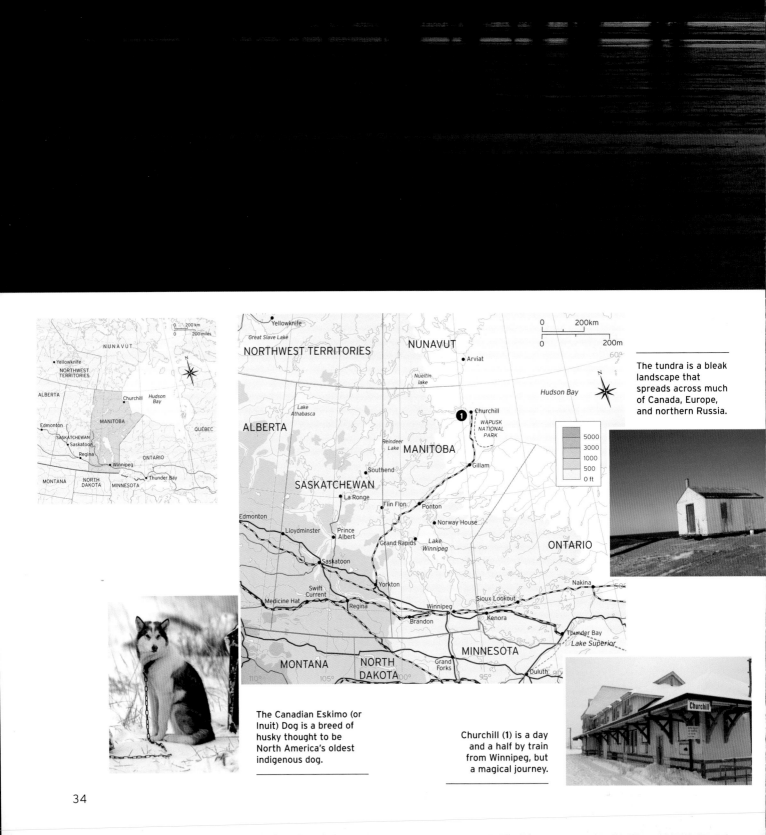

The tundra is a bleak landscape that spreads across much of Canada, Europe, and northern Russia.

The Canadian Eskimo (or Inuit) Dog is a breed of husky thought to be North America's oldest indigenous dog.

Churchill (1) is a day and a half by train from Winnipeg, but a magical journey.

Churchill (1) has more to offer than the annual polar bear migration, as this glorious shot of sunrise over the Churchill River shows.

→ FACT FILE

POPULATION 1,200

CLIMATE In July and August the temperature soars to an average of 52-54°F (11-12°C), while in January-February the average daily temperature gets down to -17°F (-27°C). These are averages, though. In summer it might reach 82°F (28°C) on a warm day, and in winter plunge so low it is painful.

WHAT TO TAKE Several layers of warm clothing. With the windchill, temperatures can seem much colder, and if you coincide with an especially cold spell, you will need all the help you can get.

BEST TIME October-November for the polar bears.

NEAREST AIRPORTS Winnipeg is 650 miles (1,046 km) away, with domestic flights to Churchill's small airport.

ACCOMMODATIONS For the polar bear season you should book an organized tour well ahead, which includes a few nights' accommodation. Because of the numbers of visitors (wildlife watching is popular in spring and summer, too), there are a surprising number of hotels, motels, inns, and lodges for such a small town.

views of the wildlife. The polar bears are the big attraction in October and November, but by exploring both the Arctic tundra and the coniferous forest, you may also see Arctic foxes, wolves, caribou, and that truly magnificent creature, the snowy owl. To see one of these birds in its silent flight, looking like it is wearing thick leggings to keep it warm, is a sight that will be remembered the rest of your life.

It is the polar bears that people want to see, however, and you probably will, but as with any wildlife-watching excursion there are no guarantees. Much depends on the time of your visit, and the weather that year, and on luck. The bears usually start to arrive in late September, but some years it is a little later. Numbers increase as you move into November, but leave it too late and the bears will be disappearing, heading over the thickening ice in search of food.

The later it gets, the colder it gets, which is fine for a polar bear but not what all humans are used to. When the temperature drops well below zero, as it can in November, and the icy wind is chipping at your cheeks, it is quite easy to question whether the lengthy journey to get to Churchill was such a good idea. But then someone shouts "bears," the doors of the buggy are thrown open and everyone squeezes out onto the observation deck for a look at these great white animals, perhaps playing, perhaps fighting, or maybe just walking by, heading for the bay. And even as your cheeks tingle and your nose turns to ice, you will know it was worth it.

Polar Bear Populations

In early 2008 the animals were placed on the "threatened" list in the neighboring United States, under the Endangered Species Act. The polar bear is also listed as "vulnerable" in the officially recognized Red List of the International Union for the Conservation of Nature and Natural Resources. This means that there is a serious threat of extinction, unless its habitat or circumstances change. As the polar bear's Arctic habitat is being reduced due to the effects of global warming, it is hard to know what the future holds for this magnificent animal. Although it is thought there may be anything from 50,000 to 100,000 around the world, the World Wildlife Fund puts their numbers as low as 22,000. They may have only a few more decades left to live, before they die out in the wild.

For this reason alone, the fact that people from all over the world go to the trouble and expense every year of getting to remote little Churchill—only reachable by train or plane—is encouraging. People care about the polar bear. It can only be hoped that the caring somehow helps protect the existence of these beautiful animals, which are so awe-inspiring and powerful, and yet so vulnerable to humankind's wasteful ways.

UNITED STATES
"Nothing so liberalizes a man and expands the kindly instincts that nature put in him as travel."

Mark Twain, American writer, 1835-1910

THE GRAND CANYON

It is true what they say: No matter how many pictures you have seen, nothing prepares you for the vastness and spectacular beauty of the Grand Canyon.

AT THE EDGE OF THE GRAND CANYON, all superlatives fail. Words such as awesome, astounding, and stupendous pale in comparison to the scene that stretches before you into the horizon. It is one of those rare places when thoughts are silenced by the raw power of nature.

The Grand Canyon runs for 277 miles (446 km) through northwestern Arizona. Its width varies from half a mile to 18 miles (0.8-29 km) across. The mighty Colorado River runs 1 mile (1.6 km) below the viewpoints on the canyon's South Rim. Though from here it looks like a thin silver ribbon, this eternal sculptor continues to chisel deeper through the plateau.

Over several million years, the river carved this enormous chasm in the Colorado Plateau, a vast geological uplift that covers much of the Southwest. The fantastic shapes of its rugged bluffs and flat-topped mesas were further sculpted by erosion, the action of wind, rain, frost, snow, and heat, revealing deeper and older layers in the rock walls. As you gaze across the striated cliffs and chiseled buttes rising up out of the canyon, you are looking at two billion years of the earth's geological history. Nowhere else in the world is such a vast cross section of time so clearly manifest than in these rainbow rock layers.

Native Americans had long lived in and around the canyon when Spanish explorers saw it for the first time in the sixteenth century. In 1869, John Wesley Powell mounted the first exploratory expedition through it by boat on the Colorado River, and gave the canyon its name. With the arrival of the railroad at the turn of the twentieth century, tourism boomed. President Theodore Roosevelt established the Grand Canyon National Monument, and in 1919 it became the country's fifteenth national park. It is now a World Heritage Site.

The park encompasses over 1.2 million acres (485,623 ha). There are three sections, each a considerable distance apart. Roosevelt, who visited

Viewpoints all along the South Rim afford stunning vistas across the Grand Canyon—but don't get too near the edge!

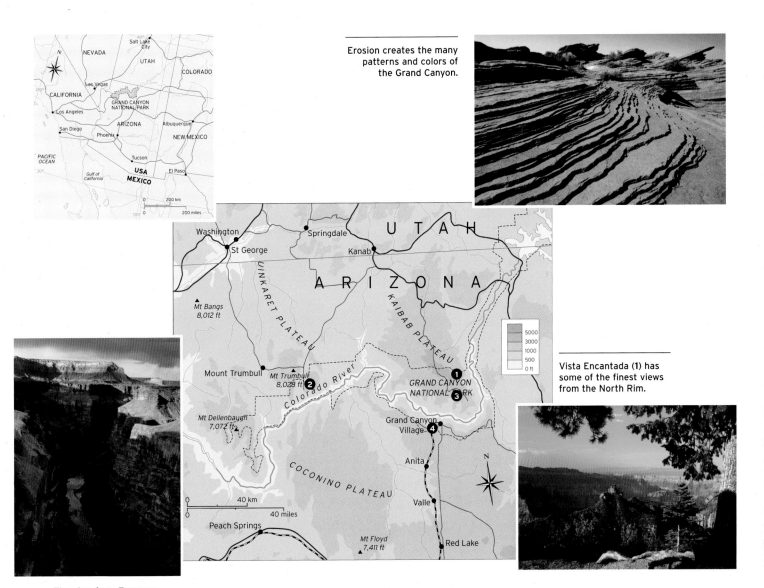

Erosion creates the many patterns and colors of the Grand Canyon.

Vista Encantada (**1**) has some of the finest views from the North Rim.

The view from Toroweap Point (**2**) shows just a small section of the Colorado River, which runs through seven states.

the canyon many times, called it "the one great sight every American should see." Each year, over 4.5 million visitors from around the world take his advice.

The South Rim

The South Rim is by far the busiest part of the Grand Canyon. It has the easiest access via Flagstaff, 85 miles (137 km) away, the most tourist facilities, and arguably the finest views. The south entrance leads into Grand Canyon Village.

From here, Hermit Road winds for 8 miles (13 km) to the westernmost viewpoint, Hermit's Rest. From March to November it is closed to cars, but a free shuttle bus takes you to eight scenic overlooks along the way. You can also hike along the flat Rim Trail, the best bet for an easy yet spectacular day hike. Desert View Drive runs for 25 miles (40 km) east of the village along the South Rim to the park's east entrance, with more stunning vistas along the way.

Take time to sit and admire the canyon from the various viewpoints, picking out the flat-topped

-> Grand Canyon Skywalk

Grand Canyon West, the most remote section of the park, lies on land belonging to the Hualapai Nation. Over 240 miles (386 km) from the South Rim, it is closer to Las Vegas, about 120 miles (193 km) away. Here you can get an eagle's eye view over the Grand Canyon from the Skywalk on its West Rim. This U-shaped, cantilever walkway extends 70 feet (21 m) out from the edge of the cliff. At its tip, nothing but the glass-bottomed bridge stands between you and the river 4,000 feet (1,219 m) below. This distance is more than twice the height of the world's tallest skyscraper (Shanghai's Taipei 101). To visit the Skywalk you must purchase a Grand Canyon West entrance package that includes a variety of tours and activities.

The Cape Royal Trail (**3**) is a short and easy hiking trail on the North Rim that leads to some stunning scenic views over the canyon.

mesas and rock formations named for ancient gods and temples. Its appearance changes almost from minute to minute, with each angle of the sun or passing cloud, so that it seems to be a living entity, alternately flirting, resting, or demanding your attention. This is the real wonder of the Grand Canyon.

There are several strenuous hikes down into the canyon. Even the fittest cannot make it to the canyon floor and back in one day. If you want to hike a short way in, remember that it takes twice as long to come back up as it does to go down! Book several months ahead if you want to take a mule trek into the canyon.

The North Rim

The South Rim can become congested in high season, and many visitors prefer the canyon's quieter North Rim. Though it is only 10 miles (16 km) away as the crow flies, it is over 200 miles (322 km) and a good five hours by road, with lovely scenery along the way. At over 8,000 feet

The area directly below Hopi Point (**4**) on the South Rim is aptly called "The Inferno."

-> FACT FILE

CLIMATE Conditions vary according to elevation. While summer temperatures on the South Rim are pleasant with highs in the 80soF (27-32oC), temperatures in the inner canyon are extreme, reaching over 100oF (37oC). Afternoon thunderstorms in summer can be severe and lead to flash floods. The North Rim is cooler due to higher elevation, with highs in the 70soF (21-26oC). Winter conditions on the South Rim can be extreme with snow and ice, though afternoon highs average in the 40soF (4-9oC) due to sunshine. The North Rim is closed in winter due to heavy snowfalls.

WHAT TO TAKE Good walking shoes or hiking boots, sunscreen, plenty of water. Be prepared for rapidly changing conditions with a rain jacket and warm clothing.

BEST TIME Summer has the warmest temperatures but is usually very crowded. Spring and fall have fewer visitors and generally pleasant weather, though be prepared for sudden changes. The North Rim is generally open mid-May to mid-October, weather permitting.

NEAREST AIRPORTS Sky Harbor International Airport in Phoenix is 220 miles (354 km) from the South Rim, 335 miles (539 km) from the North Rim, and 253 miles (407 km) from Grand Canyon West. McCarran International Airport in Las Vegas is 290 miles (467 km) from the South Rim, 277 miles (446 km) from the North Rim, and 120 miles (193 km) from Grand Canyon West.

ACCOMMODATIONS There are several good lodges as well as campgrounds in the park. Most accommodations are at the South Rim's Grand Canyon Village. Book well ahead. There are a range of hotels and motels at Tusayan, just outside the park's entrance. There is a lodge with cabins and a campground at the North Rim; otherwise the closest accommodation is 25-45 miles (40-72 km) away. There is some accommodation at Grand Canyon West and a range of hotels and motels at Kingman.

PARK ENTRANCE An entrance fee per vehicle is valid for seven days. Annual passes good at all national parks are also available.

(2,438 m), the North Rim is 1,000 feet (305 m) higher in elevation. Snowfall often closes the road during winter.

The North Rim is surrounded by a more alpine scenery, with thick forests of Douglas fir and ponderosa pine, meadows and aspen trees that turn bright gold in fall. The viewpoints afford stunning views of the Grand Canyon and the Painted Desert to the east. Several hiking trails are less strenuous and more accessible for day hikes than those on the South Rim.

Whichever part of the park you choose, try and stay long enough to experience both sunrise and sunset. The secret to visiting the Grand Canyon is to experience its ever-changing moods, from the pastel pink glow of a misty morning to the fiery red flames at sundown. Watch the play of light and color on the rocks throughout the day. Even the shadow of a passing cloud can alter the atmosphere. Each day as the light dances across this vast, variegated canvas, nature, the supreme artist, creates a new masterpiece.

MONUMENT VALLEY

The setting is familiar from old Western movies, but these magnificent monoliths are even more impressive when you see them with your own eyes.

IT IS THE QUINTESSENTIAL IMAGE of the Old West—a solitary hero on horseback, galloping across a vast red desert below towering rock monoliths, undaunted by the formidable trials of this rugged land. John Wayne personified the myth in a string of Hollywood Westerns. But the real star of these movies was the landscape in which they were filmed—Monument Valley.

Covering nearly 92,000 acres (37,231 ha), this remarkable region of lofty buttes, flat-topped mesas, and rocky spires spans the border between southern Utah and northern Arizona. It lies completely within Navajo tribal lands. The area was occupied by Paleo-Indian hunters as long ago as 12,000 B.C. Hundreds of ancient petroglyphs and the ruins and artifacts left by later Ancestral Pueblo people known as the Kayenta Anasazi, can still be seen today. These early natives named it the Valley of the Rocks, and assigned spiritual meanings to its striking geological features.

What makes Monument Valley so spectacular is the scale. The massive monoliths rise abruptly from the flat plain, their sheer walls soaring up to 1,000 feet (305 m) high. They stand in solitude, spaced out across an infinite horizon like sentries guarding the passage to another world. It seems, at times, a desolate place, with little wildlife and sparse greenery breaking the arid landscape apart from sagebrush and the occasional juniper tree. But as the sun moves across the sky, turning the sandstone walls from soft pink to fiery red, and billowing clouds frame the crumbling pinnacles while casting changing shadows on the desert floor, it becomes a place of singular, awesome beauty.

A Star Is Born

Monument Valley is part of the Colorado Plateau, which covers 130,000 square miles (336,687 sq km) of Colorado, Utah, Arizona, and New Mexico. Its flatness is deceiving, and it is amazing to realize that the valley is actually more than 1 mile (1.6 km) above sea level. It is not really a valley at all, but a geological uplift known as the Monument Upwarp.

Eons ago, this was indeed a huge lowland basin, collecting layers of shale, sandstone, and siltstone eroded from ancient mountains. Then, some 75 million years ago, the collision of the

The northern approach to Monument Valley along US 163 from Utah is one of the most memorable views of the American Southwest.

–> FACT FILE

CLIMATE Summers are hot and dry, with average highs in July of 90ºF (32ºC), though nights are cool. Due to the elevation, winters are cold and snowy. Average daytime highs in December are 42ºF (5.5ºC) with night temperatures dropping well below freezing.

WHAT TO TAKE Sunscreen, hat, sunglasses, and drinking water and snacks for touring. Warm jacket or sweater for summer nights.

BEST TIME Peak season is May to October. Spring and fall have the most pleasant temperatures and are less crowded.

NEAREST AIRPORT The nearest large airport is at Flagstaff, 175 miles (282 km) southwest of Monument Valley.

ACCOMMODATIONS Limited near Monument Valley, so book ahead, especially in peak season. There is one lodge, one hotel, and bed and breakfast establishments, as well as campgrounds. Hotels can be found in several small towns in a radius of 25-50 miles (32-80 km) from the park.

PARK ENTRANCE There is a small fee per person to enter the park.

TRAVEL TIPS Always ask before photographing local Navajos and offer a tip; many people depend on income from tourism.

The distinctive formation Merrick Butte (**3**) stands alongside the Mittens (see opposite) to make a remarkable scene in the otherwise barren landscape.

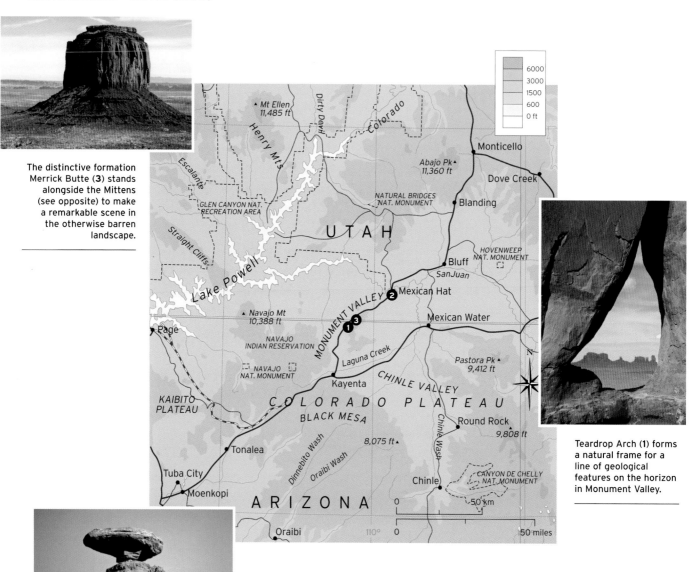

Teardrop Arch (**1**) forms a natural frame for a line of geological features on the horizon in Monument Valley.

Erosion has produced many whimsically named landmarks such as Mexican Hat Rock (**2**).

Pacific and North American continental plates pushed the entire region upward, forming the Colorado Plateau. Over time, the flow of rivers winding across the plateau slowly carved out this wide wonderland we call Monument Valley.

The sediments and minerals from different geological eras can easily be seen in the stratified layers of the buttes and mesas. The varying hardness and softness of the rocks produced the sculpted spires and pinnacles as they were chiseled away by wind and rain. The orange-red hues come from iron oxide in the exposed siltstone. Manganese oxide creates the dark bands known as desert varnish. There are remnants of volcanic activity in the surrounding area, too, such as Agathla Peak on the southern fringes of the valley.

Still, it is hard not to imagine a master sculptor at work as you admire the landmarks, many of which have been given descriptive names based on their unusual shapes. The Mittens, Elephant Butte, Camel Butte, The Thumb, Three Sisters, and the narrow column known as Totem Pole, along with Ear of the Wind Arch, are some of the highlights.

Director John Ford recognized this surreal landscape as a perfect setting for the great themes

The buttes known as East Mitten (above) and West Mitten (**3**) are two of the most distinctive rock formations in Monument Valley.

of storytelling—man against nature, good against evil—at the heart of the classic Western. After filming *Stagecoach* with John Wayne in 1939, he returned to shoot nine more Westerns here, even though some, like *The Searchers*, were set elsewhere. A popular lookout point that featured in that film has been named John Ford's Point in his honor. Long after the Western faded from Hollywood's spotlight, Monument Valley continued to be used as a television and film location (*Thelma and Louise, Forrest Gump, Mission Impossible II*) and features on everything from music albums and DVD covers to computer games.

Navajo Tribal Park

Though you can see some formations from a distance on the main road, most of the best scenery lies within Monument Valley Navajo Tribal Park. The entrance is 30 miles (48 km) north of Kayenta, Arizona, off US Highway 163. The best approach, however, is to head south on US 163 from Utah, which gives you the famous, stunning view of the long, straight road heading toward the distant towering buttes.

Opposite the turnoff for the park, the small hamlet of Goulding, established as a trading post in 1923, has a lodge, restaurant, and facilities for visitors. The post still looks much the same as it did when Harry Goulding and his wife "Mike" ran it in the 1930s. The museum is filled with mementos from their friendships with Ford, Wayne, and other Hollywood film stars.

From the park's visitor center there is a good view of three of Monument Valley's most famous peaks—East Mitten, West Mitten, and Merrick Butte. A 17-mile (27-km) self-drive scenic loop runs through the valley past many major landmarks and viewpoints. The road is unpaved, but is suitable for most cars except after heavy rains. Hiking or driving off this one road, however, is prohibited. To get a closer view (and better photographs) of the spires and arches, and to see some of the more remote formations, you have to hire a Navajo guide or take a four-wheel drive jeep, van, or horseback tour. These are arranged at the visitor center, and can include visits to a Navajo hogan as well as the chance to see ancient cliff dwellings, caves, and petroglyphs.

THE ADIRONDACKS

Less than half a day's drive from America's biggest city is the largest expanse of parkland in the lower forty-eight states, with ancient mountains, dense forests, and pristine lakes.

"NEW YORK HAS HER WILDERNESS within her own borders," wrote Henry David Thoreau in 1848, "and though the sailors of Europe are familiar with the soundings of her Hudson, and Fulton long since invented the steamboat on its waters, an Indian is still necessary to guide her scientific men to its headwaters in the Adirondack country."

He was referring to the Adirondack Mountains, whose rounded peaks and dense woodlands are today preserved in a park that covers most of the northeast region of New York State. At 6 million acres (2.43 million ha), it is the largest park in the United States outside Alaska, bigger than Yosemite, Yellowstone, Glacier, the Grand Canyon, and Great Smoky Mountains National Parks put together. Around 1 million acres (404,686 ha) is designated wilderness. Much of it is state land, part of the Adirondack Forest Preserve. But just over half of the park is privately owned, although

protected by strict regulations regarding use and development.

The park is broadly encircled by some of the great watery landmarks of the Northeast. To the west is Lake Ontario, which flows into the St. Lawrence River running north of the park. To the east, separating it from Vermont, are Lake Champlain and Lake George. To the south is the valley of the Mohawk River. The park itself is studded with 3,000 lakes and ponds. The most famous of these is Lake Placid, twice the site of the Olympic Winter Games, in 1932 and 1980.

There are also some 6,000 miles (9,700 km) of rivers and streams. Deep in these mountains the mighty Hudson River gets its start in a tiny hidden pool known as Lake Tear of the Clouds. From here it flows 315 miles (507 km) to its mouth in New York Harbor, where it feeds one of North America's leading seaports.

Saving the Wilderness

It is surprising that such a vast wilderness exists so close to New York City and the most densely populated region of the country. Although Lake Champlain, a fine natural waterway between Canada and the Hudson River, had been fought over since colonial times, the Adirondacks remained virtually unknown and untamed well into the nineteenth century. By the time Ebenezer Emmons, a geologist, finally gave them a name in 1838, Americans had already set out to conquer the West.

Emmons christened the region with an Anglicized version of a name given to a tribe of Algonquin Indians by their Iroquois enemies—"Ratirontak." It means "eaters of bark," a reference to their surviving on the interior bark of white pine during harsh winters.

The trees were a source of wealth, not survival, to the loggers who began cutting down huge swathes of virgin forest. By the 1870s and '80s, concern that wide-scale logging would result in the erosion of the mountains and the silting up of the Hudson River and Erie Canal had spread, and New York's businessmen joined with conservationists and public figures to lobby for the preservation of the region. Adirondack Park was established in 1894.

By then, many thousands of acres had also been bought up by wealthy families, the Vanderbilts and Morgans among them, for whom the Adirondacks provided a rustic getaway. They built the famous Great Camps along the shores of many lakes. Though some started out as tent camps, most were grand summer compounds of cabins where they could entertain friends and family in the style to which they were accustomed. Some still exist, including Sagamore on Raquette Lake, now listed on the National Register of Historic Places.

Mountain Playground

Definitions vary on whether or not the Adirondacks are part of the Appalachians, the huge mountain chain that runs most of the length of the eastern United States. Geologically they have more in

The idyllic mountain lake area of Chapel Pond (1, opposite) is home to birds of prey such as the pergrine falcon, migrating hawks, and ravens.

A tranquil fall scene of Lake George (2) belies the wealth of activities available, which include hiking, biking, tubing, ice-skating, skiing, camping, and more.

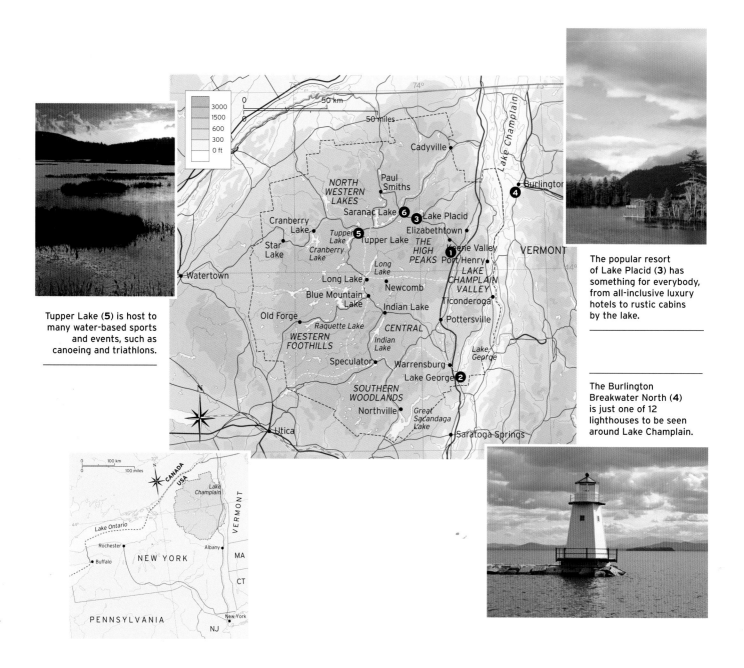

Tupper Lake (**5**) is host to many water-based sports and events, such as canoeing and triathlons.

The popular resort of Lake Placid (**3**) has something for everybody, from all-inclusive luxury hotels to rustic cabins by the lake.

The Burlington Breakwater North (**4**) is just one of 12 lighthouses to be seen around Lake Champlain.

common with Canada's Laurentian Plateau. Their rounded peaks were formed mainly by erosion over several hundred million years. Compared with their western counterparts, the Adirondacks are low as mountains go. But in primeval times their peaks reached upward of 20,000 feet (6,095 m).

Mount Marcy, at 5,344 feet (1,629 m), is the highest peak. There are magnificent views from the top, taking in Lake Champlain and Vermont's Green Mountains. Even better is the view from Whiteface Mountain, where you can also see across the valley of the St. Lawrence to Montreal. Altogether there are 42 summits topping 4,000 feet (1,219 m) in the High Peaks region of the park. The mountain slopes and valleys are blanketed in dense forests of varied woodlands, from spruce and balsam fir to hardwoods, which put on a brilliant display of fall color.

The Adirondacks are a year-round playground. Some 2,000 miles (3,219 km) of hiking trails wind through the park. Saranac Lake is a good starting point to explore the network of lakes and streams by canoe. For the more adventurous there are boat and raft rides through the Ausable Chasm gorge. Indian Pass and the Keene Valley in the center of the High Peaks are other beauty spots. Lake George is a busy tourist resort.

With its Olympic facilities, Lake Placid is the best known of the Adirondacks' dozen skiing centers, which include groomed trails for cross-country skiers. Eleven scenic byways run through or near the park. Visitors are more likely to see white-tailed deer than the park's elusive population of black bear, which keep to themselves deep in the mountains.

Saranac Lake (**6**) is more than a pretty vacation spot; it has been a pioneering health resort since 1876, when Dr. Edward Trudeau found it beneficial for treating tuberculosis.

-> FACT FILE

POPULATION 130,000 live year-round in the park's towns and resorts.

CLIMATE Temperatures and climate conditions vary according to elevation and different parts of the park. The western side is wetter than the eastern side, receiving 50 inches (127 cm) or more of rain per year. Summer temperatures usually range from the upper 70s to lower 80s°F (24-29°C). Average winter temperature is around 16°F (-9°C). Average snowfall is 90 inches (229 cm) from late November to April.

WHAT TO TAKE Good walking shoes or hiking boots, rain gear, sunscreen, insect repellent.

BEST TIME Avoid blackfly season (early June to mid-July). Midsummer to early September for swimming and summer sports; fall color is generally best mid-September to mid-October, but varies from year to year.

NEAREST AIRPORTS Albany International Airport is the closest; it is 53 miles (85 km) from Lake George and 133 miles (214 km) from Lake Placid.

ACCOMMODATIONS There is a range throughout the park, from motels and lodges to campgrounds and luxury resort hotels. Lake Placid, Lake George, and Saranac Lake are popular resorts.

THE PACIFIC COAST HIGHWAY

Travel along the rugged sea cliffs and pounding surf of California's west coast for one of the most stunning scenic drives in North America.

THE PACIFIC COAST HIGHWAY is one of America's most famous scenic drives. The dramatic stretch of Highway 1 that hugs the coast for 485 miles (781 km) between San Francisco and Los Angeles has some of California's most spectacular views: rocky sea cliffs, roaring surf, sandy coves, and pine-covered mountains. Along the way you can visit secluded beaches and bustling resorts, quaint rural towns, historic missions and mansions, and a host of attractions. There are many chances to see wildlife in the state parks, preserves, and ocean viewpoints. And at either end there are two of America's finest cities to explore.

The Golden City

San Francisco boomed during the California Gold Rush of the mid-1800s, but unlike the mines it never went bust; not even a devastating earthquake and fire in 1906 could destroy its fortunes. The city quickly rebuilt with the beautiful turn-of-the-century architecture that has made it one of America's favorite cities, picturesquely nestled on a 46-square mile (119-sq km) peninsula between the Pacific Ocean and San Francisco Bay. Its vibrant atmosphere comes from its easygoing liberalism and its status as the center of America's counterculture.

San Francisco is a great walking city. Its diverse neighborhoods are spread over some 50 hills, some of them so steep that steps are cut into the sidewalk. The city's famous cable cars are a fun way to tackle the heights. They also make up the last surviving cable-car system in the world. The two most scenic lines run from Market and Powell Streets, near Union Square, over Nob Hill with its grand mansions and hotels, to points near Fisherman's Wharf.

There are few fishermen left these days, and the wharf may be America's most famous tourist trap, but from here you can walk along the Embarcadero beside the bay to the Ferry Building with its wonderful gourmet market hall. In between is Pier 39 with its marina, carousel, and hundreds of California sea lions that have taken over its floating docks. From here you can take a sightseeing ferry to Alcatraz Island, the notorious former prison.

You will also pass North Beach, where the bohemian atmosphere that made the neighborhood a hub for the 1950's Beat generation lives on. There are fine views from the Coit Tower, which crowns Telegraph Hill. Other city highlights include Chinatown, Golden Gate Park, and the Presidio—with its historic buildings, beaches, dunes, and woodlands.

The name of the great landmark of the Golden Gate Bridge derives from the strait it crosses to connect the tip of the city with Marin County. Completed in 1937, it was once the longest suspension bridge in the world. Its orange-red towers, 746 feet (227 m) high, often rise impressively out of the rolling fog at its base. You can walk across to savor the views or drive to Vista Point at the northern end for a superb view back to the city.

Beaches and Boardwalks

South of San Francisco, several state beaches line Highway 1 between Pacifica and the marine reserve at Pillar Point. Half Moon Bay has 4 miles (6 km) of wide, sandy beach; beyond are more beaches backed by rocky bluffs, and idyllic coves with

From Alamo Square, the bright lights of San Francisco's downtown (1) shine above the Victorian houses known as the "painted ladies."

–> **FACT FILE**

POPULATION San Francisco: 765,000; Los Angeles: 3.8 million.

CLIMATE Varies from north to south, and with elevation. Average summer highs range from 70ºF (21ºC) in San Francisco to 84ºF (29ºC) in L.A. Winters are mild, ranging from 46ºF (7ºC) in San Francisco to 65ºF (18ºC) in L.A. The northern coast has more rain and fog in winter.

WHAT TO TAKE Sweater for cool nights, boat rides, mountains; rain jacket, comfortable walking shoes, sunscreen, binoculars for spotting wildlife.

BEST TIME January, April, and early May are the best times to see migrating gray whales. Winter rains can cause mudslides and road closures around Big Sur. Summer is high season everywhere, while fall (lasts from September to early December) brings fewer crowds, less traffic, and lower prices.

NEAREST AIRPORTS San Francisco International Airport is 14 miles (23 km) south of downtown on Highway 101. Los Angeles International Airport is located near Highway 1 between Marina del Rey and Manhattan Beach.

ACCOMMODATIONS Plentiful along the Pacific Coast Highway, ranging from quaint bed and breakfasts to hotels and motels in all price ranges.

Highway 1 winds around the coastal hillsides of Sonoma County (**2**), giving tantalizing vistas of the Pacific Ocean.

roaring surf, tidepools, and lagoons. Stop at the lighthouse at Pigeon Point, where sea lions are often seen offshore.

On the northern edge of Monterey Bay, Santa Cruz is a beach resort and university town with a wonderfully old-fashioned beach boardwalk more than 100 years old. Its star attractions—the Giant Dipper wooden roller coaster, built in 1924, and the handcarved carousel of 1911—have even been designated National Historic Landmarks. The Surfing Museum is set in a lighthouse along scenic West Cliff Drive.

Monterey was California's capital until 1848, and many of its old adobe homes and historic buildings can be seen on walking tours. The 1827 Custom House is the oldest public building in the state. The old sardine-packing plants of Cannery Row were made famous in John Steinbeck's novel of the same name. Today they house stores, restaurants, and the Monterey Bay Aquarium.

Some of the coast's most magnificent views lie along the 17-Mile Drive on the Monterey Peninsula. This toll road runs past pristine beaches, forests of Monterey pine, and the Lone Cypress Tree on its rocky sea ledge. Sightings of sea otters, sea lions, and many sea birds are common here.

Carmel, Big Sur, and Hearst

With its beautiful setting on the headlands of Carmel Bay, the picturesque town of Carmel-by-the-Sea has numerous art galleries and designer stores. Nearby, the Carmel Mission, dating from 1770, has been carefully restored to depict mission life.

Sea otters and sea lions can be spotted at Point Lobos State Reserve, 2 miles (3 km) south. The point is also a good place to see migrating California gray whales, especially in January, April, and the beginning of May.

The 100-mile (161-km) stretch of coast at Big Sur is the highlight of the Pacific Coast Highway. Here, Highway 1 runs dramatically along a narrow, winding route carved out of the cliffs, high above the sea. Below are rocky coves and crashing waves; inland are steep mountains, canyons, and dense forests.

Few people live in this rugged region. A cluster of restaurants and stores surrounds the resort of Nepenthe, tucked away behind oak trees. Most of the coastline is protected in a string of state parks, which offer hiking trails, campsites, wilderness areas, and access to sandy beaches and rocky shores.

After the stunning natural beauty of Big Sur comes the former port of San Simeon and the opulent Hearst Castle. Built between 1922 and 1947, it was the glamorous retreat of the media magnate

It's a thrill to drive across the Golden Gate Bridge (1), one of North America's great man-made landmarks.

Surf pounds the shore beneath the rugged cliffs of the Big Sur coastline (**6**).

Extinct volcanoes lurk among the lush hills of San Luis Obispo (**5**).

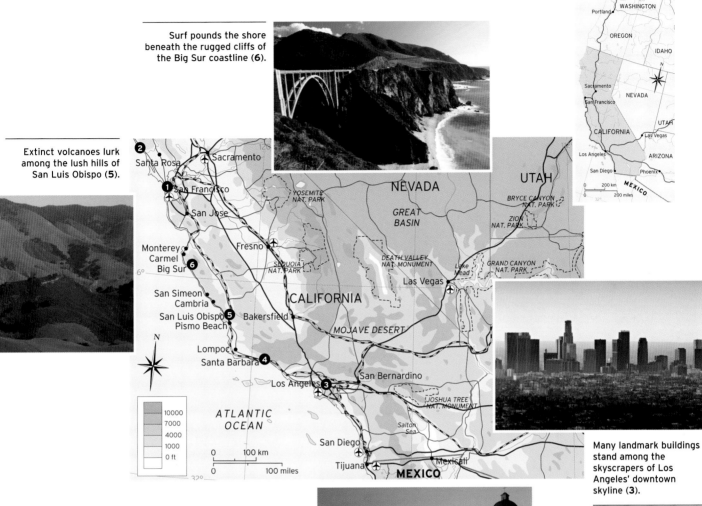

Many landmark buildings stand among the skyscrapers of Los Angeles' downtown skyline (**3**).

Santa Barbara Mission (**4**) is one of the most photographed buildings along the Pacific Coast Highway.

William Randolph Hearst. You can tour the twin-towered Casa Grande—lavishly decorated with architectural features and furnishings Hearst acquired from across Europe—and grounds.

Cambria to Santa Barbara

A few miles south, Cambria is a pleasant artists' colony with a pretty shoreline, where you may spot sea otters and other marine life. The old fishing village of Cayucos has a long pier and sandy beaches. At the fishing port of Morro Bay, the huge rock rising out of the bay is one of several extinct volcanoes along this coast; it is now a wildlife reserve protecting nesting peregrine falcons.

Highway 1 meets Highway 101 at San Luis Obispo, about halfway between San Francisco and Los Angeles. Slightly inland, the town is full of attractive architecture and has a historic mission. Back on the coast, Pismo Beach runs for several miles backed by large sand dunes. Highway 1 runs south through inland agricultural valleys of rolling countryside, skirting Vandenberg Airforce Base. At Lompoc, pick up a map of the 19-mile (31-km) Flower Drive through the valley, which identifies its many flower fields.

With its whitewashed buildings, red-tiled roofs, and palm trees, Santa Barbara's Spanish-Mediterranean style architecture makes it one of the most attractive cities in the country. Among its wealth of attractions are the County Courthouse, the restored Presidio (fort) buildings dating from 1782, and the Santa Barbara Mission, known as the Queen of the Missions. The Museum of Art has a superb collection of regional art.

Malibu and Los Angeles

From here, the 72-mile (116-km) drive through Ventura, gateway to the Channel Islands, and Oxnard brings you to another beautiful stretch of coast at Malibu. Movie stars have long colonized

With a lighthouse as its centerpiece, Fishermen's Village at Marina Del Rey is styled after a New England fishing village (3).

These pastel-painted beach houses have the perfect spot on Santa Monica's sandy shore (3).

the pricey beachfront bungalows, but there are public access points to the rolling surf, such as at Malibu Pier and the renowned Surfrider Beach. One of California's few remaining wetlands survives at Malibu Lagoon State Park.

The Getty Villa at Malibu is a stunning home for the billionaire's collection of Greek and Roman antiquities, housed in a recreated Roman villa. The Getty Center in Brentwood houses his vast collection of Western art.

Highway 1 continues through the coastal communities of the Los Angeles metropolitan area. Santa Monica, with its famous pleasure pier and old-fashioned carousel, is bordered by miles of wide, sandy beach. Its Third Street Promenade is a hotspot for bars, restaurants, and cafés. A cycle path runs to Venice Beach, where the boardwalk is lined with a parade of unusual characters, from palmreaders to jocks pumping iron on Muscle Beach. By contrast, the pretty harbor at Marina del Rey lies beyond.

Inland, Los Angeles has many attractions. Pay tribute to the stars at the Hollywood Walk of Fame

and Grauman's Chinese Theatre. Drive along the Sunset Strip and through beautiful Beverly Hills. If the budget will not stretch beyond window-shopping on Rodeo Drive, try quirky Melrose Avenue or hip West Hollywood. Universal Studios Hollywood is a popular highlight with its theme park rides and studio tours.

The city is full of excellent museums and cultural venues. Among the best are the Los Angeles County Museum of Art, the Hammer Museum in Westwood Village, and the Norton Simon Museum of Art in Pasadena. Downtown L.A. has the Museum of Contemporary Art, many landmark buildings, and the lively historic district around Olvera Street.

Back on the coast, California's beach culture started on the South Bay beaches of Manhattan, Hermosa, and Redondo, where George Freeth started the surfing craze in 1907. The drive around the Palos Verdes peninsula offers beautiful views. It carries around into Long Beach and on to the theme parks and beaches of Orange County.

–> Marine Life of the Pacific Coast

The Monterey Bay National Marine Sanctuary lies offshore along the Pacific Coast Highway, stretching 276 miles (444 km) from Marin, north of San Francisco, to Cambria and encompassing 5,322 square miles (13,784 sq km) of ocean. Established in 1992, it protects diverse habitats for a remarkable variety of marine species, from microscopic algae to great blue whales. Sea lions, sea otters, migrating gray whales, and numerous sea birds are frequently seen from many viewpoints along the shore.

Ventura is the gateway to Channel Islands National Park, approximately 40 miles (64 km) offshore. Encompassing five of the eight Channel Islands, the park preserves 145 endemic species of animals and plants found nowhere else in the world and is home to some of the largest breeding colonies of seals and sea lions in the country, as well as important nesting sites for sea birds.

VINEYARDS OF NAPA VALLEY

The rolling green hills of the Napa Valley are covered in vines, and the landscape and the wine combine to produce a dream California escape.

SOME OF THE BEST WINE in the world is produced in Napa Valley. Until 1976 the world did not know this, but in that year several Napa wines were among the California choices that beat the best French labels in a blind tasting in Paris, conducted mostly by French wine experts. What was intended as a fun event had a surprise result that really put Napa Valley on the map. Today it is one of the most popular destinations anywhere for the wine-loving traveler, with over 250 wineries in just 35 miles (56 km).

Napa History

Wine has been made in the Napa Valley since the 1850s, when the first commercial vineyard was opened. The area's Mediterranean climate appealed to immigrants, especially the many with French and Italian backgrounds, who brought their love of wine with them. It was only natural that they would want to plant vines, and try making their own New World wines.

George Yount, after whom the valley town of Yountville is named, was an early pioneer who is credited with planting the first ever grapevines in Napa Valley in 1836. They flourished, and by 1858 the first commercial vineyard had been opened. In 1879 the Inglenook Winery—still a famous name in wine—became the first Napa winery to produce Bordeaux-style wines, and even back then was winning awards at the 1889 World's Fair in Paris

(where Buffalo Bill's *Wild West* show with Annie Oakley was one of the attractions).

When the twentieth century dawned there were over 140 wineries in Napa Valley, but an outbreak of the disease phylloxera, followed by Prohibition and the Depression, all but put an end to the valley's wine production. Many vines were torn up, and a few vineyards kept going by making holy wine and wine for family consumption. It was not until the late 1930s and beyond that Napa Valley began its phoenix-like rise into what we see today.

Visiting the Valley

Even without the wine industry, Napa Valley would be a beautiful spot, with its green rolling hills, warm climate, and its general California "feel-good" factor. When you add the vineyards, though, the feel-good factor grows even bigger. The rows of vines add a pleasing pattern to the landscape, as they do around Bordeaux in France and in Italy's rolling Tuscan hills. They serve as a reminder of the land's fertility, and how humans have always worked the earth to produce both essential foods and luxuries such as wine—though many regard the latter as an essential part of this California/ Mediterranean lifestyle.

Good wine brings with it good food, and a good place to explore that relationship is at Copia, The American Center for Wine, Food & the Arts, in Napa, where there are exhibits, tours, and tastings. Throughout the valley there are many fine hotels, inns, and spas where you can indulge yourself. Calistoga, at the northern end of the valley, has natural hot springs and mud baths. The valley has some outstanding restaurants, with Yountville the culinary hot spot, but "foodies" should also check out the Saturday morning farmers' markets in every town with their wealth of local produce and artisan foods.

–> Sonoma County

Napa Valley is California's best-known wine region, but it's far from the only one. Touring the neighboring Sonoma Valley is a whole other experience, as here there are more small-scale family-run vineyards, where touring is much less organized.

Whether or not you enjoy drinking wine, the vine-covered hills of Napa Valley make this one of California's loveliest regions for touring by car.

Vineyards large and small are scattered throughout Napa Valley.

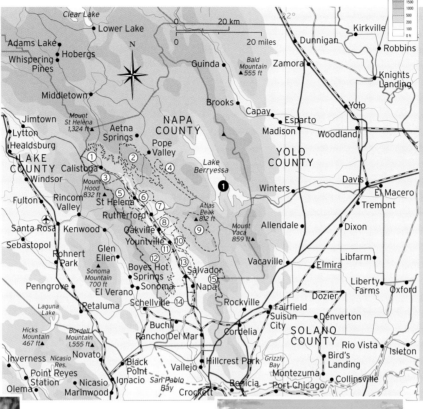

Wine-growing Districts of Napa County

1. Calistoga
2. Howell Mountain
3. Diamond Mountain District
4. Chiles Valley District
5. Spring Mountain District
6. St. Helena
7. Rutherford
8. Oakville
9. Atlas Peak
10. Stags Leap District
11. Yountville
12. Mount Veeder
13. Oak Knoll District
14. Los Carneros
15. Wild Horse Valley

Merlot grapes are just one of many varieties that thrive in the region.

Take a break from the vineyards at Lake Berryessa (1), a man-made reservoir used for swimming and boating.

Vineyard Tours

Although many of the vineyards are large commercial operations, there are still some small-scale, family-run places. They provide a chance to discover new labels and new tastes, and find some personal favorites—this sense of discovery is also part of the Napa Valley appeal. That said, you will learn more about wine and the fascinating history of Napa Valley by taking a tour of one of the larger vineyards, where they have the resources to help visitors make the most of their experiences.

One of the best tours is at the Robert Mondavi Winery. Mondavi came from an Italian background, and his were among the wines in that 1976 blind tasting that beat the French winemakers at their own game. Mondavi was a pioneer, creating the wine style of fumé blanc, and the first man to put the grape varieties on wine labels. The tours at Mondavi are not cheap, but they last for 75 minutes and upward, and are both fun and educational. The winery offers some in-depth tours, for those who may want to learn more about pairing wine with food or how to taste wine the professional way.

Other vineyards have other styles, and there is lots more to some of them than just the wine. The Hess Collection winery is owned by Swiss art collector Donald Hess, and his gallery here includes works by international names such as Francis Bacon, Andy Goldsworthy, and Franz Gertsch. It is housed in a property originally dating from 1903, when the Christian Brothers were here making holy wine. Beringer Vineyards was founded in 1876 and is the oldest continually operating vineyard in the whole valley, managing to stay open during Prohibition by also making holy wine. Sterling Vineyards provides some of the best views in the valley, while Inglenook is owned by moviemaker Francis Ford Coppola, who does oversee the wine production when he is not making movies.

Visiting Napa is an experience that is beyond wine, but it is the wine that holds it together. It courses through the valley like blood, and reminds us that humans and nature, working together, sometimes get it absolutely right!

-> FACT FILE

POPULATION Napa County 110,000.

CLIMATE Napa Valley has the typical California climate of warm, dry summers and mild winters, but its wine-favoring microclimate gives it even warmer summers than the neighboring valleys. In July–August there is a brief spell of 100ºF (37ºC) heat. Most rain falls November–March, but it is not excessive.

WHAT TO TAKE Sun protection, a jacket or umbrella in case of a shower, and plenty of money as tastings can be pricey and the wine will tempt you. Prices are usually good at the cellar door.

BEST TIME There is no bad time but September–October is best, when the grapes are ready for harvesting.

NEAREST AIRPORT San Francisco International Airport is about 60 miles (97 km) due south of Napa.

ACCOMMODATIONS Plenty of choice in Napa, and some in other valley towns such as Yountville, St. Helena, and Calistoga, though prices can be high. Book ahead.

Barrels of Napa Valley wine aging in the cellars are a popular sight on most vineyard tours.

THE LIGHTS OF LAS VEGAS

The odds are in your favor in Las Vegas—you are guaranteed to have a good time at this crazy, extravagant showplace in the Nevada desert.

WHEN MEXICAN MERCHANTS traveling from Santa Fe named this place Las Vegas in 1829, they did not know what they were starting. The name means "The Meadows," because here at one time, surrounded by desert, was an oasis of lush grassland, watered by artesian wells. Pickings are pretty lush for some today, watered by the gambling industry that has helped turn Las Vegas into the Entertainment Capital of the World.

The bedazzling Las Vegas we know today began with the building of the Hoover Dam, which brought a huge jump in the town's population, and coincided with the legalization of gambling in 1931. Illegal gambling had long been commonplace in Nevada, as in other frontier states, and in the 1930s the first legal casinos arrived, mostly downtown on Fremont Street. In time Fremont Street became known as Glitter Gulch, thanks to all the sparkling lights whose power source was the new Hoover Dam.

Fremont Street glitters more than ever now. The spectacular nightly light show known as the Fremont Street Experience uses 12.5 million lightbulbs, 220 speakers, 8 robotic mirrors, and 10 computers to illuminate the canopy over a stretch of Fremont Street, where the Las Vegas New Year's Eve party is also held. With several different themed shows a night, it is an amazing display of electronic ingenuity.

The Strip

Fremont Street is no longer the focal point of Las Vegas, which has shifted southward to The Strip. Officially known as Las Vegas Boulevard South, this 4-mile (6.5-km) stretch of highway is what the world thinks of when it thinks of Las Vegas. A walk or trolley ride down The Strip is like a quick tour of the world, too, with miniature—and not so miniature—versions of the canals of Venice, the Eiffel Tower, the New York skyline, even the Egyptian pyramids, in its signature hotels. It is a sensory overload, as you pass spectacular fountain

Glitter Gulch lives up to its name with the 12.5-million LED display lighting up the Fremont Street Experience (1).

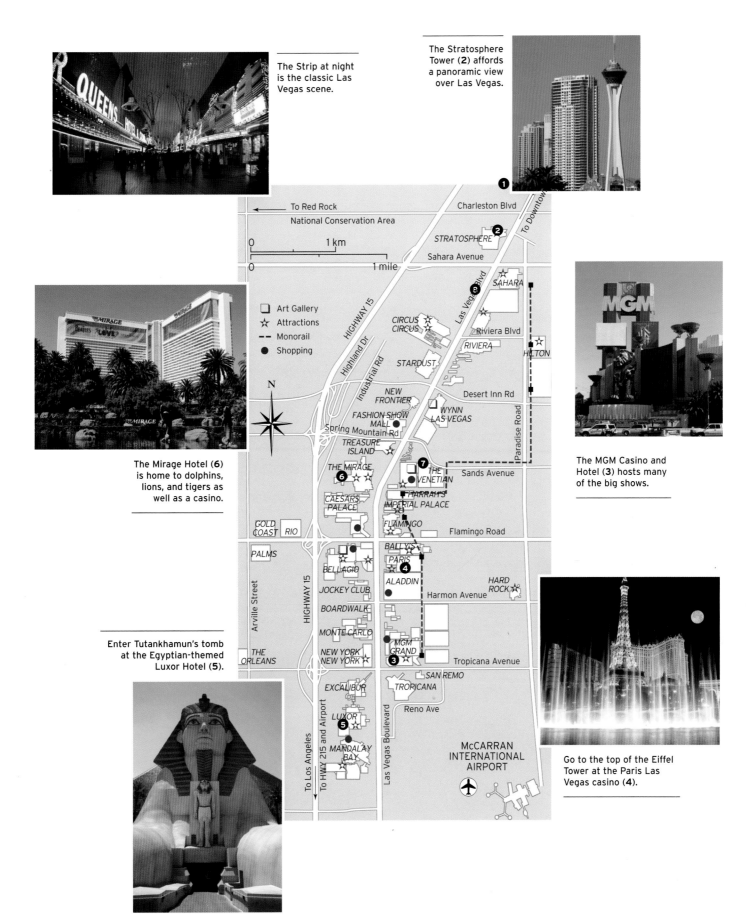

The Strip at night is the classic Las Vegas scene.

The Stratosphere Tower (2) affords a panoramic view over Las Vegas.

The Mirage Hotel (6) is home to dolphins, lions, and tigers as well as a casino.

The MGM Casino and Hotel (3) hosts many of the big shows.

Enter Tutankhamun's tomb at the Egyptian-themed Luxor Hotel (5).

Go to the top of the Eiffel Tower at the Paris Las Vegas casino (4).

Map labels:

To Red Rock National Conservation Area
Charleston Blvd
To Downtown
STRATOSPHERE
Sahara Avenue
SAHARA
Art Gallery
Attractions
Monorail
Shopping
CIRCUS CIRCUS
Riviera Blvd
RIVIERA
HILTON
STARDUST
HIGHWAY 15
Highland Dr
Industrial Rd
Las Vegas Blvd
Paradise Road
NEW FRONTIER
Desert Inn Rd
FASHION SHOW MALL
WYNN LAS VEGAS
Spring Mountain Rd
TREASURE ISLAND
THE VENETIAN
Sands Avenue
THE MIRAGE
HARRAH'S
IMPERIAL PALACE
CAESARS PALACE
FLAMINGO
Flamingo Road
GOLD COAST
RIO
BALLY'S
PALMS
PARIS
BELLAGIO
ALADDIN
HARD ROCK
Arville Street
JOCKEY CLUB
Harmon Avenue
BOARDWALK
MONTE CARLO
MGM GRAND
NEW YORK NEW YORK
Tropicana Avenue
THE ORLEANS
SAN REMO
TROPICANA
EXCALIBUR
Reno Ave
To Los Angeles
To HWY 215 and Airport
LUXOR
Las Vegas Boulevard
MANDALAY BAY
McCARRAN INTERNATIONAL AIRPORT

N

0   1 km
0   1 mile

displays, pirate ships, quickie-wedding chapels, monumental neon kitsch, and over a dozen of the biggest hotels in the world. You can visit quirky museums or impressive art collections, be entertained by topless showgirls or the world's top superstars, and eat in restaurants run by the world's best chefs.

At the northern end of The Strip is the Stratosphere, whose 1,149-foot (350-m) tower is the second-highest freestanding building west of the Mississippi. It is so tall permission had to be granted by the Federal Aviation Administration to build it. From the top, which is not for vertigo sufferers, are spectacular views not just of The Strip and downtown, but also of the surrounding desert and hills in which Las Vegas sits. It is strange to think that only 150 years ago this sprawling city was green meadows. Of course, if you take one of the thrill rides up here, like the aptly named Insanity, which hangs you over the edge of the building, there is not much chance of quiet thought.

Life Is a Circus

Back down to earth and a little further south along The Strip is the Circus Circus Hotel and Casino, which has the world's biggest permanent big top. All day long top circus performers show off their juggling, acrobatic, and trapeze skills, and apart from the fact that the shows themselves are breathtaking, equally impressive is that, like much of the entertainment in Las Vegas, they are free. Of course you pay big bucks to see top stars such

Shop along the Grand Canal or take a gondola ride at St. Mark's Square at the Venetian (7).

as Elton John, Bette Midler, Cher, and Rod Stewart, but most of the hotels also lay on free public shows, whether they be fountains, fireworks, or sirens seducing pirate buccaneers.

Along The Strip you may sometimes wonder if you are in a hotel, casino, zoo, or theme park. Many of the hotels are a mix of them all. Along with its exploding volcano, the Mirage has dolphins and white tigers in its Secret Garden; the MGM Grand keeps a pride of lions; Mandalay Bay entertains families with its water park and Shark Reef aquarium; and the Imperial Palace has an antique Auto Collection.

You can travel around New York–New York on the Manhattan Express rollercoaster, marvel at the Luxor's re-creation of King Tut's tomb, and experience the atmosphere of Venetian and Parisien Las Vegas. Two Vegas classics are the Flamingo, with its tropical birds and pool, where mobster Bugsy Siegel was shot in 1947, and across the street, Caesars Palace, which re-creates the decadence of ancient Rome with its columns, arches, statues, and pools.

The Fountains of Bellagio are one of the top free attractions. The Bellagio hotel has a 9-acre (3.5-ha) man-made lake in front of it, separating it from the bustle of The Strip. Here the fountains dance their way through a show choreographed to music, in the afternoons and evenings. It is the nighttime shows that are the most spectacular, with 4,500 lights coming into play as the waters jump and sway to tunes such as "Singin' in the Rain" or, naturally, Elvis singing "Viva Las Vegas."

It is stars such as Elvis Presley and Frank Sinatra who helped make Las Vegas into the Entertainment Capital of the World. Some people spend days here and hardly ever leave the casinos. Others visit and never set foot in the casinos, settling instead for the beautiful Nevada sunshine by day and the dancing lights of Las Vegas at night.

-> FACT FILE

POPULATION 550,000

CLIMATE The Las Vegas desert climate provides plentiful sunshine all year round, with very hot summers, cold winter nights, and little rainfall.

WHAT TO TAKE Sunscreen, in winter something warm for the evenings, comfortable shoes, lady luck.

BEST TIME In June–August the heat peaks and Vegas is best avoided if you plan to spend time outside, but any other time of year should be fine.

NEAREST AIRPORT McCarran International Airport is 5 miles (8 km) south of the center.

ACCOMMODATIONS All types, all prices, including some of the world's top hotels, but few bargains to be had as conventions keep hotels operating at about 90 percent capacity all year.

Vegas is renowned for its quirky walk-in wedding venues (**8**).

MANHATTAN'S MAGNIFICENT SKYLINE

Individually they are architectural masterpieces. Together, the skyscrapers of Manhattan form North America's most famous skyline, the glittering face of New York City.

The spire of the Chrysler Building (1) is a Manhattan icon.

YOU RECOGNIZE IT INSTANTLY. The forest of gleaming buildings soaring skyward along the shore of Manhattan is known around the world through its portrayal in countless films, books, and news stories. It is more than just the cover shot for New York. It is the most iconic cityscape in the United States. Although New York extends across five boroughs, for most visitors it is synonymous with Manhattan, the city's pulsating, shining star. Its skyscrapers stand like sentries to a tantalizing world. Behind the façade lies power, wealth, culture, glamor, fame, and fun.

Manhattan's skyline is made all the more dramatic by its island location, squeezed together between the Hudson and East Rivers on a narrow strip of land 13 ½ miles (22 km) long and just

2 ¼ miles (3.5 km) wide. The solid bedrock beneath the surface enabled the city to be built ever higher; limited space compelled it to be so. Over the course of a century, the development of architectural techniques and styles created a vertical metropolis unlike any other.

Although the skyscraper was invented in Chicago in 1885, in New York it came into its own. Here this practical, steel-framed monument to progress was imbued with a flamboyant face that captured the public's imagination. The bases of Manhattan's early skyscrapers, designed to impress at ground level, were richly decorated with sculpted stone, ornamental friezes, grand entrances, and other elements of the Beaux Arts style. They were topped with spires, pyramids, and shapes that announced

The Empire State
Building (2) is an
Art Deco masterpiece
towering above the city.

Times Square (3)
lies at the heart of
the Broadway
Theater District.

The United Nations
buildings (4) look out
across the East River.

The Statue of Liberty stands
proud on Liberty Island (6),
southwest of Manhattan.

The Flatiron Building (5), one
of Manhattan's earliest and
best-known skyscrapers.

The view of the densely
packed island from above
shows that Manhattan has
nowhere to grow but up.

their corporate identity. In between the buildings formed slender, elegant columns sporting arched windows and faced with terra-cotta, brick, granite, and limestone.

Early Landmarks

Unsurprisingly, some of the first skyscrapers were built in Lower Manhattan, where they forged the atmospheric concrete canyons along the narrow streets of the Financial District. Though many early skyscrapers have been demolished in New York's continual drive for real-estate redevelopment, others have survived as important landmarks.

One of the oldest is the 13-story Bayard-Condict Building at 65 Bleecker Street. Built in 1898, it is New York's only building by the renowned Chicago architect Louis Sullivan. Further uptown near Madison Square, Daniel Burnham's Flatiron Building is wedged into the triangular plot at Fifth Avenue and Twenty-third Street that gave it its distinctive shape and name. At 285 feet (87 m) it would hardly be called a skyscraper today, but when it was built in 1902 cynics called it "Burnham's folly," believing that high winds would blow it down.

A decade later, skyscraper height had more than doubled with Cass Gilbert's Woolworth Building (1913) at 233 Broadway rising to 792 feet (241 m). It was the world's tallest building for 27 years and is still considered one of New York's most beautiful, topped by its narrow, neo-Gothic tower set back from the base. This set the standard for the high-rise boom of the 1920s. Faced with such massive heights, the city passed zoning laws in 1916

-> The Twin Towers

From their completion in 1972 and 1973, the 110-story Twin Towers of the World Trade Center were the tallest buildings in New York. They were destroyed in the horrific aerial terrorist attacks of September 11, 2001. The site is being rebuilt with a memorial and the 1,776-foot (541-m) tall Freedom Tower, whose height (in feet) represents the year of America's birth.

It was not the first time New York's skyscrapers were struck by airplanes. In the 1940s a light aircraft hit the pyramid of the former Bank of Manhattan, and in 1945 a B-25 bomber crashed into the 79th floor of the Empire State Building during heavy fog, killing 14 people. But neither had such large-scale tragic consequences as the attack on the Twin Towers, which left an unforgettable hole in the Manhattan skyline.

requiring the upper stories of new skyscrapers to be stepped back to allow light and air to reach the street below. Among the first was Raymond Hood's striking American Standard Building (1924) at 40 W. Fortieth Street.

One early skyscraper, built in 1903–1905, still holds its place in an annual American ritual. At midnight on December 31, millions of TV viewers see in the New Year by watching the silver ball drop from the former Times Tower at 1 Times Square.

Signature Towers

The Art Deco era of the 1920s and early 1930s brought some of the city's best-loved skyscrapers. Some of the more ornate examples of the style can be seen in the Paramount Building (1926), 1501 Broadway, Times Square; the Fred F. French Building (1927), 521 Fifth Avenue; and the Chanin Building (1929), 122 E. Forty-second Street.

In the race to be the "world's tallest," the soaring heights of the buildings were matched only by the vision of their architects—and the egos of their backers. Even as H. Craig Severance's 70-story Bank of Manhattan at 40 Wall Street claimed the title in April 1930, his rival William Van Alen was secretly constructing a 125-foot (38-m) stainless steel spire inside the Chrysler Building, 405 Lexington Avenue. It was raised through the roof a month later, stealing the crown. With its clever automotive motifs—the spire is patterned after a car's radiator grille—the 1,047-foot (319-m) Chrysler Building is an Art Deco masterpiece and a favorite New York skyscraper. But it was surpassed in height only a year later.

Built in just two years (1929–1931) during the Great Depression, the Empire State Building, 350 Fifth Avenue, has 102 stories and reaches a height of 1,453 feet (443 m) at its pinnacle. It was the world's tallest skyscraper for 41 years until the construction of the World Trade Center in 1972. The upper stories are floodlit at night, changing colors according to seasons and events, adding to the building's iconic status. It has two famous observation decks from which to admire the Manhattan skyline by day or night.

Rockefeller Center was also built during the Great Depression. Its centerpiece is the elegant G. E. Building at 30 Rockefeller Plaza, where the three-tiered Top of the Rock observation deck provides more fine panoramas of the city, including the only public view of Central Park from above. From this vantage point 70 stories high, you can take in important skyscrapers of the modern era, from Ludwig Mies van der Rohe and Philip Johnson's Seagram Building (375 Park Avenue) to the postmodern Citygroup Center (153 E. Fifty-third Street).

-> FACT FILE

POPULATION 8.25 million New York City, 1.6 million Manhattan.

CLIMATE Ranges from hot and humid (82°F/28°C and above) in summer to subfreezing temperatures and occasional snowfall in winter.

WHAT TO TAKE Good walking shoes and a jacket for rainy days or chilly nights. Casual but smart attire is appropriate for most occasions. Don't overpack–save room for the city's great shopping bargains.

BEST TIME Weather is best in the fall, with warm temperatures well into October. Spring is variable, with more chance of showers. Post-Christmas and midsummer sales are also a draw.

NEAREST AIRPORTS International flights arrive at John F. Kennedy (JFK) airport in Queens and Liberty International Airport in Newark, New Jersey. Both are about 15 miles (24 km) from the city. LaGuardia Airport in Queens handles domestic flights.

ACCOMMODATIONS New York hotels are expensive in all categories; consider booking a package deal.

WHAT TO DO The best way to see the Manhattan skyline is on a Circle Line sightseeing cruise around the island and New York Harbor. For details visit *www.circleline42. com*. The Skyscraper Museum, 39 Battery Place, *www.skyscraper.org*, has a range of exhibits on Manhattan's high-rise heritage.

The view from the observation deck of the Empire State Building (2) sweeps across the skyscraper tops of Manhattan.

ALASKA'S MAJESTIC MOUNTAINS

Take to the skies and soar among the peaks of the breathtaking Alaska Range, landing on the snowpacked glaciers of North America's highest mountain—Mount McKinley.

ALASKA IS A LAND OF THE GIANTS. The largest state in the U.S., it covers 656,425 square miles (1,700,075 sq km), and if you split it in half it would still make up the two largest states in the country. Alaska's 39 mountain ranges contain 17 of the 20 highest peaks in the country. This includes Mount McKinley (Denali), which at 20,320 feet (6,194 m) is North America's highest mountain. Eighteen other Alaskan peaks top 14,000 feet (4,267 m).

The five largest U.S. national parks are in Alaska. These parks contain some of North America's biggest animals: moose, caribou, polar and grizzly bears, and the giant Kodiak brown bear. Even the vegetables are huge—a prize-winning cabbage at the 2000 Alaska State Fair measured 6 feet (1.8 m) wide and 4 feet (1.2 m) high and weighed over 105 pounds (48 kg). No wonder this vast state is nicknamed "The Last Frontier."

Outside of the Alaskan capital, Juneau, some of the first things you will encounter are beavers and otters. These are not furry, river-dwelling animals but nicknames for the small airplanes that are the main mode of transportation for much of the state. While the Lower 48 (as the rest of the country is called) cherish their SUVs, up here plane culture thrives. Due to Alaska's huge distances and remote settlements, for many residents it is the only way to get around. For visitors, it can provide the thrill of a lifetime.

Flightseeing Thrills
Talkeetna is a drive of about 110 miles (177 km) north of Anchorage, and one of the main southern gateways

into Denali National Park. It is the perfect rustic community you imagine backwoods Alaska to be, with a café, a few stores, bars where locals hang out with visiting mountaineers and hikers, a historic downtown made up of buildings from the early 1900s, and an annual Moose Dropping Festival.

Talkeetna is also the takeoff point for an exciting flightseeing trip over the mountains of Denali National Park culminating in landing on a glacier on the slopes of Mount McKinley itself. You take off from Talkeetna on wheels, but land on skis that drop down from the plane to allow for a slightly bumpy and slithery landing on ice and snow. In between, the pilot swoops the beaver past snow-covered peaks for an awesome bird's-eye view of the landscape, descending to fly through gorges and giving you a close-up look at the glaciers below.

The thrills only get better as the skis come down and you slide to a halt and step out onto the Ruth Glacier, on top of the deepest gorge in North America. The air up here bites at your nose and cheeks, and the thousands of years of glacial ice force the cold up through the soles of even the thickest boots. The Ruth Glacier is estimated to be about 3,800 feet (1,158 m) thick, and it is cradled in the Great Gorge. Without Ruth's presence the gorge, at some 9,000 feet (2,743 m) deep, would dwarf even the Grand Canyon, a thought that is hard to comprehend as you stand in silence and gaze around, awed by the summit of Mount McKinley peeking through the clouds above. It must be a similar experience to landing on the moon, for here there is the sound of silence and the eerie feeling of being in an alien landscape.

The full moon shines over the shoulder of Mount McKinley, mirrored in Reflection Lake in Denali National Park (1).

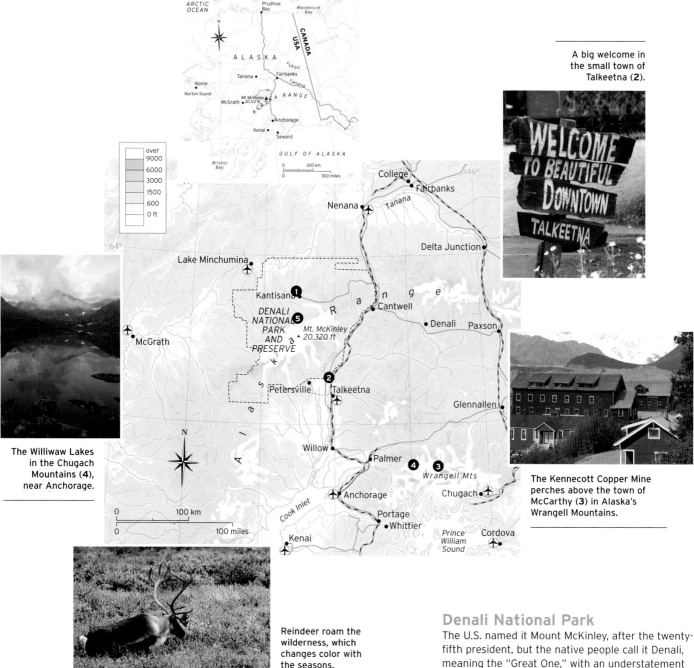

A big welcome in the small town of Talkeetna (**2**).

The Williwaw Lakes in the Chugach Mountains (**4**), near Anchorage.

The Kennecott Copper Mine perches above the town of McCarthy (**3**) in Alaska's Wrangell Mountains.

Reindeer roam the wilderness, which changes color with the seasons.

-> Up, Up, and Away

On the outskirts of Anchorage, Lake Hood is the world's busiest seaplane base. On a peak summer's day it averages 800 takeoffs and landings. The annual average from late spring to early fall—when the lake is not frozen over—is 90,000. Alaska has six times as many pilots and 16 times as many airplanes per capita as the rest of the country.

Denali National Park

The U.S. named it Mount McKinley, after the twenty-fifth president, but the native people call it Denali, meaning the "Great One," with an understatement that speaks with respect. The national park in which it stands is the most famous in Alaska, and covers an area of 9,492 square miles (24,583 sq km), an area almost as big as the state of Vermont. Among its spectacular landscapes are vast, sweeping expanses of tundra, set against the majestic Alaska Range.

There is just one road into the park, open only to park shuttles. By keeping it wild you are more likely to see its wildlife: Dall sheep, moose, herds of caribou, the golden eagles soaring and silhouetted against a sky of the deepest blue. There are bears here too, both black bears and grizzlies, but unlike in some of the national parks in the Lower 48, the bears here are not used to humans. They need to be respected and treated with caution. If startled or threatened they can kill, and have done so.

Flightseeing is one of the main attractions of the area, here seen heading toward Mount McKinley (5).

->FACT FILE

So too has Mount McKinley, where altitude sickness sometimes takes people unawares. In this northerly latitude the air is thinner, and on McKinley's steep slopes this, combined with the altitude and the exertion, can quickly cause problems. The sheer bulk and size of the mountain also surprises. Comparing the Alaskan landscape to the Himalayas is not fanciful, as McKinley rises higher to the eye than Mount Everest. From the plateau on which it stands, McKinley climbs over 18,000 feet (5,486 m) into the sky to reach its final height, but Everest is only about 12,000 feet (3,658 m) from base to summit.

Alaska constantly impresses, and surprises. It truly has one of the greatest landscapes in the world. But to fully experience its magnificence, you have to take to the skies.

CLIMATE The climate in the Denali National Park is, like most of Alaska, one of extremes. The summers are short but temperatures can reach the 70sºF (low 20sºC) in summer, and well below 0ºF (-18ºC) in winter. The average daily temperature in Talkeetna in January is 10ºF (-12ºC). Rain falls steadily all year, mostly from June to October. The Denali National Park also straddles the Alaskan Range of mountains, and on the north side it is drier but with warmer summers and colder winters, while to the south it is wetter but with less extremes.

WHAT TO TAKE Layers of clothing, sun protection, sturdy shoes or hiking boots, a willingness to rough it a little.

BEST TIME Spring and fall are good times, when there is less rain than in summer but you avoid the bitter winter temperatures.

NEAREST AIRPORTS There is a small airport in Talkeetna for local flights; the nearest international airport is at Anchorage, 110 miles (177 km) to the south.

ACCOMMODATIONS There are hotels, wilderness lodges, and campgrounds around the park; the main centers are Talkeetna, Healy, and the area known as Glitter Gulch to the north of the park. The choice is not great, though, and it is wise to book ahead.

PARK ENTRANCE An entrance fee per vehicle is valid for seven days. Annual passes good at all national parks are also available.

THE ALASKA HIGHWAY

A controversial wartime road became a legendary highway of adventure through one of the last great wilderness regions of North America.

An intense display of the Northern Lights casts an eerie glow over Whitehorse (1) in the Yukon Territory.

TO RESIDENTS OF THE LOWER 48, the Alaska Highway holds the promise of adventure. It leads through some of the last places on the continent that are still wild, still remote, and still teeming with a landscape that disappeared south of the Canadian border a century ago. Conceived during the Great Depression and built during World War II, the construction of this great wilderness road was one of the great engineering feats of all time.

The Alaska Highway is 1,422 miles (2,288 km) long. The majority of the road runs through Canada; only 15 percent of it is in Alaska itself. It begins in Dawson Creek in northern British Columbia as Highway 97 and meanders 613 miles (987 km) northwest into the Yukon Territory, where it becomes Highway 1. After crossing several hundred miles of the southern Yukon, it reaches the border at Port Alcan, entering Alaska at Historical Mile 1221.8. Here it becomes Highway 2 for the final

200 miles (322 km) to its official end at Delta Junction. Highway 2 then joins the Richardson Highway and carries on for another 98 miles (158 km) to Fairbanks.

To drive the Alaska Highway is to realize just how far away Alaska is. Between Edmonton and Fairbanks, there are no large cities for some 1,400 miles (2,253 km). The land becomes wilder and the towns become smaller the further north you go. Alaska was not yet a state when the road was built. It was America's last frontier. Many of its settlements could only be reached on foot, in a canoe, or by dog sled. Its people, native and white alike, lived off the land.

Then, in 1942, 11,000 U.S. soldiers and 7,500 civilian workers poured into this northern wilderness. In just eight months they built the highway, connecting Alaska to the Lower 48 and ending its isolation. In doing so, they changed forever the life of the people in small communities along the way.

From Skyway to Highway

Routes for an overland road to Alaska had been surveyed in the 1930s, but nothing ever came of the plans until the bombing of Pearl Harbor in December 1941 launched the U.S. into World War II. As Japan took control of the Pacific, many people feared Alaska would become the next target. Keeping the supply lines open became a matter of military urgency. Canada granted right-of-way, the U.S. paid for construction and maintenance of the highway, with Canada regaining control of its sections after the war. But to the chagrin of residents in the Pacific Northwest, the military chose a longer route much further east, away from the ports and through country that had never even been surveyed. Why? Their primary aim was to resupply a series of isolated airfields that had been established before the war, and their chosen route connected this Alaska skyway.

Construction began in March 1942. Seven engineering regiments along with teams of civilian workers started at either end and points in between. Time was of the essence, and the initial road was not graded or even well planned, often following rivers or old Indian trails. Workers bushwhacked and bulldozed their way through

-> FACT FILE

CLIMATE Varies along the length of the highway. In general, summers are mild with temperatures ranging from 50°F (10°C) into the 70s°F (low 20s°C). Much of the region receives high rainfall. Anchorage is rainiest in August-September, Fairbanks in July-August, Juneau in September-October. Winters are cold and snowy with temperatures well below freezing.

WHAT TO TAKE Pack for variable weather, from hot and sunny to cold and rainy. Good rain gear and waterproof footwear is essential, and warm clothing for cold nights. Pack food, water, and emergency supplies as there are long wilderness stretches of the road.

BEST TIME Most people travel June-August, when the weather is warmer (though wetter) and there are long hours of daylight. Spring and fall often bring beautiful clear, sunny days, though the weather can be variable. Accommodation and campgrounds are less busy, too. Driving is more hazardous in winter and there can be as little as three hours of daylight in the north.

NEAREST AIRPORTS Anchorage International Airport is the nearest to the Alaska Highway. The international airports at Edmonton and Vancouver are on the east and west access routes to the start of the highway at Dawson Creek, where there is also a regional airport.

ACCOMMODATIONS There are hotels, motels, and campgrounds in towns all along the Alaska Highway. These can fill up during the busy summer season, so it is wise to call ahead and reserve. Some businesses operate seasonally.

TRAVEL TIP *The Milepost* is the bible of North Country travel and nearly as thick. Published annually, it has mile-by-mile logs of the Alaska Highway and other major routes. A valuable trip planner.

A traveler on the Alaska Highway leaves the St. Elias Mountains behind as the road enters Kluane National Park (**2**).

6 miles (10 km) of wilderness a day. They battled great hardships, from mosquitoes and black flies to subzero temperatures to melting permafrost that turned the ground to ditches of mud.

By late fall they had opened the pioneer road and the Alaska Highway was officially dedicated in November 1942. Another year was spent improving and rebuilding much of this first rough road into a usable highway.

Driving the Highway

After the war, the highway, which had cost $140 million, remained closed to tourists until 1948. The military warned of its rough conditions, but by then the allure of the far North had captured people's imagination and thousands embarked on the road trip of a lifetime.

Driving the Alaska Highway is still a great adventure. Just getting to its start at Dawson Creek is a week-long, 2,300-mile (3,701-km) journey from Seattle. Though the two-lane highway is now surfaced in asphalt, there are rough patches, frost heaves, and gravel sections; repairs are ongoing in this harsh climate. There are long stretches of wilderness, and towns on a map often turn out to be little more than pit stops for food and gas. It is a road to take your time on, a place where you should be prepared for anything.

The mileposts along the highway were put up in the 1940s to help guide travelers, and they became a tradition, often used as mailing addresses and location points. But since numerous repairs and improvements have altered the highway over the years, they no longer represent an accurate driving distance. Matters were further complicated in the 1970s, when Canada went metric and the mileposts were changed to kilometerposts. The term "historic milepost" is often used to avoid confusion.

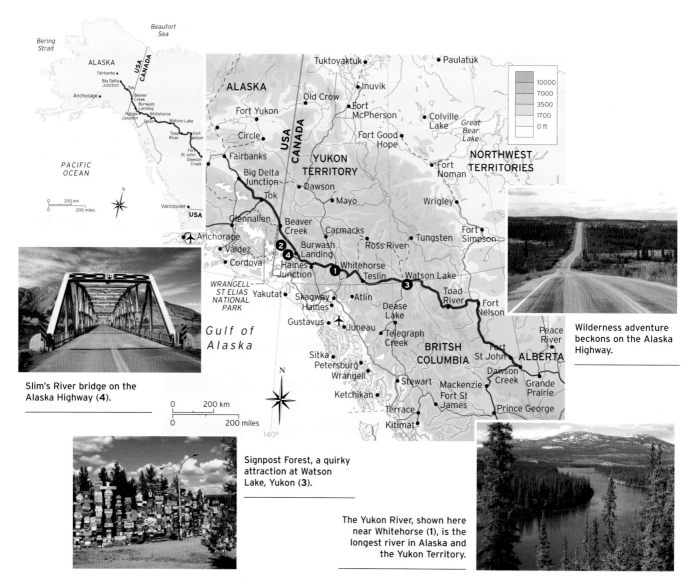

Slim's River bridge on the Alaska Highway (4).

Wilderness adventure beckons on the Alaska Highway.

Signpost Forest, a quirky attraction at Watson Lake, Yukon (3).

The Yukon River, shown here near Whitehorse (1), is the longest river in Alaska and the Yukon Territory.

The main towns along the way include Dawson Creek, Fort St. John, Fort Nelson, Watson Lake, Whitehorse, Haines Junction, Tok, and Delta Junction. They are pleasant towns, service centers, and gateways into the backcountry; there is not a lot of sightseeing. That is not the point of the Alaska Highway. The biggest sight is the road itself. Watch out for wildlife—you are likely to see bears, moose, and bison grazing along the highway. Contemplate this vast and abundant landscape. Get out of the car—often—to breathe in the crisp, clean air. Listen to the magnificent silence. Although much has changed, much remains timeless on this great wilderness road.

Watson Lake, on the outskirts of its namesake town, is a popular recreation spot along the Alaska Highway (**3**).

-> Naming the Highway

Some people refer to the highway as the ALCAN, an acronym used by the military for the pioneer road. But the term (short for Alaska-Canada) was unpopular with northerners, who resented the military restrictions and bureaucracy. Many alternatives, ranging from the Canalaska to the Laskadian Highway, were proposed. Americans were sensitive to the fact that most of the highway lies in Canada. But everyone recognized the established tradition of naming roads for their destination, rather than the land through which they passed. In 1943, both the United States and Canada officially named the road the Alaska Highway.

ALASKA'S MIGHTY GLACIERS

The ice age still reigns in Alaska. The sight and sound of its massive glaciers crashing into the sea is awesome to behold.

NEARLY EVERY ROAD IN ALASKA could be considered a scenic byway, such is the endless beauty of the state's majestic mountains, shoreline, and river valleys. But the official scenic byway, the northernmost in America, is the Seward Highway, which runs 127 miles (204 km) from Anchorage, south to Seward on the Kenai Peninsula. This road is also the quickest and easiest way to see Alaska's incredible glaciers—a highlight of a visit to the state.

Glaciers carved Alaska's most familiar landscapes and seascapes. The deep, narrow coastal fjords, now filled with seawater, and the steep-sided islands of the Gulf of Alaska, inland canyons, and mountain valleys are all glacier-born. An estimated 100,000 glaciers exist in Alaska today, covering nearly 30,000 square miles (77,697 sq km), or about 5 percent of the state. Many are fed by vast ice fields such as the Bagley Icefield in Wrangell-St. Elias National Park, the largest subpolar ice field in North America.

Bagley is the starting point for the Bering Glacier, the longest in North America, which stretches over 126 miles (203 km) to the Gulf of Alaska. It also feeds the massive Malaspina Glacier, which measures 40 miles (64 km) wide and 28 miles (45 km) long. Fanning out across 1,500 square miles (3,885 sq km) of a broad plain, this glacier is so large it can be seen in its entirety only from space.

The most exciting glaciers are tidewater glaciers, which flow into the sea. As they reach the water, enormous chunks of ice break off from the glacier wall and plunge into the sea, forming icebergs. This is known as calving. The Hubbard Glacier, which begins in Canada and flows 76 miles (122 km) to Alaska's Yakutat Bay, is the largest tidewater glacier on the continent. It is one of the few glaciers that is advancing, rather than retreating, with a calving face over 6 miles (10 km) across. At times it has blocked the outlet of Russell Fjord, turning it into a lake.

Kenai Fjords National Park

Heading south from Anchorage, the Seward Highway (Highway 1) winds around the Turnagain Arm, a long, narrow tidal inlet. Even on a cloudy day it is atmospheric, with swirling waters, rippled gray mudflats, and stunning views across to the

-> FACT FILE

CLIMATE The region has a temperate maritime climate. Summer highs average 50-60ºF (10-15ºC). Even in summer, temperatures are cool on the water, especially at the glaciers where they average 40ºF (4ºC). The region receives high amounts of rain and snow that in turn produce the many large glaciers in this area.

WHAT TO TAKE Good rain gear is essential. Dress in layers; for cruises, bring warm clothes, a hat, gloves, and rainproof jacket for the outside deck, as well as sunglasses and sun cream for sunny days. Wear good walking shoes with rubber soles.

BEST TIME April-June are usually the driest months at Glacier Bay. September and October are the wettest. Summer sees long hours of daylight; there can be long periods of continuous rain. In winter the roads may be closed due to heavy snowfall.

NEAREST AIRPORTS Anchorage is the main international airport.

ACCOMMODATIONS Anchorage has the widest range of accommodations, but there are hotels and guesthouses in Seward and other towns along the Seward Highway, and lodges in Barlett Cove and Gustavus at Glacier Bay.

PARK ENTRANCE There are no entrance fees for visitors at either national park.

The mighty glaciers that reach down to the shoreline in Glacier Bay National Park (1) dwarf even a large cruise ship.

Ships sailing into Glacier Bay National Park (1) enjoy this close-up view of the Margerie Glacier.

Tidewater glaciers calve into the icy waters of Prince William Sound (2).

Glacier-carved mountains line the Seward Highway (3), south of Anchorage.

–> Rivers of Ice

What creates these great rivers of ice? Glaciers form in areas that have high snowfall in winter and cool temperatures in summer, so that snowfall accumulates faster than it can melt. As the snow builds up, the underlying layers become compressed. Eventually the pressure produces a solid mass of ice. When it reaches a critical thickness, the force of gravity causes the glacier to move slowly, or "flow." Glaciers often appear blue because the ice absorbs all the other colors of the spectrum, but reflects the blue.

mountains beyond. You can often spot beluga whales feeding on salmon in the inlet from Beluga Point. As you round the tip of the Arm and begin climbing the 1,000-foot (305-m) Turnagain Pass, you can see the first of many glaciers in the distance, their icy blue fingers spilling down the mountain crevasses. At the end of the highway, the small town of Seward sits on the edge of the Kenai Fjords National Park. From here you can take cruises into the park's glacier-lined bays.

Dall sheep and mountain goats perch on the cliffs, colonies of steller sea lions sun themselves on the rocks, while in the waters there are harbor seals, sea otters, orcas (killer whales), and playful porpoises who race alongside the boat. Finally, you come face to face with a stunning tidewater glacier.

As you sail into the fjord, you are approaching a living, breathing white giant. The captain cuts the engine—not too close—for glaciers can calve underwater, sending icebergs bursting up through the surface. As you stand on the outer deck, the boat bobbing silently as chunks of ice float eerily past, you hear a low groaning like a voice from another world. Suddenly a gunshot crack shatters the air, and with a thunderous roar a block of ice as big as a house crashes into the sea. To watch this awesome spectacle in a remote and timeless land is to know the raw power of the earth.

Before or after your trip, pay a visit to the Alaska SeaLife Center. Dedicated to research

The Hubbard Glacier, North America's largest tidewater glacier, crashes into the sea at Disenchantment Bay (**4**).

and the rehabilitation of marine animals, it has underwater viewing galleries where you can watch sea lions, giant Pacific octopuses, and seabirds diving for food. It is a wonderful place to learn about the amazing creatures you can see along the stunning coastline.

Prince William Sound and Glacier Bay

A side road from the Seward Highway runs southeast to Whittier, on the shores of Prince William Sound. The town is an embarkation point for glacier cruises into Prince William Sound, and ferries across to Valdez. Dozens of tidewater glaciers calve into these waters. The largest is the Columbia Glacier, flowing more than 40 miles (64 km) down from the Chugach Mountains and filling the bay with huge bergs of ice. The sound is home to humpback and killer whales, Dall's porpoises, sea lions, and harbor seals.

Glacier Bay National Park can be reached only by boat or seaplane. It is a popular spot for cruise ships sailing up the Inside Passage along Alaska's long southeastern shore. But 250 years ago, this bay did not even exist. It was completely filled by the Grand Pacific Glacier, thousands of feet thick. Over this short—in glacial terms—space of time, the glacier calved enormous quantities of ice, leaving a 65-mile (105-km) long fjord in its wake. The surrounding national park is one of the largest internationally protected biosphere reserves and a UNESCO World Heritage Site.

Today, 16 tidewater glaciers flow into the icy fjords of Glacier Bay from the soaring coastal mountains of the Fairweather Range. One is named for the naturalist John Muir, who visited by canoe in 1879. He was among the first to notice the rapid retreat of these glaciers. Their prodigious calving is creating not only a spectacular landscape, but a laboratory in which to observe the remarkable life cycle of the glacial world.

NIAGARA FALLS

For nearly two centuries, the romantic beauty of this spectacular trio of waterfalls on the U.S.-Canadian border has attracted dreamers, daredevils, and honeymooning couples.

Visitors are in for a drenching on the popular Cave of the Winds tour, which leads to the Hurricane Deck at the base of Bridal Veil Falls (1).

WELL BEFORE YOU SEE THEM, you will hear their roar. The mist on your face adds a tingle of excitement as you approach the viewpoint overlooking one of the most famous beauty spots in North America–Niagara Falls. Straddling the border between Canada and the United States, the Niagara River cuts a channel across a strip of land called the Niagara Escarpment, connecting Lake Erie and Lake Ontario. About midway along, it plunges over the falls in a thundering torrent, sending up clouds of white-water foam and spray as it drops into the 7-mile (11-km) long Niagara Gorge.

Niagara Falls comprises three separate cataracts. Like the Great Lakes themselves, they were formed by ice-age glaciers and the subsequent process of erosion as the river began pouring over the escarpment around 12,000 years ago. The river split into two channels around the point now known as Goat Island. On the eastern side it formed the American Falls, 180 feet (55 m) high and 1,060 feet (323 m) wide, and the smaller Bridal Veil Falls. On the western side the river angled ninety degrees to form the even more dramatic Horseshoe Falls, 170 feet (52 m) high and 2,200 feet (671 m) wide, which captures 90 percent of the flow.

These magnificent waterfalls are among the largest in the world. Their volume and breadth make them the most powerful on the continent. More than 6 million cubic feet (169,860 cu m) of water flows over the edge of the falls every minute during peak viewing hours. This figure is even more incredible when you realize that this is only half of the river's actual flow; the rest is diverted to hydroelectric power plants.

Visiting the Falls

The falls face toward Canada, so you will get the most panoramic view from the Canadian side. The best place to see them is from the platforms in Queen Victoria Park, landscaped with lovely gardens. The observation decks of the Minolta Tower and the higher Skylon Tower offer impressive views from above. To get up close to the thundering power of the falls, take a *Maid of the Mist* tour boat. Journey Behind the Falls is an attraction that lets you walk behind the torrent of Horseshoe Falls in a series of tunnels.

Rainbow Bridge connects the Canadian and American sides of the falls. Downstream, alongside the Whirlpool, there are more attractions, including the Great Gorge Adventure, with a tunnel leading to a boardwalk for a close-up view of the Whirlpool Rapids. You can also ride across the river in the Whirlpool Aero Car, an antique cable car that affords an overhead view of the swirling waters.

On the American side, most of the falls are contained within Niagara Falls State Park. This is the oldest state park in the country, created as the Niagara Reservation in 1885 after lobbying to preserve the area. The Free Niagara conservation movement was led by such figures as Frederick Law Olmsted, designer of New York's Central Park, and the architect Henry Hobson Richardson.

Prospect Point, at the edge of the American Falls, is the best viewpoint. It is especially delightful mid-morning when rainbows sometimes arc across the mist. The Observation Tower alongside takes you 200 feet (61 m) above the falls in glass-sided elevators for more impressive views. Far below you will see the *Maid of the Mist* bobbing around in the churning waters. These tour boats, which have been operating since 1846, are the most thrilling way to see the waterfalls as they take you right up to the base, sometimes close enough to reach out and touch the cascade. Stand on deck for a drenching but exhilarating experience.

There are more great views from Goat Island, which lies above the falls. From here the Cave of the Winds tour takes you down to the base of Bridal Veil Falls.

Over the Falls

Niagara Falls was America's first big tourist attraction, and it was long ago dubbed the Honeymoon Capital of the World. One of the earliest honeymooners was Napoleon Bonaparte's brother, Jérôme, who came here with his American bride from New Orleans in 1804. Some say it is the ions generated by the surging waters that give couples that elated feeling, and tens of thousands check it out each year.

Niagara Falls has also attracted its share of daredevils. The first on record was Sam Patch, who jumped into the gorge below the falls in 1829; the self-proclaimed "total idiot" survived. Tightrope

An aerial view of the American Falls (**2**, foreground) and adjacent Bridal Veil Falls (background).

-> FACT FILE

CLIMATE Average high temperatures in summer are 77ºF (25ºC). Winter high temperatures (November-March) average 21-39ºF (-6-4ºC) with much snowfall. The falls affect local weather conditions.

WHAT TO TAKE Waterproof jacket or poncho, dry clothes and footwear, warm clothing as breezes near the falls can be chilly.

BEST TIME Summer is the warmest and sunniest time, when you can also visit the falls in the evening. From mid-March-December the falls are illuminated at night. Spring and fall are less crowded, but temperatures can be chilly in April and October. Winter is cold and snowy, but the frost and ice can make for a magical scene.

NEAREST AIRPORTS Buffalo International Airport on the New York Side is 24 miles (39 km) away. Hamilton International Airport and Toronto International Airport on the Canadian side are 50 miles (80 km) and 81 miles (130 km) away respectively.

ACCOMMODATIONS There is a range in all price categories in the city of Niagara Falls, including bed and breakfast places, historical inns, and some overlooking the falls.

CROSSING THE BORDER American and Canadian citizens should carry proof of citizenship if they wish to visit both sides of the falls. A valid passport is the best form of identity. Requirements vary for citizens of other countries. Regulations change, so check the situation before you go to ensure you have the right documents with you.

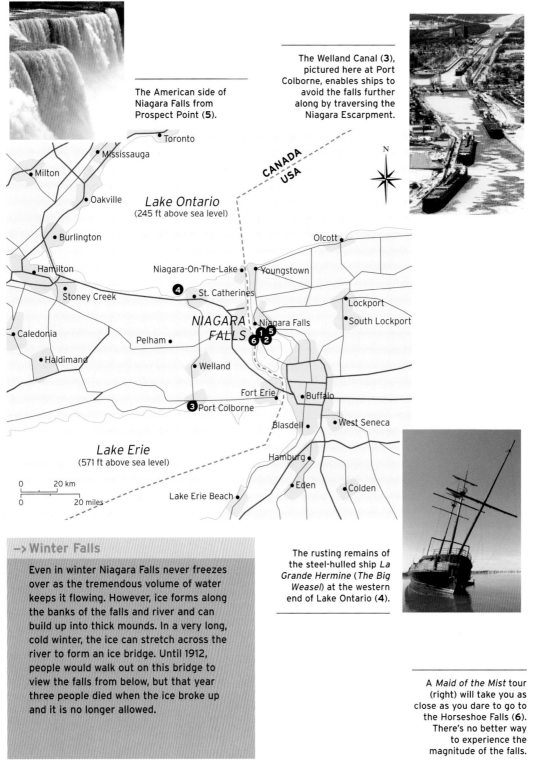

The American side of Niagara Falls from Prospect Point (**5**).

The Welland Canal (**3**), pictured here at Port Colborne, enables ships to avoid the falls further along by traversing the Niagara Escarpment.

Toronto
Mississauga
Milton
Oakville
Lake Ontario
(245 ft above sea level)
Burlington
Olcott
Hamilton
Niagara-On-The-Lake
Youngstown
Stoney Creek
❹ St. Catherines
Lockport
NIAGARA FALLS
Niagara Falls
South Lockport
Caledonia
❶❺
Pelham
❻❷
Haldimand
Welland
Fort Erie
Buffalo
❸ Port Colborne
Blasdell
West Seneca
Lake Erie
(571 ft above sea level)
Hamburg
0   20 km
0   20 miles
Eden
Colden
Lake Erie Beach

CANADA
USA

N

→ Winter Falls

Even in winter Niagara Falls never freezes over as the tremendous volume of water keeps it flowing. However, ice forms along the banks of the falls and river and can build up into thick mounds. In a very long, cold winter, the ice can stretch across the river to form an ice bridge. Until 1912, people would walk out on this bridge to view the falls from below, but that year three people died when the ice broke up and it is no longer allowed.

The rusting remains of the steel-hulled ship *La Grande Hermine* (*The Big Weasel*) at the western end of Lake Ontario (**4**).

A *Maid of the Mist* tour (right) will take you as close as you dare to go to the Horseshoe Falls (**6**). There's no better way to experience the magnitude of the falls.

walker Jean François Gravelet, known as Blondin, made the first of several crossings over the gorge in 1859, near the present Rainbow Bridge. He competed with Signor Fanini, a.k.a. William Hunt, in performing ever more daring stunts here.

The first person to go over the falls in a barrel was Annie Edson Taylor, a 63-year-old schoolteacher, who did it as a publicity stunt in 1901. She emerged in one piece, saying "No one should ever try that again." Since then at least 14 people failed to heed her warning and threw themselves over the falls in various contraptions. Some did not make it out alive. Most of those who did were hit with fines, or even jail time.

YOSEMITE NATIONAL PARK

With its awesome peaks, ancient trees, and the highest waterfall in North America, nowhere outshines Yosemite for sheer mountain majesty.

The writings of environmentalist John Muir (1838-1914) still inspire nature lovers to explore and protect the wilderness.

"THE CLEAREST WAY INTO THE UNIVERSE is through a forest wilderness," wrote the conservationist John Muir. And no wilderness is more majestic than Yosemite National Park in California's Sierra Nevada Mountains. Muir likened Yosemite to a mountain mansion in which, "Nature had gathered her choicest treasures, to draw her lovers into close and confiding communion with her." These treasures include plunging cascades, clear lakes, scenic rivers, wildflower meadows, towering peaks, stunning rock monoliths, and groves of giant sequoias.

Native Americans had lived peacefully in the Yosemite Valley for thousands of years, but it was only discovered by white men in 1851, when a volunteer militia chased a band of Ahwahneechee Indians into their refuge here. Muir, a Scotsman, first came here soon after arriving in San Francisco in 1868. Four years earlier, President Lincoln had signed the Yosemite Grant, which was the first federal legislation to set aside parkland for preservation and public use. This paved the way for the creation of the first U.S. national park–Yellowstone (see pages 88-91)–in 1872. Muir continued to lobby for further protection for Yosemite, and it became the third U.S. national park in 1890.

Yosemite could not have had a finer champion than Muir. A naturalist, writer, scientist, explorer, and environmentalist, he hiked through the Sierra Nevada for weeks at a time, seeking to experience the raw power of nature. He campaigned hard to save Yosemite from development, and inspired millions with the sense of well-being and spirituality he found in the mountains and forests. Lauded as the Father of our National Parks, Muir also cofounded the Sierra Club, a leading environmental organization that continues to protect natural resources.

Today Yosemite National Park encompasses nearly 1,200 square miles (3,108 sq km) and is a World Heritage Site. Nearly 95 percent is designated wilderness, and much of the park is accessible only on foot. This is a good thing, for around 3.5 million visitors descend on the park each year, seeking the inspiration and natural bliss enjoyed by Muir and numerous artists, writers, and photographers such as Albert Bierstadt, Wallace

Stegner, and Ansel Adams. To find spiritual bliss during high season you might have to get away from the cars and crowds and take to the hiking trails that offer a splendid escape. Use the park's shuttle buses to avoid the traffic jams on the few main roads.

Exploring the Valley

The heart of the park is the Yosemite Valley. Although it is just 7 miles (11 km) long and 1 mile (1.6 km) wide, it contains the park's most famous landmarks and beauty spots. Muir was the first to realize that the valley's spectacular

–> FACT FILE

CLIMATE Temperatures vary according to elevation; the high country is generally 10-20ºF (6-11ºC) lower than those in the valley. Summer highs in the valley average 90ºF (32ºC) in July-August. Winters are mild with average highs reaching 48ºF (9ºC) in the valley in December-January. There is heavy snowfall in the high country. Winter also sees the most rain in the valley, from 5 ½-6 ¼ inches (14-15.7 cm) per month.

WHAT TO TAKE Jacket or poncho for waterfalls as well as showers; warm clothes for cool nights and high elevations; hiking boots or sturdy shoes with good grip; sunscreen; insect repellent.

BEST TIME Each season has its high points: in spring, the waterfalls are at their finest (many are down to a trickle by late summer), but roads and trails in the high country may be closed until early June due to snow. Tioga Road is open only in June-October. Summer has the warmest temperatures but largest crowds. September and October have fewer visitors and cooler temperatures for hiking, with fall colors in the valleys. High country roads are closed in winter, but the snowy scenery is magical.

NEAREST AIRPORTS The closest major airports served by international carriers are in San Francisco, Oakland, and San Jose, all about 200-250 miles (322-402 km) from Yosemite. The closest airport to the park is Fresno-Yosemite International Airport, 90 miles (145 km) southwest of Yosemite.

ACCOMMODATIONS Lodging within the park ranges from campgrounds to tent cabins to motel-grade rooms to luxury and historic hotels. All fill up quickly and you need to reserve months in advance for high season.

BEAR NECESSITIES Bears have an incredibly keen sense of smell, and they break into hundreds of cars and camps each year looking for food. Never leave food, snacks, or even scented toiletries in your car (including the trunk). Use the food storage facilities available in the parks.

PARK ENTRANCE An entrance fee per vehicle is valid for seven days. Annual passes good at all national parks are also available. Wilderness permits are required for overnight trips into the backcountry.

features were formed by glaciers. During the last ice age, enormous glaciers carved their way through these granite mountains, slicing off great slabs of rock, gouging out bowls and hanging canyons, and rounding and polishing the peaks and ridges. When the glaciers melted, they left behind this fertile valley, 4,000 feet (1,219 m) above sea level.

The Merced River runs through the center of the valley, one of the park's two designated wild and scenic rivers (the other is the Tuolumne). Entering from the west, you come to Bridalveil Falls, a lovely, almost delicate cascade that blows in the wind as

The view from Glacier Point (1) sweeps across the Yosemite Valley, taking in some of its most famous landmarks such as Half Dome (seen on the right) **(2)**.

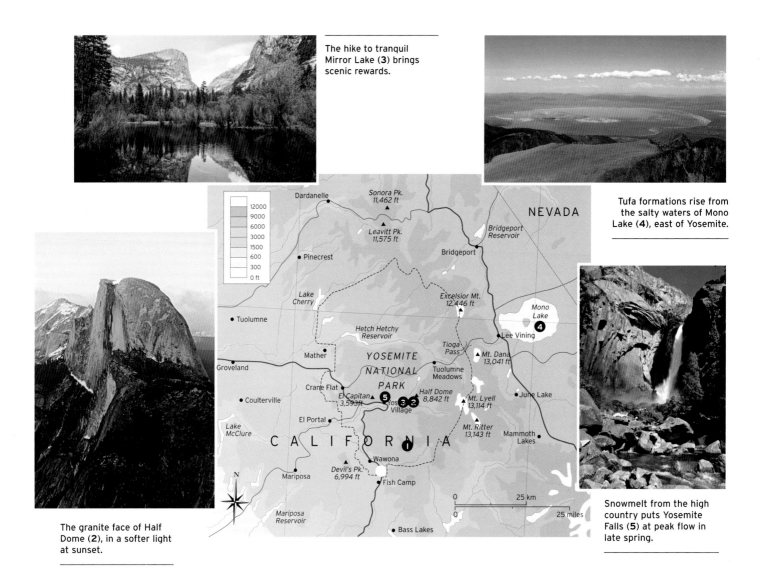

The hike to tranquil Mirror Lake (**3**) brings scenic rewards.

Tufa formations rise from the salty waters of Mono Lake (**4**), east of Yosemite.

The granite face of Half Dome (**2**), in a softer light at sunset.

Snowmelt from the high country puts Yosemite Falls (**5**) at peak flow in late spring.

it tumbles 620 feet (189 m). Opposite, the massive granite face of El Capitan, one of the largest rock monoliths in the world, rises nearly 3,600 feet (1,097 m) from the valley floor. East of the falls are the striking formations of Cathedral Rocks and Cathedral Spires.

There is a relatively easy hike to the top of the 8,122-foot (2,476-m) Sentinel Dome. The climb up Half Dome is much more arduous, but this 8,842-foot (2,695-m) summit is Yosemite's most distinctive mountain. Rivaling the granite domes are the park's magnificent waterfalls. The triple cascade that makes up Yosemite Falls is the highest waterfall in North America, measuring 2,425 feet (739 m).

Beyond the Valley

Throughout the park there are 800 miles (1,287 km) of hiking trails, leading to remote corners and stunning panoramic views. Along with the famous beauty spots, Vernal Falls, Mirror Lake, and Tuolumne Grove are popular hikes.

South of the valley, the Wawona Road leads to Tunnel View, a splendid vista that takes in Yosemite Falls, Half Dome, and El Capitan. Beyond, a winding side road leads to another fabulous overlook at Glacier Point. Muir brought Theodore Roosevelt here to show him the grandeur of Yosemite. Near the southern entrance is the Mariposa Grove, the largest of the park's three groves of giant sequoias. Among its 500 or so trees is the Grizzly Giant, with a 92 1/2-foot (28.2-m) girth. More than 2,700 years old, it is one of the oldest trees on Earth.

Yosemite's highest peaks, some topping 13,000 feet (3,962 m), lie further north and east. Tioga Road, open only in summer and fall, is a breathtaking drive through the high country.

Tuolumne Meadows is the highlight in summer, with its subalpine landscape of thick grasses and bright wildflowers. From here numerous trails lead into glorious backcountry.

Yosemite was named after the Native American word for grizzly bear, and while these giants have long since vanished, their cousins, the black bears (which are often brown), are prevalent in the park. You may also spot mule deer, bobcats, coyotes, marmots, pikas, birds of prey, and some of the park's 300 other bird species. Amid the beauty of Yosemite you may wish that you, like they, could call the park home.

–> The Big Trees

Yosemite's giant sequoias are the largest living things on earth. The western slopes of the Sierra Nevada, between 5,000 and 7,000 feet (1,524 and 2,134 m) in elevation, are the only place where they grow naturally. Though the coastal redwood trees grow taller, the huge girth of the sequoias gives them greater volume. The world's biggest sequoia is the General Sherman tree, soaring 274.9 feet (83.8 m) high with a circumference of 102.6 feet (31.3 m). It stands south of Yosemite in Sequoia National Park, which became the country's second national park one month before Yosemite in 1890.

Visiting the giant sequoia trees in Mariposa Grove (**6**) or nearby Sequoia National Park is like entering the land of the giants.

YELLOWSTONE NATIONAL PARK

Early explorers called Yellowstone "the place where hell bubbles up," but volcanic activity created a heavenly domain in the world's first national park.

Descendants of America's last wild bison herd graze in Yellowstone's grasslands.

EVERY NINETY-ONE MINUTES (give or take) the show begins. A few small jets splash through a crusty cone in the ground. Soon they erupt into a boiling fountain of water and steam, spouting up to 184 feet (56 m)—higher than Niagara Falls. During the next two-five minutes, Old Faithful will expel up to 8,400 gallons (38,178 L) of scalding water, which has been superheated by molten rock 2 miles (3.2 km) below the surface. Then the world's most famous geyser retreats back underground to the silent applause of the awestruck crowd.

Old Faithful is the star attraction of Yellowstone National Park, which covers 3,472 square miles (8,992 sq km) in the northwest corner of Wyoming and spilling over into Montana. There is no other place quite like it in the world. Vast expanses of pristine wilderness support a wealth of wildlife, including the largest bison herd in North America. Yet it sits atop a supervolcano—a seething hot spot whose phenomenal geothermal features

remind us that it could erupt again at any time, maybe in 10 years, maybe in 10,000. Between 1,000 and 3,000 earthquakes are recorded here every year.

In the early 1800s the first white men to see Yellowstone were fur trappers and explorers such as John Colter, who called it a place of "fire and brimstone." Few people took their tales of boiling mud lakes, petrified forests, and water spouting upward seriously, but later expeditions confirmed the wonders of Yellowstone and lobbied for its protection. In 1872 it was preserved as the world's first national park.

A Primordial Landscape

Yellowstone contains more than 10,000 hydrothermal features, half of all those on earth. They are fueled by searing temperatures from the hot spot miles below ground. There are bubbling mudpots, simmering paintpots, and steaming fumaroles, sometimes accompanied

The magnificent Rocky Mountains surround the shores of Yellowstone Lake (**2**).

Old Faithful (**1**), the world's most famous geyser, puts on its show.

The Screaming Man is a natural formation found in the terraces at Mammoth Hot Springs (**3**).

Small hydrothermal pools formed the vast travertine terraces of Mammoth Hot Springs (**3**).

Morning Glory Pool (**1**) in the Upper Geyser Basin shows off Yellowstone's brilliant natural colors. It can be reached on a 1¹/₂-mile (2.4-km) walk from the Old Faithful Inn.

by the putrid smell of sulfur and noxious gases. There are hot springs edged in lurid pools of lime green, orange, yellow, and blue, with algae, bacteria, and mineral deposits responsible for the brilliant hues. Throughout the park there are extraordinary scenes of surreal beauty. To walk out along the boardwalks amid the primeval surroundings of the Grand Prismatic Spring or Porcelain Basin is an amazing feeling. It is as if you are looking back to the origins of the world.

Despite its fame, Old Faithful is not the biggest or even the most consistent geyser in the park. Yellowstone contains two-thirds of all the geysers in the world. They number over 300, and many of them can be seen in a series of geyser basins along the Firehole River north of Old Faithful. Further on, Norris Geyser Basin is the hottest geothermal area in the park. Here you will find the swirling Whirligig Geyser and the world's tallest geyser, Steamboat,

-> **Grand Teton National Park**

Directly south of Yellowstone rise the jagged peaks of the Grand Tetons, some of the most impressive on the continent. Their granite spires soar steeply up out of the flat grasslands and are reflected in clear glacial lakes along their base. This national park stretches along the range, a haven for wildlife and a paradise for high-country hikers and climbers. Jackson Hole Mountain Resort, adjacent to the park, is a prime ski area.

which spurts as high as 400 feet (122 m), though its eruptions are infrequent.

At Mammoth Hot Springs a different sort of geothermal action is at work. Here, hot springs flowing through limestone have left deposits as they hit the cooler air, creating the massive travertine terraces, another of Yellowstone's famous sights. Boardwalks lead around the terraces and to lovely Palette Springs and Canary Springs.

Rivers, Lakes, and Canyons

Resting on a high plateau in the Rocky Mountains, most of Yellowstone lies above 7,500 feet (2,286 m) in altitude. It is bordered by mountain ranges with

peaks up to 11,358 feet (3,462 m) high. The Continental Divide runs diagonally through the southern part of the park, near many of the geothermal features. But there is much more to see, from lakes, forests, grassland, and canyons to dramatic rivers and waterfalls.

When the park was founded, the hunting of large grazing animals was still rife. In 1886 the army was brought in to patrol the park and stop the slaughter. Yellowstone then became the last refuge of the buffalo, which had been wiped out on the Great Plains. Today Yellowstone is one of the best places in the country to see large animals; its herd of wild bison is 3,000 strong, and there are large herds of

Some of Yellowstone's most impressive geothermal features lie in the primeval landscape of Norris Geyser Basin (4).

elk and antelope, as well as grizzly bears, moose, bighorn sheep, and many other animals. Wolves have also been successfully returned to the park.

Yellowstone's scenery is so grand and its atmosphere (away from the crowds) so peaceful that it is easy to forget its violent beginnings, formed by the catastrophic explosion of a supervolcano some 640,000 years ago. It left the Yellowstone Caldera in its wake, 30 miles (48 km) wide, 45 miles (72 km) long, and thousands of feet deep. Yellowstone Lake fills much of the crater today and is among the world's largest high-altitude lakes.

The Grand Canyon of the Yellowstone clearly shows the volcano's handiwork. This deep gorge was carved by the Yellowstone River through layers of ancient lava flows, exposing the yellow-hued rock that inspired the park's name. Two viewpoints near Canyon Village overlook the Upper and Lower Falls plunging into the gorge. The fire lookout on Mount Washburn offers another fine panoramic vista.

Yellowstone is always crowded in high summer. The only way to escape is to get out of the car and onto the many hiking trails. Then you will discover the majesty of the natural wilderness those early explorers found here.

–> FACT FILE

CLIMATE Weather is unpredictable at any time of year due to the park's high elevation. Winters are cold with daytime temperatures ranging from 0-20ºF (-18--7ºC). Summers are mild with average daytime temperatures in the 70sºF (24ºC) or 80sºF (29ºC) at lower elevations, cool nights, and afternoon thunderstorms. Snowfall can occur in spring and fall. Average annual rainfall is 15¼ inches (39 cm), average annual snowfall is 72 inches (183 cm).

WHAT TO TAKE Rain gear and a warm jacket, even in summer; sturdy shoes or hiking boots.

BEST TIME Summer has the best weather but also the most crowds. Spring is normally rainy with snow at higher elevations, but a good time for wildlife viewing. September is a good month for wildlife and fall color. Most park roads are closed from November, reopening in April or May depending on conditions.

NEAREST AIRPORTS Yellowstone Airport in West Yellowstone is the closest to the park, with regional flights via Salt Lake City in summer. Jackson Hole Airport, 8½ miles (13.7 km) from Jackson, is inside Grand Teton National Park. Larger airports in Montana include Gallatin Field at Bozeman and Logan International Airport at Billings.

ACCOMMODATIONS The Old Faithful Inn and Lake Yellowstone Hotel offer atmospheric lodging in the park, and there are also cabins and campgrounds. More park lodging is available in Grand Teton National Park. They are often fully booked months in advance, especially in summer, so reserve as early as you can.

PARK ENTRANCE An entrance fee per vehicle is valid for seven days. Annual passes good at all national parks are also available.

CALIFORNIA DESERTS

Far from being barren wasteland, southern California's deserts contain a variety of intriguing mineral patterns and fascinating plants and wildlife.

DEATH VALLEY CONJURES UP images of cattle skulls and parched prospectors diving into a mirage pool only to find a mouthful of sand. It was named by a band of pioneers who got lost in this harsh desert on their way to the California gold fields in 1849. In fact, they all made it out alive except for one elderly man who was failing before they had even reached Death Valley. But it came to symbolize the extreme hardships of settling the West. Today, rather than scaring them off, Death Valley attracts curious travelers to its stark beauty and extraordinary natural features.

While the southern California coast is lush with palms and orange groves, inland it is a different story. The Sierra Nevada and San Bernardino mountains soak up most of the rain falling beyond. But this arid landscape still supports an amazing variety of life.

More than a thousand plant species live in Death Valley, including some not found anywhere else on earth. California's deserts have an array of spiny cacti and striking Joshua trees, while in springtime wildflowers explode into brief, but brilliant bloom. These plants have found a variety of ways to adapt to this environment. Most wildlife is nocturnal and therefore hard to see, but there are coyotes, kit foxes, bobcats, owls, peregrine falcons, kangaroo rats, ground squirrels, rabbits, and other small mammals. You can sometimes spot elusive desert bighorn sheep at higher elevations.

Three deserts meet in southern California—the Great Basin, the Mojave, and the Sonoran. Within their 39,000 square miles (101,000 sq km) are the hottest and driest places in the United States. In 1994 three federal parks were preserved under the California Desert Protection Act—Death Valley National Park, Joshua Tree National Park, and Mojave National Preserve.

Hottest, Driest, Lowest

Death Valley National Park covers over 5,000 square miles (12,950 sq km) of the Great Basin, a vast desert that sprawls from western Utah across Nevada to eastern California and Oregon. This valley was once a narrow, ancient sea, running 140 miles (225 km) long between two rugged mountain ranges. The sea evaporated long ago, leaving behind salt pans, briny ponds, and cracked mudflats that, along with mineral deposits spread out in alluvial fans, give the landscape its fascinating patterns and textures. Undulating sand dunes, snow-dusted peaks, ribbons of multicolored rock, and the play of shadows across the deep red and orange hues at sunset make this a place of surreal, haunting beauty.

Death Valley is regularly the hottest place in the country, with summer temperatures frequently topping 120ºF (48ºC); it reached a record high of 134ºF (56ºC) in July 1913. It is also one of the driest places on earth with less than 2 inches (5 cm) of rainfall a year, compounded by a high evaporation rate. At Badwater Basin you can stand on the lowest point in North America, 282 feet (86 m) below sea level. The park's highest point is the 11,049-foot (3,368-m) Telescope Peak in the Panamint Mountains. The vertical drop from here to Badwater Basin is twice as deep as the Grand Canyon.

The Furnace Creek Visitor Center is a good starting point for tours and information. Nearby Zabriskie Point hosts sunrise views over variegated peaks and ridges. High up in the Black Mountains, Dante's View offers a panorama across Death Valley. From here you can see the lowest (Badwater) and highest (Mount Whitney) points in the contiguous United States. Artist's Drive is one of the valley's most scenic loops.

Joshua Tree National Park (1) is named for these eerie inhabitants of the Mojave Desert, which reminded early pioneers of Biblical prophets.

Beavertail prickly pear cactus (*Opuntia basilaris*) brightens up the desert when it blooms in springtime.

Scotty's Castle (5) provides an ornate contrast to the stark landscape of Death Valley.

DEATH VALLEY
NATIONAL PARK

The beehive-shaped Wildrose Charcoal Kilns (2) once produced charcoal for ore smelters in the Panamint Range at the western edge of Death Valley National Park.

Badwater Basin (3) is as low as you can go in the continental United States.

Stovepipe Wells Dunes (4), a classic view in Death Valley National Park.

Until the 1930s, mining was the main activity and ghost towns are scattered throughout Death Valley. The main ore to come out of this region was borax, used for soap and industrial compounds. Twenty Mule Team Canyon is named for the massive wagon teams that hauled 36-ton loads across the desert. A drive through Titus Canyon passes Leadville ghost town and petroglyphs at Klare Spring. In the north of the park, Scotty's Castle is a villa built in the 1920s and looked after by a colorful prospector called Death Valley Scotty. Rangers give tours of the opulent interior. A rough dirt road leads to Racetrack, where rocks mysteriously slide of their own accord across a dry lakebed.

The Mojave Desert

Most of the 1,234 square miles (3,196 sq km) of Joshua Tree National Park is wilderness, a paradise for hikers and rock climbers. Its distinctive plants were named by pioneers, in this case a group of Utah-bound Mormons who thought the outstretched arms and beardlike tufts resembled the Old Testament prophet leading them across the desert to the promised land. These desert giants can grow to 50 feet (15 m) and live 200 years. Their habitat is the Mojave Desert, which covers most of the park.

The Mojave meets the Colorado Desert in the southeast corner of the park, and here you will see cholla and ocotillo cacti typical of that terrain. Elsewhere the park has five fan palm oases, good places for birdwatching and wildlife spotting. In addition to numerous hiking trails, there are paved and dirt roads, one of which leads to the magnificent Keys View overlook. The famous San Andreas Fault, responsible for so many of California's earthquakes, runs along the south side of the park and can be seen from here.

In between these two parks is the Mojave National Preserve, which encompasses a range of desert environments. You can climb "singing" sand dunes at Kelso Sand Dunes, one of the highest dune systems in the country, explore an eerie landscape of volcanic cinder cones, and tour Mitchell Caverns, a network of 40,000 limestone caves.

CLIMATE Average highs in December–January are around 65ºF (18ºC). In July, average highs are 115ºF (46ºC). Average annual rainfall in Death Valley is 1³/₄ inches (4.67 cm), slightly higher elsewhere.

WHAT TO TAKE Sunscreen, hat, sunglasses, lightweight clothing, jacket or sweater for cool nights; sturdy shoes or hiking boots.

BEST TIME Winter's cooler temperatures make it the best time for hiking. Spring is the most popular time to visit; if there have been sufficient winter rains, wildflowers bloom from late March to mid-May. From late October, temperatures are also pleasant and it is less crowded, apart from holiday times. From May onward, summer temperatures are extremely hot and most visitors stick to points of interest accessible by car.

NEAREST AIRPORTS Las Vegas Airport is about 150 miles (241 km) from Death Valley, about a two-hour drive. Los Angeles Airport is 140 miles (225 km) east of Joshua Tree National Park.

ACCOMMODATIONS There are several lodges and resorts within Death Valley National Park, in or near Furnace Creek and Stovepipe Wells. During high season (November–March) make reservations one month or more ahead.

PARK ENTRANCE An entrance fee per vehicle is valid for seven days. Annual passes good at all national parks are also available.

SAFETY TIPS Take plenty of water—3 gallons (13.6 L) per person per day, plus water for the car radiator.

Salt formations spread across the low-lying pools of Badwater Basin (**3**), the most visited spot in Death Valley National Park.

THE NA PALI COAST OF KAUAI

Rising steeply from the sea, the rugged, velvet green cliffs of Na Pali on the Hawaiian island of Kauai form one of North America's most scenic coastlines.

HAWAII IS FILLED WITH BEAUTIFUL scenic spots, but one place near the top of everyone's list is the Na Pali coast, along the northwest shore of Kauai. Its name in the native tongue literally means "the cliffs," and these fluted giants rise spectacularly out of the ocean from a base thousands of feet below the waves.

What makes them so striking is not simply their sheer, rugged power, standing 4,000 feet (1,219 m) high and forming a 16-mile (26-km) barrier to the inner island. It is their brilliant green color and lush hanging valleys, towering above the pristine beaches and deep blue sea, that give this remote coastline an aura of paradise lost. This photogenic coast has been a backdrop for numerous films, including *Raiders of the Lost Ark*, *Jurassic Park*, *King Kong*, and *The Thorn Birds*.

Kauai is called the Garden Isle. It is the oldest of the Hawaiian Islands, which were formed over millions of years by the build-up of lava from volcanoes erupting on the ocean floor. The surface of Kauai is thought to have emerged about 5.6 million years ago. Its mother volcano, Mount Waialeale, stands 5,148 feet (1,569 m) high at the center of the island. Even the road atlases mark this as the "world's wettest spot." Waialeale is drenched, on average, by 460 inches (1,168 cm) of precipitation each year and its crater is filled by some 30 square miles (78 sq km) of the Alakai

Swamp, an ominous place blanketed by fog, mist, and rain. But the rivers and waterfalls that pour down its sides have carved out Kauai's dramatic cliffs, canyons, and valleys, and draped the island in its verdant landscape.

Valley Dwellers

Kauai is a largely rural island, with small towns and a smaller population than the other major islands in the chain. It is thought that the Na Pali coast was the first area of Kauai to be settled by the ancient Hawaiians, who sailed 2,000 miles (3,219 km) from Polynesia in double-hulled outrigger canoes, arriving around A.D. 1200. Although these remote valleys might seem an unlikely choice in which to set up home, in fact they offered all the basic necessities—fresh water, fish, taro, and fertile land for growing breadfruit, sweet potatoes, and other crops. The valleys provided protection for the islanders, and they traded along the coast by canoe and footpath.

Though there are no written records before the arrival of Western explorers, it is thought that several hundred islanders once lived along the Na Pali coast. Kalalau is the largest of its five major valleys. When missionaries set up a school here in the middle of the nineteenth century, they recorded a population of around 200. The Western influence took its toll as people slowly gravitated toward the ranches and towns, and the valleys were largely deserted by the early 1900s.

Today there is little left but archeological sites, but it is fascinating to see them and imagine life in these idyllic surroundings. Some of the most impressive remains are at Nualolo Kai, an ancient fishing village backed by steep cliffs. It was occupied continuously for some 800 years. Access is only by boat with a special permit, with tours of the site and snorkeling in the protected reef.

Exploring the Na Pali Coast

The cliffs are protected in the 6,175-acre (2,499-ha) Na Pali Coast State Park, which runs along the coast and into the Kalalau Valley. Its northern end is at Ke'e Beach, which is also the northern terminus for the one main road that runs clockwise around the perimeter of the island.

Hanalei Bay (1), the largest on Kauai's north shore, is a departure point in summer for excursion boats touring the Na Pali Coast.

The road ends at Polihale State Park on the west coast. Closing the gap between them is the 22-mile (35-km) roadless stretch of the Na Pali coast.

The only way into the park is by foot, boat, or helicopter. The 11-mile (18-km) Kalalau coastal trail runs along the top of the sea cliffs, winding across and into the five main valleys and many smaller ones. Beginning at Ke'e Beach and ending at Kalalau Beach, it follows the original trail used by the early Hawaiians who lived in these valleys.

While fit, experienced hikers can make the entire distance in a day, for most people the trail is a challenge, with steep uphill climbs and descents, and sections that are in turn slippery, rocky, muddy, and very narrow with sheer drops. The majority opt for the beginning 2-mile (3-km) stretch to Hanakapiai Beach. Although rip currents make the beach dangerous for swimming, the hike

–> Waimea Canyon

Kauai's other great natural wonder is Waimea Canyon, often called the "Grand Canyon of the Pacific." The 13-mile (21-km) long, 2,500-foot (762-m) deep chasm was formed by volcanic activity and subsequent erosion exposed the striated lava cliffs. The Waimea River, the longest on the island, runs far below. The canyon is protected in a state park. Waimea Canyon Drive, 19 miles (31 km) long, has several scenic lookouts, and there are trails into the canyon.

The most dramatic views of Na Pali's rugged, plunging cliffs is from the sea, and you can travel along the coast by kayak, raft, or tour boat.

View from Kalalau Lookout
(**2**) across the lush valley
toward Kalalau Beach.

0   20 km
0   20 miles

Kilauea Point

Waigiha
1 Hanalei
Kilauea

2 Kalalau
Lookout

Kahala Point

Anahola
K A U A I
Kealia

3 ▲ *Waialeale
5148 ft*
Kawaikini ▲
5208 ft

Kapaa

Mana

Kaulakahi Channel

22°

4

Hanamaulu

Kekaha
Walmea
Lihue

Puhi

Kaumakani
Hanapepe
Koloa
● Eleele
Kukuiula

Kauai Channel

5000
3000
1000
500
0 ft

PACIFIC
OCEAN

Verdant landscape
surrounds the
birthplace of Kauai,
Mount Waialeale (**3**).

Waves crash along the
secluded shores of the
Na Pali coast of Kauai.

NIIHAU
KAUAI
Lihue
Kauai Channel
OAHU
Honolulu
Kaiwi Channel
MOLOKAI
N
LANAI
MAUI
KAHOOLAWE
Alenuihaha Channel

P A C I F I C
O C E A N

HAWAII
Hilo

0   100 km
0   100 miles

gives you a chance to experience the landscape of
the valleys. A permit is needed to continue on the
trail from here, whether or not you are camping.

An easier way to explore the coast is by boat,
and several companies run tours. These give you
some of the best vistas of the magnificent cliff
scenery. The best views are in the early morning,
before the clouds roll in. Kayaking is also a popular
and traditional way in. Raft tours stop at safe
beaches for swimming and for snorkeling in a
protected reef.

The Na Pali coast has some of the best
snorkeling in the islands. One-third of its colorful
fish species are found nowhere else, and you may
also see the Honu, or Hawaiian green sea turtle
here. These waters are also home to several pods of
dolphin, the endangered Hawaiian monk seal, and
migrating whales.

POPULATION Kauai 63,000.

CLIMATE The average temperature on the island is 75-85°F (24-29°C). Summer (April-November) is warmer and drier; winter (December-March) is cooler with much rain but also sunny spells.

WHAT TO TAKE Hiking boots, rain poncho, sunscreen, insect repellent, drinking water.

BEST TIME Anytime is good to visit, though summer is drier. The beaches on the Na Pali coast are sandy in summer but rocky in winter as storms sweep the sand out to sea.

NEAREST AIRPORT Lihue Airport on the southeast side of the island; the drive to the park takes about 1½ hours.

ACCOMMODATIONS There is a range of accommodations around the island. The nearest accommodations to the Na Pali coast are on the north coast around Hanalei. There are campgrounds for hikers within the park.

In the island's wet interior, waterfalls pour over the lush, rugged cliffs of Waimea Canyon (**4**), the largest in the Pacific.

HAWAII VOLCANOES NATIONAL PARK

Walk amid two of the world's most active volcanoes,
which have created the fiery backdrop to this unique
and dramatic national park.

MOST PEOPLE RUN AWAY FROM, not toward, an erupting volcano. Not in Hawaii Volcanoes National Park. Here you can get closer to one of the most explosive, deadly forces in nature than anywhere else in the world. The park contains two of the most active volcanoes on the planet. While Mauna Loa has been sleeping peacefully for the past 25 years, Kilauea, in the East Rift Zone, has been putting on a fiery spectacle since 1983, the longest series of ongoing eruptions in recorded history. Between them they have destroyed entire villages and produced vast lava fields up to 3 miles (5 km) wide, dotted with craters, cinder cones, pumice heaps, steam vents, and fragile islands of vegetation.

Red-hot lava is ever bubbling beneath Kilauea's crust, straining to burst through into flaming fireworks of molten rock. When it does, people rush to witness the show. At night, the eerie orange glow from the magma fountains creates a supernatural vision as creeping channels of fire spread down the mountainside, blackening everything in their path, twisting and hardening rock and debris into an otherworldly landscape. Eventually the molten mass flows over bare cliffs into the sea, billowing up into dramatic clouds of gas and steam.

Ancient Origins

Hawaii Volcanoes National Park, established in 1916, is unlike any other park in North America. Designated as a World Heritage Site and International Biosphere Reserve, it lies on the eastern side of the Big Island of Hawaii, and covers 333,000 acres (1,348 ha) at present, but it is still growing. Kilauea's lava flows have added 600 new acres (243 ha) in less than 20 years.

Visiting the park is to step into an amazing world created by 70 million years of volcanism and evolution. The Hawaiian Islands is one of the most geographically isolated places in the world, over 2,000 miles (3,219 km) from the nearest continent. Comprised of eight large islands and 124 small islands and atolls, they stretch across 1,640 miles (2,639 km) of the central Pacific.

We think of Hawaii as a lush tropical paradise, but these islands were born of the same fiery eruptions we witness in the park. They consist of billions of tons of magma, built up from volcanoes

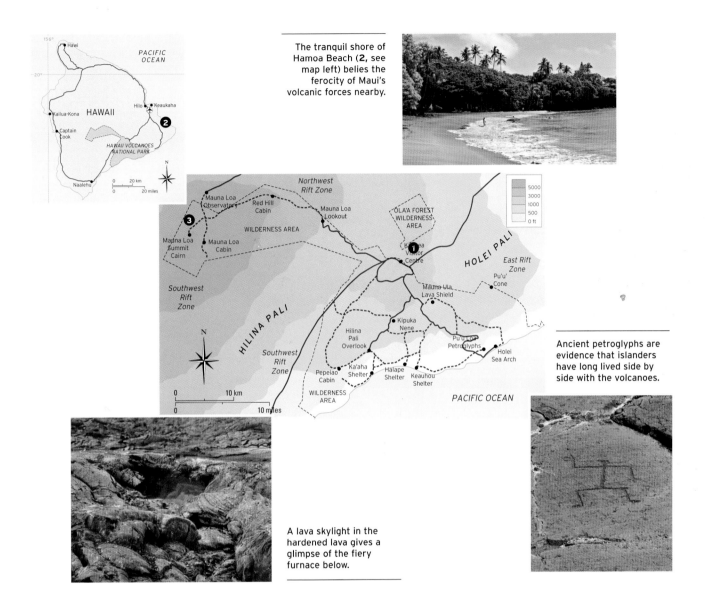

The tranquil shore of Hamoa Beach (**2,** see map left) belies the ferocity of Maui's volcanic forces nearby.

Ancient petroglyphs are evidence that islanders have long lived side by side with the volcanoes.

A lava skylight in the hardened lava gives a glimpse of the fiery furnace below.

on the ocean floor over thousands of millennia. A new island, already named Loihi, is developing by the same process, 3,000 feet (914 m) deep and 20 miles (32 km) south of Big Island, destined to emerge in about 10,000 years.

The islands emerged as bare and lifeless as the lava fields we see today, but a unique biosystem developed slowly over the years from spores and seeds carried by ocean currents, jet streams, and migratory birds. It is estimated that one new species gained a foothold every 40,000 years. Today the park contains a great range of endemic flora and fauna, including many endangered species such as the nene, or Hawaiian goose.

Unique Volcanoes

Famous volcanoes such as Vesuvius and Krakatoa are known for their violent eruptions, blasting lava and ash for miles around through their steep cones.

Hawaii's volcanoes are different. Known as fissure, or shield volcanoes, they have a steady flow of molten rock beneath the surface, rather than explosive gases. This magma is hotter–around 2,000°F (1,082°C)–and more fluid, producing slow-moving streams of lava that can flow 20 miles (32 km) before cooling and hardening, leaving rounded mountains behind.

You will see two types of lava in the park. The crusty lava fields with sharp, angular chunks are known as *a'a* lava, or *scoria*. *Pahoehoe* is a smooth lava that hardens like a skin, often with undulating shapes or a surface wrinkled like coiled rope. A tunnel of hot lava can sometimes flow underneath.

Mauna Loa, in the western quarter of the park, is the most massive mountain on earth. It has grown by around 300 acres (121 ha) each century. Its summit is 13,677 feet (4,169 m) above sea level. But if measured from its base on the seabed, it

A fountain of fire erupts from Kilauea Crater (**1,** opposite) as scientists observe the molten river of lava from a safe distance above.

The vast crater of Mauna Loa (**3**) is like the mouth of a sleeping giant and no one can predict when we will next hear it roar.

rises 56,000 feet (17,068 m)—nearly twice as high as Mount Everest. Mauna Loa has erupted 18 times in the past 100 years, and could awaken again at any moment, perhaps triggered by one of the 1,200 earthquakes that are recorded on the island every week.

Both of the park's volcanoes are crowned with wide calderas. The 11-mile (18-km) Crater Rim Drive circles the 4,000-foot (1,219-m) summit of Kilauea, taking you through luxuriant rain forest and barren lava desert. Among the strange volcanic features

are the Sulfur Banks, where foul-smelling fumes envelop delicate crystals, and the Steaming Bluff, where vapor from boiling rainwater rises up through grassland. You can walk upright through the Thurston Lava Tube, a tunnel formed by magma. Other viewpoints and hiking trails bring you up close to this fascinating landscape.

The Chain of Craters Road is a thrilling descent past huge pit craters to remarkable black lava cliffs, sea arches, and waterfall shapes formed by hardened lava, and the Pu'u Loa petroglyphs carved

-> FACT FILE

CLIMATE The island's climate is diverse, with 12 different climate zones ranging from hot deserts and tropical beaches to mountain snowfields. Elevation is more a factor than season as far as temperature, which can vary considerably from sea level to the volcano's summit. Annual rainfall at the park averaged 108 inches (274 cm) over the last five years.

WHAT TO TAKE Rain gear and layers of clothing to accommodate changing weather and elevation; sturdy hiking boots for rough trails.

BEST TIME Summer (May–October) tends to be drier with temperatures in the 70s°F (21+°C) and winter (November–April), rainier with temperatures in the 50s and 60s°F (10+°C to 15+°C).

NEAREST AIRPORT Keahole Airport in Kona, 100 miles (161 km) from the park, is served by interisland carriers and major airlines.

ACCOMMODATIONS There is lodging in the park at Volcano House, near the rim of Kilauea's crater, as well as park campgrounds. There are guesthouses and lodges at nearby towns including Hilo, Volcano, and Honaunau.

PARK ENTRANCE An entry fee per vehicle that covers all passengers is valid for seven days.

Between fiery eruptions, clouds of noxious gases billow up through the crater atop Kilauea (1) from the ever-bubbling cauldron far below.

-> The Legend of Pele

Ancient Hawaiian legends tell of Pele, goddess of the volcano, who makes her home in the Halemaumau Crater at the summit of Kilauea. She hurls fire, melts rocks, and builds mountains with her magic, and is known as "the woman who devours the land." Seen as the life force of the island, people leave ceremonial offerings for her at the crater's edge, from ti leaves and ohelo berries to her favorite tipple, gin. Liquid lava that is blown through the air into thin strands of volcanic glass is known as Pele's hair.

by ancient islanders. The park contains a great variety of differing terrain. You can sunbathe on volcanic black sand beaches or climb to snowfields on Mauna Loa's summit. Explore some 140 miles (225 km) of hiking trails through this fascinating island world.

HISTORIC HOMES OF CHARLESTON

Stately houses, narrow alleyways, ornamental gates, magnolia-lined paths, and oaks dripping with Spanish moss give this historic city a distinct Southern feel.

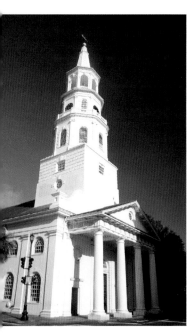

The steeple of St. Michael's Episcopal Church (1) rises 186 feet (57 m) high. It sank by 8 inches (20 cm) during an earthquake in 1886.

CHARLESTON IS THE GRAND DAME of the South. With her white-columned antebellum mansions, lacy wrought-iron balconies, and graceful church steeples, she is always dressed up for the ball. Sea breezes rustle through her exotic coif of palmetto trees. Sweet scents of gardenia, jasmine, and honeysuckle waft from her gardens. The clip-clop of horses' hooves on cobbled streets signals another carriage full of suitors come to admire her beauty.

Founded by English colonists in 1670, the original settlement was called Charles Towne (after the English king) and was located a few miles upstream on the west bank of the Ashley River. The historic landing site can be visited today. Ten years later, it relocated to its present peninsula, set between two rivers on a natural harbor, surrounded by a network of islands, deepwater creeks, and salt marshes. This watery landscape was perfect for growing rice, and soon large plantations worked by slaves were spread through the surrounding Low Country.

By the mid-eighteenth century Charleston was a prosperous port, the largest and wealthiest in the South. Much of its trade was with the Caribbean. It attracted settlers from many different ethnic backgrounds and became known as the Holy City, as much for its religious tolerance as for the number of church spires. The well-to-do built fine mansions with fine furnishings, and Charleston became the showcase of society, where wealthy planters and merchants threw lavish balls during the social season.

The first shots of the Civil War were fired in Charleston harbor in 1861. Confederate soldiers captured Fort Sumter, which stands on an island, and held it throughout the war until 1865. It is now a national monument. After the war, the old aristocracy remained in the city. But with the basis of their economy and society gone, their handsome homes became shabby and neglected. In 1886 the city was struck by a disastrous earthquake. Many buildings are studded with the round heads of earthquake bolts, with iron rods running through the walls between them to hold up the damaged structures. In 1931 Charleston passed the country's first preservation ordinance and began to restore the historic district to its former glory.

Charleston's Historic Heart

The historic center covers 4 square miles (10 sq km) at the southern end of the peninsula by the harbor. It is best to explore on foot, by horse-drawn carriage tour, or use the streetcars that loop through town. There are several fine museums, and many of the grand mansions are open to visitors.

A unique form of architecture to look for is the Charleston single house, built to accommodate the hot and humid summer climate. Typically tall and narrow, three stories high with two main rooms per floor, the narrow end faces the street. Long verandas, called piazzas, run the length of each floor, usually overlooking side gardens, allowing breezes to circulate easily through the house.

Start at White Point Gardens at the tip of the peninsula, a lovely spot with enormous live oaks and a gazebo. The promenade that curves along the Battery is lined with splendid antebellum homes, their elaborate piazzas perfectly poised to catch the sea breezes. Fort Sumter, far out in the

Now a luxurious bed and breakfast inn, the beautiful Palmer Home on East Bay Street (**2**) was once voted "The Home with the Best Front Porch."

-> FACT FILE

POPULATION City 118,000, metro area 603,000.

CLIMATE Charleston has a subtropical climate with hot, humid summers and mild winters. Average highs in July are 91ºF (32ºC), in January 59ºF (15ºC). Rainfall, significant year-round, is highest in summer, and hurricanes are possible from summer through early fall.

WHAT TO TAKE Rain jacket, walking shoes.

BEST TIME Fall temperatures remain warm into November. Spring is a beautiful time to visit when flowers are in bloom. The Spoleto and Piccolo Spoleto music and arts festivals are held over 17 days in May–June.

NEAREST AIRPORT Charleston International Airport is about 10 miles (16 km) north of downtown.

WHAT TO BUY Sweetgrass baskets made by Gullah women are a traditional Charleston souvenir.

ACCOMMODATIONS Hotels in the historic district are more expensive, but prices vary greatly depending on the season. Small bed and breakfast inns are charming options, but many have only a few rooms. Book well ahead for these, and during festivals and events.

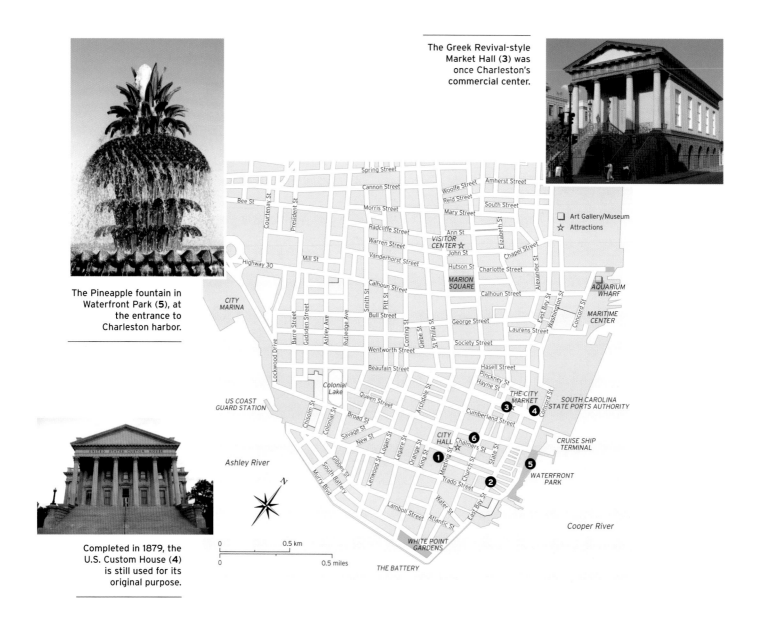

The Greek Revival-style Market Hall (**3**) was once Charleston's commercial center.

The Pineapple fountain in Waterfront Park (**5**), at the entrance to Charleston harbor.

Completed in 1879, the U.S. Custom House (**4**) is still used for its original purpose.

harbor, can be seen from the commemorative brass marker in the sidewalk. Continue along East Battery to the Edmondston-Alston House (1828), a Regency mansion with stunning views of the harbor. Further on is Rainbow Row, a colorful stretch of 14 houses dating from before the Revolution.

Many of the finest antebellum homes lie between the Battery and Beaufain and Hasell Streets. The neoclassical Nathaniel Russell House (1808) has an amazing "flying" staircase that spirals through three floors with no supports. The Calhoun Mansion (1876), an Italianate manor house with a grand ballroom and stunning interiors, is among the greatest post-Civil War houses in the South. The owner of the Heyward-Washington House (1772) signed the Declaration of Independence. In contrast, the nearby stretch of tenements on Church Street,

→ Low Country Plantations

Several historic plantations can be visited within a short drive of Charleston. Drayton Hall on the Ashley River was one of the few in the area to escape destruction in the Civil War. The magnificent gardens at Magnolia Plantation are some of the country's oldest, dating from around 1680. There are more lovely gardens and a house museum at Middleton Place. A stunning avenue of oaks leads to Boone Hall, still a working plantation.

known as Cabbage Row, was home to poorer African-Americans.

Meeting Street, and parallel King Street, are the main north-south thoroughfares. The intersection of Meeting and Broad Streets is called the Four Corners of the Law, as each corner had a different branch of government—city, state, and federal. On the fourth corner—God's law—is the city's oldest church, St. Michael's Episcopal, built in 1761. Further east along Broad Street at the waterfront is the Old Exchange and Provost Dungeon (1771), one of the most important colonial buildings in America. Pirates and patriots were imprisoned here.

Gullah is a distinct dialect that evolved among African and Caribbean slaves in colonial times.

You can hear traces of it today at Old City Market (1841), where their descendants weave the beautiful sweetgrass baskets that are a Charleston tradition. Several tours and museums give further insight into Charleston's African-American heritage.

More historic sights can be seen around Marion Square. The Old Citadel (1842) was the original site of one of the country's first military colleges. The Joseph Manigault House (1803) is an outstanding Federal-style mansion. The Aiken-Rhett House (circa 1818), the only surviving urban plantation, depicts life before the Civil War. The Charleston Museum has exhibits on life in the city and surrounding Low Country and is well worth a visit.

The Pink House Gallery (**6**) on Chalmers Street is housed in the oldest standing tavern building in the South, built in 1694.

SAVANNAH'S HISTORIC SQUARES

From its leafy, mansion-lined squares to its lively riverfront, this fun-loving former cotton port is brimming with Southern charms.

"IF YOU GO TO ATLANTA, the first question people ask you is, 'What's your business?' In Macon they ask, 'Where do you go to church?' In Augusta they ask your grandmother's maiden name. But in Savannah the first question people ask you is, 'What would you like to drink?'"

John Berendt's character Miss Harty relayed this old Savannah adage in *Midnight in the Garden of Good and Evil*, the 1994 novel that put this gracious Georgia city firmly on the tourist map for visitors from around the world. And they do indeed find that, amid the handsome historic homes and buildings, the live oaks dripping with Spanish moss, and the slow-moving pace, Savannah likes a good party. This Southern belle is a bit like Scarlett O'Hara, the heroine from that "other" book—well bred but with a wild streak.

Savannah was the first settlement in Georgia, founded as a colony to give debtors languishing in England's jails a second chance while establishing a barrier to Spanish expansion from Florida. It was America's first planned city, designed by James

Oglethorpe, the colony's founder, and laid out on a grid plan in 1734. It was based around 24 leafy public squares, 21 of which remain today. They form the heart of Savannah's historic district, where more than 800 buildings have been restored. Covering 2½ miles (4 km), it is one of the largest National Historic Landmarks in the country.

In the latter eighteenth century, the surrounding area and the Low Country in neighboring South Carolina became a rich cotton-growing region. Eli Whitney invented the cotton gin on a plantation outside Savannah in 1793. Situated at the mouth of the Savannah River, 18 miles (29 km) from the Atlantic, the city became the South's biggest cotton port. Wealthy planters and traders built lavish houses here, and Savannah's social season rivaled that of Charleston.

The city escaped ruin during the Civil War. It is said that the slash-and-burn Union general, William Tecumseh Sherman, found it too beautiful to destroy. So did the women who formed the Historic Savannah Foundation in the 1950s, which has saved hundreds of outstanding buildings from the wrecking ball. Many have been restored by the Savannah College of Art and Design (SCAD), whose students have injected fresh energy and color into this historic center.

Around the Squares

Take a leisurely stroll through the Historic District to admire the handsome Greek Revival and Regency mansions. Look for decorative details, such as

The Mercer Williams House (1) is filled with beautiful antiques and artwork, and is open for guided tours.

—> The Garden of Good and Evil

The Mercer House was built by the great-grandfather of singer Johnny Mercer. It was beautifully renovated by antique dealer Jim Williams, but in 1981 Williams shot his young male companion here in mysterious circumstances. The story of his four murder trials was the subject of John Berendt's bestseller and a Hollywood movie. It paints a portrait of Savannah full of intriguing customs and characters.

beautifully scrolled wrought-iron balconies, or foot scrapers and drainpipes in the shape of fish or animals. Horse-drawn carriage tours are also an atmospheric way to explore.

If the heat gets overwhelming, shady benches in the squares provide a respite and a good spot for people watching. Each square has its own character and distinctive features, from ornamental fountains to memorial statues. Some have flower gardens and curtains of Spanish moss hanging from ancient live oaks. When the squares were laid out, settlers were granted house lots on the north or south sides. The east and west sides were reserved for the public good, and many squares have churches there today.

Bull Street runs north to the river and connects several of the loveliest squares. It begins at Forsyth Park, which marks the district's southern border. Several blocks long, this wide rectangle is Savannah's playground, and includes a monumental fountain that is modeled after Paris's Place de la Concorde.

Opposite the park, Montery Square is the most famous of them all thanks to what locals call "the Book." On its west side, the Mercer Williams House Museum, the setting for John Berendt's bestseller, is open for tours.

On the south end of Lafayette Square is the childhood home of Flannery O'Connor, one of the South's best-known writers. She was born here in 1925, and two floors have been restored with period furnishings. Savannah was also the birthplace of Juliette Gordon Low, who founded the Girl Scouts of America. Her birthplace, a handsome mansion built in 1821, is now the Scouts' national headquarters and is open for tours.

Lovely Wright Square is one of the city's original squares and contains the grave of Tomochichi, the Native American chief who welcomed the settlers. To the west around Telfair Square are the Telfair Museum of Art, housed in a beautiful Regency mansion, and the Jepson Center for the Arts. To the east at Oglethorpe Square is the Owens-Thomas

The two-tiered fountain at the north end of Forsyth Park (2) was erected in 1858 as the focal point of a grand vista down Bull Street.

South of the squares is another historic district of ornate Victorian houses dating from the 1870s and 1880s.

–> FACT FILE

POPULATION City 128,000, metro area 320,000.

CLIMATE Savannah has a subtropical climate, with hot, humid summers and mild winters. July is the hottest month with average highs 92ºF (33ºC). January is the coldest month with average highs 60ºF (15ºC). Average annual rainfall is 49 3/4 inches (126 cm). Most rain falls in summer.

WHAT TO TAKE Light rain jacket or umbrella in summer. Casual clothes, good walking shoes.

BEST TIME Savannah is prettiest in the spring when everything is in bloom. It has the largest St. Patrick's Day (March 17) celebration in the South. The Savannah Music Festival is also held in March.

NEAREST AIRPORT Savannah/Hilton Head International Airport is 5 miles (8 km) west of downtown.

ACCOMMODATIONS There are a few luxury bed and breakfast inns in the old homes of the Historic District. A string of motels near the Visitors' Center offer less expensive options. Book far ahead for visits during events and festivals.

House, a stunning 1819 Regency house by British architect William Jay. This and the nearby Federal-style Davenport House were two of the first to be protected and restored and are open for tours.

Along the River

Near the river, free summer jazz concerts are held in Johnson Square. Between here and Franklin Square, City Market is a lively area for dining and nightlife.

The riverfront area has all the bustle and atmosphere of the old port, with its cobbled streets and cotton warehouses now converted for restaurants and entertainment. Factors Walk is lined with handsome nineteenth-century buildings such as the U.S. Customs House and Old Cotton Exchange. The 1794 Pirate's House serves up smugglers' tales with its steaks and seafood. Stroll along River Street, watching the passing cargo ships, listening to street musicians, and browsing in the gift stores. Or take a sightseeing cruise on a paddlesteamer, reliving Savannah's glory days.

Mermen statues surround the Parisian-style fountain in Forsyth Park (**2**).

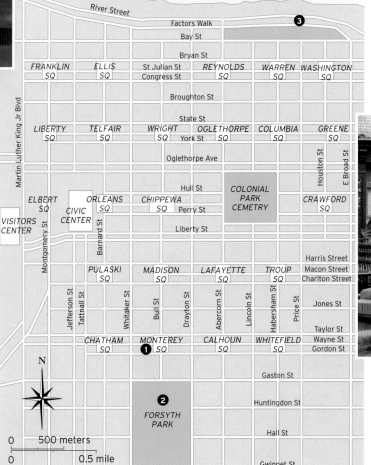

Old warehouses beside the port lend great character to Savannah's riverfront (**3**).

Time moves at a languid pace in "Slowvannah"—as the locals call their city.

Fountain at the Old Cotton Exchange along Factors Walk, at the riverfront (**3**).

ROCKY MOUNTAIN NATIONAL PARK

Drive across the Continental Divide on America's highest continuous paved road, through the glorious landscape of Rocky Mountain National Park.

During the fall mating season, the astonishing rutting calls of the bull elk (seen here crossing Sprague Lake, 1), known as bugling, echo through the park.

THE ROCKY MOUNTAINS ARE THE LARGEST mountain range in North America, stretching across some 3,000 miles (4,800 km) of the western United States and Canada, from northwestern British Columbia to New Mexico. They encompass dozens of smaller individual ranges that display a striking array of scenery, from rugged snow-capped peaks to alpine lakes and wildflower meadows to slopes covered in slender, white-barked aspen trees. One of the finest places to appreciate this magnificent landscape is in this national park in Colorado.

The Rockies are the backbone of the continent. They straddle the Continental Divide, a meandering line that separates the watersheds for the Pacific and Atlantic Oceans. Although there is no visible sign marking its location, it creates an interesting

phenomenon—all rivers, streams, and the water from rain and snowmelt on the western slopes run toward the Pacific Ocean, while water on the eastern side runs toward the Atlantic. A whirlpool or vortex will likewise spin in opposite directions on either side of this mountain spine.

The Continental Divide also gives each side of the park a different character. The west side is wetter and greener, covered in dense forest. The drier east side contains more of the bowl-shaped hollows known as cirques, gorges, and the glacier sculpting that is a defining feature of this park.

Established in 1915 as the country's tenth national park, Rocky Mountain National Park lies northwest of Boulder and covers 414 square miles (1,072 sq km) along Colorado's Front Range.

Different seasons and times
of day give Longs Peak (**2**),
the park's highest summit,
its changing character.

—> FACT FILE

CLIMATE Weather is changeable and varies widely
with the elevation. High temperatures in July-
August reach 70–80ºF (21–26ºC). In winter, the high
country sees Arctic conditions with deep snow.

WHAT TO TAKE Be prepared for rapidly changing
weather. Take a rain jacket and warm sweater or
jacket for high altitudes, which can be windy and
cold. Bring sunscreen, sunglasses, plenty of drinking
water, and food, as there is none in the park except
for the snack bar at the Alpine Visitor Center.

BEST TIME The park is open year-round, but Trail
Ridge Road is closed in winter. Summer has the
warmest weather but often sees afternoon
thunderstorms. Spring often comes late and there
can be snow at high elevations into May and June.
Wildflowers bloom at lower elevations from late
April through May, and higher elevations from June
through early August. Fall color is at its best from
mid-September to mid-October, though conditions
vary year to year.

NEAREST AIRPORT Denver International Airport is
80 miles (129 km) away.

ACCOMMODATIONS There is a range of hotels at
Estes Park and at other nearby communities on the
eastern side of the park. On the west side you will
find accommodations at the resort town of Grand
Lake and further beyond at Granby and Winter
Park. There are five campgrounds within the
national park.

SAFETY TIP When hiking in high elevations in
summer, it is advisable to get back below treeline by
mid-afternoon, as there is a danger of lightning
strikes from sudden thunderstorms.

PARK ENTRANCE An entrance fee, valid for seven
consecutive days, is charged per vehicle, or per
person for pedestrians, bicycles, etc. Annual passes
covering the entire national parks system are also
available at any park entrance.

Rocky Mountain National Park, a gateway across the Continental Divide.

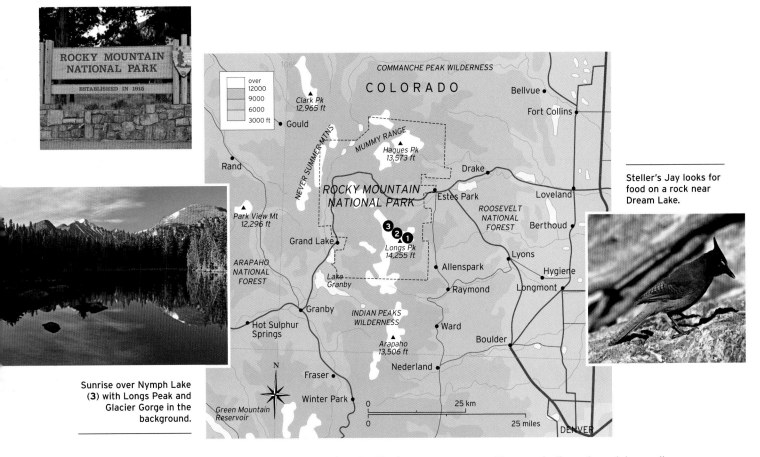

Steller's Jay looks for food on a rock near Dream Lake.

Sunrise over Nymph Lake (3) with Longs Peak and Glacier Gorge in the background.

Nowhere else in the American Rockies has so many high peaks concentrated in such a compact area. More than 60 of them have elevations of 12,000 feet (3,658 m) or more. The highest is Longs Peak at a lofty 14,255 feet (4,345 m). There are higher peaks elsewhere in the country and indeed in Colorado, but nothing quite compares to this mass of granite slopes and frosted summits, a vista that is simply breathtaking.

–> Rocky Mountain Wildlife

The park has many species of wildlife, but is best known for its large animals, from its 3,000-strong elk herd to mule deer and a small moose population. The cliffs are home to around 800 bighorn sheep, while the backcountry harbors more elusive animals such as black bears, cougars, and coyotes. You may spot an eagle or hawk soaring overhead, or catch sight of delightful small creatures such as marmots and pikas.

These majestic peaks and deep valleys were carved by glaciers during the ice age. You can still see some small, permanent glaciers at the higher elevations, and the ridges of rock debris they left behind, known as moraines. With over a third of the park above treeline, this is the highest national park in the country, protecting a stark and fragile landscape of alpine tundra where only hardy mosses and tiny alpine flowers can survive. It is the only ecosystem of its kind south of the Arctic Circle.

Below there are sapphire lakes, verdant valleys, and groves of aspen trees that turn bright yellow in the fall. In summer, the mountain meadows are blooming with purple columbine, red Indian paintbrush, and hundreds of other wildflowers.

The High Road

Rocky Mountain National Park has two main gateways. Estes Park, 71 miles (114 km) northwest of Denver, leads to the park's eastern entrance. At the western boundary of the park is the resort town of Grand Lake. In between, Trail Ridge Road follows an old Native American trail through some of Colorado's most awesome scenery. Also known

as U.S. 34, this is the highest continuous paved highway in America. It runs 48 miles (77 km) through the park from east to west, ranging in elevation from 8,000 feet (2,438 m) to over 12,000 feet (3,658 m). A leisurely drive from end to end with stops to admire the superb scenery or view wildlife will take three to four hours.

Apart from the mountain scenery, highlights along Trail Ridge Road include Horseshoe Park, a couple of miles beyond the Falls River eastern entrance. There is a bighorn sheep crossing here, allowing the animals to reach the meadow and Sheep Lakes from the ridges above—see them in the mornings in spring and early summer.

As the road climbs above treeline, look for Rock Cut, where you can take a self-guided trail for an hour-long hike through the alpine tundra. Beyond, you will often see a large herd of mule deer grazing near the side of the road.

Trail Ridge Road reaches it highest point at 12,183 feet (3,713 m) shortly before reaching the Alpine Visitors Center, which has interpretive displays about this fascinating environment. Walk up the windy path through the tundra, surrounded by magnificent views of the mountain peaks and snow bowls. From here, the road descends through gentler terrain into a greener landscape of lush forests.

The headwaters of the Colorado River, which flows through seven southwestern states on its way to the sea, is contained within the park boundaries. It is hard to imagine that the gentle stream you see here becomes the mighty force that carved out the Grand Canyon. A pleasant hike along the Colorado River Trail follows the infant river to the ghost town of Lulu City.

With many miles of hiking trails to explore, it is worth spending a full day or more, and there are other areas of interest elsewhere in the park. Bear Lake Road beckons with more grand scenery on the eastern side, a 9-mile (14-km) drive that winds past glaciers, waterfalls, and stunning views of Longs Peak to the picturesque mountain lake. From here you can hike into Glacier Gorge for a closer look at some of the park's classic glacial features.

The stunning peaks of Rocky Mountain National Park are reflected in the pristine waters of its 150 lakes.

SANTA FE: CITY OF COLOR AND LIGHT

Beautiful adobe architecture, world-class art, and the mix of Native American, Hispanic, and Anglo cultures make this historic southwest city a perennial favorite.

Colorful Native American pottery is a popular souvenir, found in markets and shops throughout the city.

SANTA FE IS A CITY OF COLOR AND LIGHT. Red strands of chile *ristras* hang from the timbers of ancient buildings. Adobe towers on old mission churches gleam in the sunshine against a sheer blue sky. Brightly woven Navajo rugs are piled high on a corner market stall. All senses are heightened in the crisp, clear light that bathes this charming city, sitting 7,000 feet (2,134 m) high on a plateau against the Sangre de Cristo Mountains.

This wonderful light has drawn artists to this region of northern New Mexico since the nineteenth century, most notably Georgia O'Keeffe, who is honored here with a museum dedicated to her works. Today around a sixth of the population works in the arts, and the city is brimming with outstanding museums and galleries. In 2005, Santa Fe became the first city in the U.S. to be designated a UNESCO Creative City, one of only a handful in the world. The artists have been followed in recent years by film crews. The Coen brothers' *No Country for Old Men* is among the many acclaimed productions filmed in and around Santa Fe.

Long before it was discovered by Anglo artists, Spanish conquistadors traveled north from Mexico to establish a farming and ranching colony in the Rio Grande Valley. They founded Santa Fe as their capital in 1610. It is both the oldest and the highest state capital city in the country. The land was home to the native Pueblo people, and eight of New Mexico's nineteen Native American pueblos lie north of the city on the road to Taos. Pueblo artisans are renowned for their beautiful and distinctive pottery and jewelry. After Mexico won independence from Spain in 1821, traders and settlers from the U.S. began to arrive via the Santa Fe Trail. The blending of three distinct cultures— Hispanic, Native American, and Anglo—make Santa Fe a vibrant southwestern crossroads.

Around the Plaza

The heart of Santa Fe is the Plaza, which dates back to the founding of the city. Its landscaped lawn and benches are a good spot for people watching. Along the north side is the Palace of the Governors, a

Striking Pueblo Revival-style architecture is reminiscent of dwellings once built by Native Americans in the Southwest.

Weaving and rugmaking are traditional Native arts that date back to prehistoric times.

one-story adobe building that housed the colonial and regional governments for 300 years. Built in 1610, it is the oldest public building in continuous use in America. Since 1909 it has housed the New Mexico History Museum, a fascinating collection of artifacts from colonial times. Beneath the timbered arcade, Native American artists spread their blankets to sell beautiful jewelry and crafts in the daily market. Stores, galleries, and cafés surround the Plaza.

Next door to the palace, the Museum of Fine Arts is housed in an early Pueblo Revival-style adobe building built in 1917. It displays paintings, sculpture, photographs, and other works by southwestern artists from the early twentieth century to the

present, with an emphasis on New Mexico. Nearby, the Georgia O'Keeffe Museum is the only place where you can see an extensive collection of her works under one roof. Many famous paintings were inspired by the landscape around her New Mexican house at Abiquiu.

To the east of the Plaza in a pink Pueblo Revival building is the Institute of American Indian Arts. It displays a huge array of works by contemporary Native American artists alongside traditional arts, and has a wonderful sculpture garden. St. Francis Cathedral, with its striking, honey-colored Romanesque façade, stands opposite the museum. Built in 1869, it houses a venerable statue of the Virgin Mary carved in Mexico in 1625.

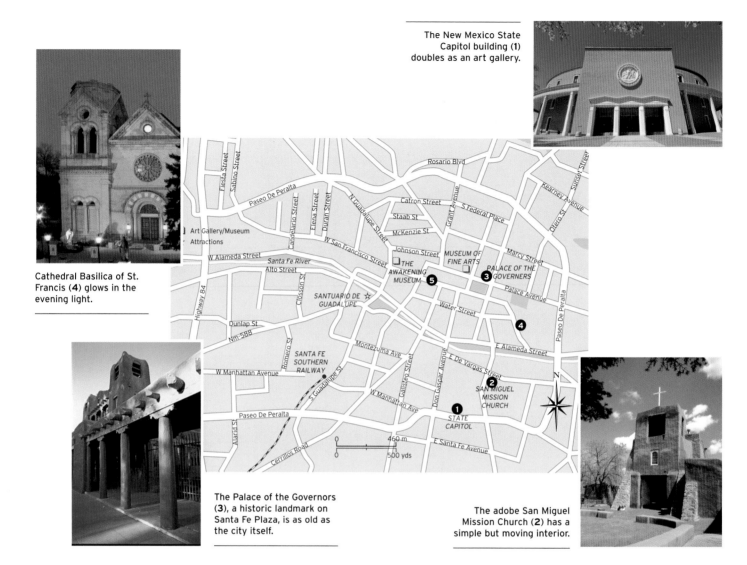

The New Mexico State Capitol building (1) doubles as an art gallery.

Cathedral Basilica of St. Francis (4) glows in the evening light.

The Palace of the Governors (3), a historic landmark on Santa Fe Plaza, is as old as the city itself.

The adobe San Miguel Mission Church (2) has a simple but moving interior.

Two more famous religious sites are south of the Plaza along Old Santa Fe Trail. The Loretto Chapel dates from the 1870s and contains the "miraculous staircase," built for the nuns by a mysterious carpenter to give access to the choir loft. The elegant spiral makes two complete turns but has no nails or central support. San Miguel Mission is the city's oldest church, first built by Tlaxcala Indians around 1610. The carved wooden altarpiece is priceless.

–> Museum Hill

More outstanding museums are a short drive southeast of the center on Museum Hill. The Museum of International Folk Art is the largest collection of its kind in the world. The Museum of Indian Arts and Culture and the Wheelwright Museum of the American Indian both focus on Native American traditions. Also here is the Museum of Spanish Colonial Arts.

Capital of Art

Santa Fe is such an arts city that even its seat of government is a museum. Just beyond the mission, the circular New Mexico State Capitol building, built to resemble a Zia Pueblo sun symbol, is filled with contemporary works by New Mexican artists on four levels.

With more than 250 art galleries and dealers in town, Santa Fe is considered the second largest art market in the country. Nearly half of them lie along Canyon Road. This was once an ancient Indian track between the pueblos, and the city's first irrigation channel, the Acequia Madre or "Mother Ditch," still runs alongside. A few quaint, colorful, adobe houses are dotted among the upscale galleries, sculpture gardens, cafés, and restaurants.

El Santuario de Guadalupe, at the west end of Santa Fe River Park, marked the end of the old Camino Real trading route from Mexico. The adobe church of 1795 is dedicated to the Virgin of Guadalupe. The newest development in this historic district is south of the shrine at the Santa Fe Railyard. It includes a public plaza, outdoor performance area, artists' studios, park, promenade, and the farmers' market.

The Spanish Renaissance style of the Lensic Performing Arts Center (5) makes an atmospheric home for music, dance, and theater.

–> Fact File

POPULATION 68,000

CLIMATE Four distinct seasons. Due to the city's high elevation, temperatures can vary greatly within a day. June is the hottest month with highs in the mid-upper 90sºF (32+ºC). Winter brings some snow but is generally sunny, with average January highs 47ºF (8ºC). Average annual rainfall is 14 inches (35.5 cm).

WHAT TO TAKE Warm sweater or jacket for chilly nights, casual clothes.

BEST TIME April-October are the most popular months; July, August, and October are peak times. Check out the many local events and festivals.

NEAREST AIRPORTS Albuquerque Sunport is the closest major airport to Santa Fe, about 66 miles (106 km) from downtown. Santa Fe's municipal airport handles some domestic flights.

ACCOMMODATIONS Hotels in the city center are beautiful and historic, but more expensive. Many cheaper chain hotels and motels can be found along Cerrillos Road. Book well ahead during festivals, events, and conventions.

WHAT TO EAT Santa Fe cuisine is in a class of its own—the cooking methods and combination of ingredients are very different from Tex-Mex. Be sure to try some of its distinctive dishes, such as blue corn tortillas, red and green chile, and *carne asada* (roasted meat).

CARLSBAD CAVERNS

Beneath the dry, flat plains of southeast New Mexico lies a subterranean world of magical cave formations formed by an ancient inland sea.

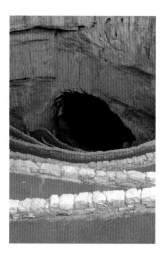

Walking down into Carlsbad Caverns through the Natural Entrance (1) is the most atmospheric way to approach this amazing underground world.

THE RANCHLANDS OF SOUTHEASTERN New Mexico seem to roll like tumbleweeds into the endless expanse of West Texas. Scan the horizon and you will not see anything remarkable, save for the rocky cliffs of the Guadalupe Mountains that rise above the Chihuahuan Desert. But there is more to this sparse landscape than first meets the eye. Deep underground is one of the largest cave systems in the world, and well over half a million visitors come here each year to marvel at its amazing limestone formations.

There are more than 300 known caves in this remote area, and over one-third of them are protected in Carlsbad Caverns National Park. Covering 46,766 acres (18,926 ha), it became a national park in 1930 and a World Heritage Site in 1995. Around two-thirds of the park is a designated wilderness area, with hiking trails through the desert solitude.

It is hard to imagine that this arid terrain was once an enormous, shallow inland sea. In fact, the caves are part of the 400-mile (644-km) long Capitan Reef, created by algae, sponges, and other living sea creatures over 200 million years ago. It became a horseshoe-shaped limestone bank of rock, over 1,800 feet (549 m) thick. Over time, the sea evaporated and the reef was buried under layers of sediment. Over the past 20 million years, the geological forces that uplifted the Guadalupe Mountains above the caves also caused the

sediments to wear away, exposing the reef beneath. Sulfuric acid in rainwater seeped through the cracks, dissolving the limestone and carving out great caverns and passageways.

It is impossible to date the cave formations, or speleothems, but scientists believe they began forming half a million years ago, when the climate was much wetter. As drops of water trickled into the caverns, they hit the drier air and evaporated, leaving behind tiny deposits of calcite and other minerals. Drip by drip, this process created a vast natural art gallery of popcorn, soda straws, flowstone, draperies, lily pads, and other whimsically named decorations.

Finding a Wonderland

Native Americans did not venture beyond the mouth of Carlsbad Cavern, using it for shelter and leaving painted pictographs on the walls. The cave has long been home to a huge colony of Mexican free-tail bats, which roosts in a passage off the Natural Entrance from early spring through October. The nightly flight of thousands of these creatures swarming out of the cave in search of food is a spectacle watched by visitors from the park's amphitheater. At one time they numbered one million strong, but their numbers have dropped by around half, due, it is thought, to the use of DDT in Mexico, where they migrate for the winter.

The bats led to the discovery of these magnificent caverns. In 1898, 16-year-old Jim White was one of several cowboys who lowered themselves into the cave in buckets, mining the bat guano to sell as fertilizer for the California orange groves. White ventured further in and found the ornate chambers. Few people took him seriously until 1915, when he took a photographer with him. Excitement spread, and the caves were protected as a national monument in 1923.

White explored 19 miles (31 km) of the caverns, using only kerosene and a wick in a coffeepot. He later became the park's chief ranger. White named many of the formations, memorizing them as a way to get in and out. If you have trouble remembering the difference between the two main forms, try his descriptions. He called stalactites "hangy-downys," while "sticky-uppies" were the stalagmites rising from the cave floor.

–> Lechuguilla Cave

In May 1986, cavers broke through an old mining pit in the park's backcountry to discover one of history's most exciting caves. Over 120 miles (193 km) of Lechuguilla Cave have so far been mapped, making it the fifth longest in the world. At 1,604 feet (489 m), it is the deepest limestone cave in the country. Its size and beauty surpasses even Carlsbad Cavern, with enormous chandeliers, long delicate soda straws, and amazing speleothems never seen before. But this pristine cave, untouched by man, has yielded something even more important. Rare microorganisms have been found that may help humans in the fight against cancer. It is only open to researchers.

Formations such as the Twin Domes in the Hall of Giants, which can be seen on the Big Room (**2**) tour, highlight the enormity of this ancient cave system.

–> FACT FILE

CLIMATE Temperature in the cave is a constant 56ºF (13ºC) all year round. Outside, summer temperatures soar to 100ºF (37ºC) while cold temperatures and occasional snow are the norm in winter.

WHAT TO TAKE Sweater or jacket, long trousers, and sturdy walking shoes with nonslip soles for the cave; hiking boots for outdoor trails.

BEST TIME Spring and fall are less crowded than summer and outdoor temperatures are at their best. Spring can be windy.

NEAREST AIRPORTS El Paso, 165 miles (265 km) away; Albuquerque 275 miles (442 km) away.

ACCOMMODATIONS There is a resort and motel at White City, nearest to the park entrance. More lodging options are found 20 miles (32 km) northeast at the town of Carlsbad.

PARK ENTRANCE Entry tickets per person are required and are valid for three days. Prices for guided tours vary and reservations are strongly recommended.

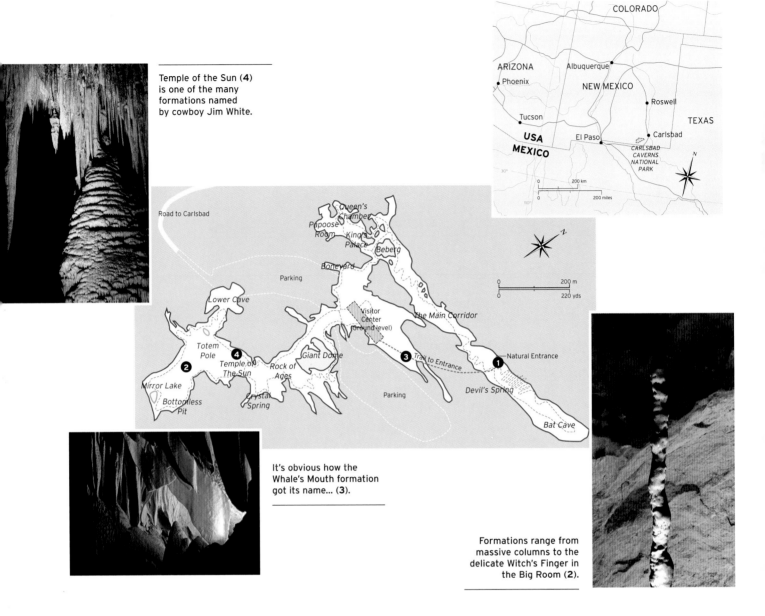

Temple of the Sun (**4**) is one of the many formations named by cowboy Jim White.

It's obvious how the Whale's Mouth formation got its name... (**3**).

Formations range from massive columns to the delicate Witch's Finger in the Big Room (**2**).

Exploring the Caverns

The first visitors were lowered into the cavern in guano buckets, just like the cowboys. It is much easier today. There is an elevator down into the central lunchroom, 750 feet (230 m) deep. But it is much more rewarding to walk in via the Natural Entrance, along a steep but paved 1-mile (1.6-km) trail. From here there is a self-guided walk through the Big Room, the largest known cavern some 24 stories high. You will see some of the most famous formations here, such as the huge stalagmites called the Twin Domes, the Giant Dome column—62 feet (19 m) high, the Rock of Ages, Fairyland, and the Bottomless Pit.

Here, too, is Crystal Spring Dome, the largest active speleothem in the cave today. Some areas of the caverns are still growing, though at a far less rapid pace—1 millimeter per year is the normal growth rate. Because the climate is drier, only about 5 percent are active today.

You can visit other parts of the caverns on guided tours. The King's Palace tour takes you to the deepest accessible point, 830 feet (250 m) below ground, as well as the Queen's Chamber with its 40-foot (12-m) tall draperies and cobweb-like helictites, the Papoose Room, and the Green Lake Room, with its calcite lily pads. Other tours go to more remote caves, such as Lower Cave or the wilder Slaughter Canyon Cave. While more than 100 miles (161 km) of cave passages are now open, there are many more that have not been explored, or even discovered.

When Jim White led the first surveyor into the caverns in 1923, he stopped with awe and said "I have neither the words nor the instruments to describe this place." Such is the beauty of this fragile, hidden world, created with the infinite artistry and patience of nature over such a great span of time.

Around every turn, Carlsbad Caverns reveals rooms full of magical formations created by mere drops of mineral-laden water.

THE BLUE RIDGE PARKWAY

Often called "the most graceful road in America," this spectacular drive through Virginia and North Carolina highlights the history, wildlife, and beauty of the Appalachian Mountains.

Sunset lights the fall leaves with a warm, rosy glow across the forested mountains bordering North Carolina's Blue Ridge Parkway (1).

THE BLUE RIDGE PARKWAY IS ONE of North America's most beautiful drives. It follows the backbone of the southern Appalachian Mountains for 469 miles (755 km), from Shenandoah National Park in Virginia, through North Carolina to Great Smoky Mountains National Park on the Tennessee border. Around 20 million visitors drive this road every year, making it the most visited unit of the U.S. National Park System.

At its northern end, the parkway connects with Skyline Drive, a 105-mile (169-km) road that runs the length of Shenandoah National Park. Together they make up one of the longest scenic drives in the country. There are numerous overlooks where you can stop to take in the fantastic views sweeping across the mountain ridges, forests, and valleys. Mileposts numbered north to south help you locate the hiking trails, picnic areas, historic sites, and points of interest along the way. From bright spring wildflowers to lush summer meadows to fiery fall foliage, the route is a kaleidoscope of natural beauty, with deer, wild turkeys, and even black bears among the woodland wildlife that may cross your path.

–> FACT FILE

CLIMATE Conditions can vary greatly from the valleys to the high mountains, where temperatures can be 10ºF (6ºC) or cooler. Summers in the lowlands are hot and humid, with pleasant temperatures in the mountains, but be prepared for rain. Winters bring snow and ice at higher elevations.

WHAT TO TAKE Sweater or jacket and rain gear at all times of year; hiking boots or good walking shoes.

BEST TIME Spring for the wildflowers, summer for the best temperatures, and late September–October for brilliant fall foliage, though the latter is a particularly busy time. The road is not maintained in winter, and sections of the route at high elevations and near tunnels may be closed in winter due to snow and ice.

NEAREST AIRPORTS Dulles International Airport in Chantilly, Virginia, is the closest airport to the northern end of Skyline Drive. There are regional airports near the parkway at Roanoke, Virginia and Asheville, North Carolina. Charlotte Douglas International Airport is a 2$1/2$-hour drive from Asheville.

ACCOMMODATIONS There are four park lodges along the parkway and several campgrounds. A variety of accommodations from chain motels to hotels and bed and breakfast inns are located in towns just off the parkway.

TRAVEL TIP Sections of the parkway may occasionally be closed for repairs. Check the National Parks website for updates.

PARK ENTRANCE There is no fee to travel on the Blue Ridge Parkway. There is an entrance fee for Skyline Drive.

Skyline Drive

Though it is barely an hour's drive from the nation's capital, Washington, D.C., 40 percent of Shenandoah National Park is designated wilderness. Skyline Drive is the park's thoroughfare, running northeast to southwest along the crest of the Blue Ridge Mountains. Most of its 75 overlooks peer out over wilderness covered in hardwood forest, with the Shenandoah Valley to the west. The narrow and winding road has a speed limit of 35 miles (56 km) per hour, making for a leisurely drive of about three hours end to end.

From the northern entrance at Front Royal, Skyline Drive winds up through the trees to a stunning viewpoint overlooking the Shenandoah Valley. Shortly beyond, the Dickey Ridge Visitor Center has exhibits about the area's history and natural features. The Hogback Overlook has splendid views over several bends in the Shenandoah River, meandering through the valley. After Thornton Gap, Mary's Rock Tunnel runs 670 feet (204 m) through solid granite.

Watch for the face of Stony Man outlined on the 4,011-foot (1,223-m) peak around milepost 39.

The "Star City of the South," hub of the Roanoke Valley (2).

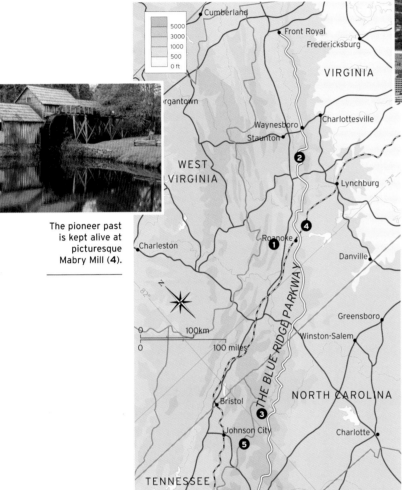

The pioneer past is kept alive at picturesque Mabry Mill (4).

Just beyond is the highest point of the drive, 3,680 feet (1,122 m), at Skyland Resort where trails lead to the summit. Nearby, White Oak Canyon is a popular half-day walk, featuring huge boulders, steep gorges, waterfalls, and pools. Further on, Dark Hollow Falls is a closer walk from the road. Big Meadows is the halfway point of the drive, a good place to see the park's white-tailed deer, birds, and many of its 66 rare plant species. From Loft Mountain, the drive slowly descends to its southern terminus at Rockfish Gap.

On the Road

Originally called the Appalachian Scenic Highway, the Blue Ridge parkway took more than 52 years to complete, its final section laid in 1987. It passes through 26 tunnels, all but one of them in North Carolina. They were dug through the rock by hand in the 1930s, providing employment during the Great Depression. The longest is the Pine Mountain Tunnel, at 1,434 feet (437 m). The parkway also incorporates 6 viaducts and 168 bridges.

A great variety of plants, animals, reptiles, and birds thrive in its diverse climate zones. Nearly 100 tree species grow along the parkway, about as many as on the entire European continent. Most eastern migratory species use the Appalachian Mountains as a flyway, making it an excellent place for birdwatching.

The speed limit on the parkway is 45 miles (72 km) per hour, less on some stretches. Allow several days to drive the route and enjoy its historic sites and hiking trails.

–> The Appalachian Trail

Another way to see these glorious mountains is on foot along the Appalachian Trail, a 2,175-mile (3,500-km) hiking route that runs from Maine to Georgia. A 70-mile (113-km) stretch of the trail runs through Great Smoky Mountains National Park, at the southern end of the Blue Ridge Parkway. At 6,643 feet (2,025 m), Clingmans Dome on the North Carolina–Tennessee border is the highest peak in the Smokies. The highest section of the Appalachian Trail runs just below the summit.

The Gothic-style Jackson Building at Pack Square, Asheville's first skyscraper (3).

The stunning views from Waterrock Knob (**5**) make it a challenge to keep your eyes on the road along one of the most scenic stretches of the parkway.

The Blue Ridge Parkway begins at Rockfish Gap, near Waynesboro, Virginia. Humpback Rocks is a good first stop, with its collection of nineteenth-century cabins and farm buildings. More historic homesteads are set in a forest clearing at the Peaks of Otter, with impressive views of Flat Top and Sharp Top peaks. Roanoke is the largest city off the parkway, and there are splendid views over the valley from the summit drive around Roanoke Mountain. Pioneer skills are demonstrated at Mabry Mill, with its working waterwheel. The Blue Ridge Music Center near Galax has weekend concerts, demonstrations, and a museum dedicated to old-time regional music.

In North Carolina the parkway becomes higher and more rugged. The parkway began at Cumberland Knob, near the state line, in 1935. The open meadows at Doughton Park are one of the best places to see deer, raccoons, and other wildlife. Near Blowing Rock, Flat Top Manor in Moses H. Cone Memorial Park houses the Parkway Craft Center. Linn Cove Viaduct, the final piece of the parkway to be built, is an engineering triumph that curves around Grandfather Mountain. The dramatic Linville Falls plunge into a deep gorge.

Beyond Crabtree Meadows, the parkway leaves the Blue Ridge Mountains and continues through other Appalachian mountains and forest. At Asheville you can visit the Folk Art Center, home of the Southern Highlands Craft Guild, which displays traditional mountain handicrafts along the parkway, and the opulent Biltmore House, built by George Vanderbilt in 1888-1895. After Mount Pisgah, the road climbs to 6,047 feet (1,843 m) on Richland Balsam Mountain, the highest point on the parkway. Waterrock Knob has panoramic views that stretch into four states. The parkway descends to its final milepost on the edge of the Indian reservation at Cherokee. Beyond rise the Great Smoky Mountains and their surrounding national park, with vast stretches of untamed wilderness.

FLORIDA EVERGLADES

Southern Florida's exotic Everglades are an enormous river of grass, teeming with endangered wildlife and rare plants found nowhere else in the world.

The freshwaters of the Big Cypress Swamp (1) play a vital role in supporting the habitat of the neighboring Everglades.

"HERE ARE NO LOFTY PEAKS seeking the sky, no mighty glaciers or rushing streams wearing away the uplifted land. Here is land, tranquil in its quiet beauty, serving not as the source of water but as the last receiver of it." President Harry S. Truman spoke these words at the dedication of Everglades National Park in December 1947.

The Everglades form the only subtropical wilderness in North America. The park, which covers 1,508,538 acres (610,475 ha) at Florida's southern tip, is only one small portion of this amazing ecosystem that once encompassed the entire peninsula south of Lake Okeechobee. In fact, it begins much further north near the theme parks of Orlando, where the Kissimmee chain of lakes

forms the headwaters to the Everglades. From here, water flows along creeks, levees, and the Kissimmee River to Lake Okeechobee, where the watershed begins.

Native Americans called the Everglades "Pa-hay-okee" meaning "the grassy waters." Their elevation is never higher than 8 feet (2.4 m) above sea level, but the only source of water throughout the region is rainfall. This remarkable ecosystem depends on the annual cycle of wet and dry seasons. Although the landscape appears flat as far as the eye can see, its limestone base slants ever so gradually southward to the coast. After the summer rains, water flows from Lake Okeechobee in a great, slow-moving sheet over 60 miles (97 km) wide

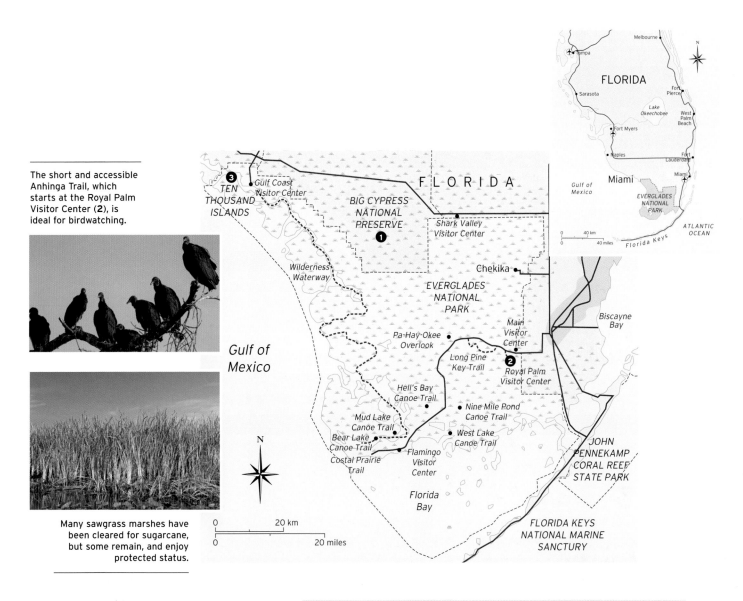

The short and accessible Anhinga Trail, which starts at the Royal Palm Visitor Center (**2**), is ideal for birdwatching.

Many sawgrass marshes have been cleared for sugarcane, but some remain, and enjoy protected status.

but only a few inches deep, rejuvenating the rich plant and animal life of the Everglades before draining into Florida Bay. The landscape then dries up until the following season.

Early Native American tribes lived in harmony with the Everglades, as did the Seminoles who fled here from the north to escape military persecution in the 1800s. Their descendants still live here today. But in the late nineteenth century, as Florida settlement grew, people began draining the Everglades for farmland, flood control, and urban development. The building of US 41—the Tamiami Highway—across the Glades in the 1920s severely disrupted the flow of water and wildlife. In less than a century, humans destroyed 50 percent of a unique environment that had thrived for thousands of years.

Everglades National Park

When Everglades National Park was founded in 1947, it was the first time a large area of wilderness was set aside for the conservation of its plants,

-> The Real Mermaids?

Manatees are native to Florida and live in rivers, inlets, and bays. These gentle giants can grow up to 10 feet (3 m) long and weigh 3,500 pounds (1,588 kg), with a sweet face and broad rounded tail. Though they spend much of their time underwater, they are mammals and must surface to breathe. For centuries sailors on long voyages have reported seeing lovely creatures who were part woman, part fish. It is believed that they were actually seeing manatees, not mermaids.

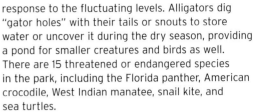

The Salt Water Crocodile can be found lurking in the Everglades...

Great blue heron is in its element wading through Florida's wetlands.

animals, and habitat, rather than for its scenic beauty. It is the third-largest U.S. national park outside Alaska, after Death Valley and Yellowstone. In recognition of its global significance, it has been designated an International Biosphere Reserve, a UNESCO World Heritage Site, and a Wetland of International Importance.

There is nowhere else on earth like the Everglades. At first glance they may appear to be a monotonous swamp, with an endless expanse of the sharp-edged sawgrass writer Marjory Stoneman Douglas first dubbed the "River of Grass." But these still waters are teeming with a rich diversity of life that includes 40 mammal species, more than 360 bird species, 300 species of fish, and 50 reptile species from tiny lizards to giant crocodiles.

Wildlife has long adapted to the water cycles of the Everglades, often moving over some distance in response to the fluctuating levels. Alligators dig "gator holes" with their tails or snouts to store water or uncover it during the dry season, providing a pond for smaller creatures and birds as well. There are 15 threatened or endangered species in the park, including the Florida panther, American crocodile, West Indian manatee, snail kite, and sea turtles.

Altogether there are more than 1,000 species of plants in Everglades National Park, including 45 endemic species that exist only here. They thrive in nine distinct but interrelated habitats. Clinging to the limestone bed is a thin layer of decayed vegetation, called "marl," which acts as soil for the sawgrass prairie. This sweeping expanse is broken by hardwood hammocks, the small islands that rise a few inches above the high water level and support mahogany, red maple, and other trees and plants. There are also smaller mounds called bayheads, mangroves, cypress swamps, freshwater sloughs, and a few pinewoods at higher elevations.

Seeing the Everglades

From the main park entrance west of Florida City, a 38-mile (61-km) road runs through the southern section of the park. There are trails and boardwalks along the way where you can get close-up views of this fascinating environment. An easy introduction is the short Anhinga Trail at the Royal Palm Visitor Center, where you are practically guaranteed to see alligators. It is named for a notable Everglades bird, often seen drying its black-and-white wings after diving for fish. Heron, egrets, bald eagles, and perhaps the rare snail kite may be spotted at the Pa-hay-okee Overlook Trail. There are more good trails at Long Pine Key and Mahogany Hammock. At the end of the road is Flamingo, a former fishing village misnamed for its multitude of pink-feathered roseate spoonbills. There are canoe trails here and tour boats to Cape Sable, the most southerly point on the U.S. mainland.

From the north you can enter the park at Shark Valley, where you can see wildlife from the bike trail, tram, or observation tower. From Everglades City you can see the park only by canoe or boat tours, which will take you to the Ten Thousand Islands area, part of the largest stand of protected mangrove forest in the western hemisphere. To the north, the protected swamplands at Big Cypress National Preserve are another vital part of the Everglades ecosystem.

The Everglades remain under threat, but a 30-year, multibillion-dollar plan to redress the damage done by human activity began in 2000. Though progress is slow, over time it is hoped that this unique and fragile environment will be preserved.

Roughly 200 species of
fish and over 190 species
of birds take refuge in the
Ten Thousand Islands (**3**).

-> FACT FILE

CLIMATE The Everglades have two seasons: wet and dry. The rainy season is June-October, with annual rainfall 60 inches (152 cm) per year. Summers are hot and very humid, with high temperatures around 90ºF (32ºC) and afternoon thunderstorms. Hurricane season is June-November. Winters are mild and pleasant with highs averaging 77ºF (25ºC) December-April, though there are occasional cold fronts.

WHAT TO TAKE Insect repellent, rain jacket, light clothing with long sleeves and trousers to deter insects; sunscreen, sun hat, sunglasses.

BEST TIME Winter (November-March) is the best time to see wildlife when birds and animals gather near water spots during the dry season; however the park is busy and prices are higher. Mosquitoes and other insects can make summer visits uncomfortable. Spring and late fall are good times to balance the weather, wildlife, and crowds.

NEAREST AIRPORTS Miami International Airport is about 35 miles (56 km) from Everglades National Park.

ACCOMMODATIONS There are campgrounds but only one hotel in the park, at Flamingo. A range of hotels, motels, bed and breakfasts, and resorts can be found in nearby towns and cities.

PARK ENTRANCE An entrance fee per vehicle or per cyclist is valid for seven days. Annual passes good at all national parks are also available.

ART DECO MIAMI

Sultry nights and Latin rhythms give Miami its sizzle;
the brightly colored Art Deco hotels of South Beach
give it its style.

As in their 1920s' heyday, the hotels of the Art Deco District, South Beach (1), are a mecca for Hollywood stars and the rich and famous.

MIAMI IS SYNONYMOUS WITH SUN and fun, conjuring up images of sandy beaches, luxury yachts, flashy cars, and beautiful people. It also has the largest group of Art Deco buildings in the world, clustered in an 80-block district in South Beach.

In the 1920s, Miami Beach was the Las Vegas of its day. Gangsters and gamblers saw out the dark days of Prohibition in its swanky hotels, where gaming, girls, and bootleg liquor were in plentiful supply. It became a winter playground for the wealthy set. A decade later, they were followed by middle-class sunseekers who sparked a new tourist boom. Rather than see the South Beach shoreline cluttered with lackluster budget hotels, city

Before there was South Beach, there was Biscayne Boulevard; travel across the causeway (west) and you'll reach Biscayne Boulevard, downtown Miami.

Just one of the many lifeguard towers that line the shore at South Beach.

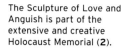

The Sculpture of Love and Anguish is part of the extensive and creative Holocaust Memorial (**2**).

Miami's trendy hub: it all happens on Ocean Drive (**3**), especially at night.

planners took the enlightened decision to impose a distinct building style: Art Deco.

The style had been launched in Paris in 1925 at the Paris Exposition Internationale des Arts Décoratifs et Industriels Modernes. It was the designers' answer to the burgeoning Machine Age, an attempt to join industrial mass production with the decorative arts. Art Deco architecture amalgamated a variety of early twentieth-century forms and influences, from the geometric shapes of Cubism to the elaborate swirls of Art Nouveau, using man-made materials such as glass, aluminum, and stainless steel. Interestingly, it was only nicknamed Art Deco retroactively in the 1960s.

It was perfect for Miami's South Beach. The city's wooden buildings had been flattened by a hurricane in 1926, and the new concrete structures were better able to withstand fierce storms. Their original exteriors—stark white with only the trim and details in color, in keeping with Art Deco style—reflected Florida's harsh sun. The clean lines and stylish

-> Other Architectural Styles

Two more styles are frequently seen in the Art Deco Historic District. Mediterranean Revival is a whimsical version of Old World architecture, with features such as rough stucco walls, bell towers, clay-tile roofs, and carved stonework. A prime example is the Versace Mansion. Miami Modern, or MiMo, was a 1950s style incorporating futuristic shapes, asymmetry, tiled mosaic walls, and open balconies.

details were cheerful and uplifting, an optimistic contrast to the pall of the Great Depression. Inexpensive to construct and ultramodern in appearance, hundreds of Art Deco buildings soon spread across South Beach.

Art Deco Miami-style

Art Deco architecture took on its own special style in Miami. Its early form, dubbed Tropical Deco, drew on the city's climate and seaside location. Decorative reliefs featured flamingos, palms, and foliage, or nautical motifs such as portholes and anchors. Windows sported "eyebrows"—small ledges above to provide shade. Long bands of windows, which often wrapped around curved corners, brought in sunlight and ocean breezes.

Architects used a variety of new construction materials, from glass blocks to terrazzo (an imitation marble) floors. Neon lighting was another striking new feature. Interior spaces were also adorned with murals, iron, and glasswork.

The later Streamline Moderne form smoothed out some of Art Deco's stark, geometric lines. Architects borrowed elements from industrial designs for ocean liners and automobiles. They aimed to create a sense of movement with vertical central pillars that soared above the roofline, resembling a ship's funnel, or colored bands painted round corners, known as racing stripes.

Some of the best Art Deco buildings are concentrated along Ocean Drive, Collins Avenue, and Washington Avenue, parallel to the ocean. But the entire district runs south from Dade Boulevard to Fifth Street, and west to Lenox Avenue. Stop by the Art Deco Welcome Center for maps and information. Some of the outstanding hotels to look for are the Cardozo, Leslie, Cavalier, Breakwater, Clevelander, Marlin, and Delano.

In Miami, designers adopted themes and colors to the Art Deco style that reflected the breezy, seaside character of the city.

-> FACT FILE

POPULATION City 377,000; county 2.25 million.

CLIMATE Tropical, with hot and humid summers and warm temperatures year-round. Average highs range from 76ºF (24ºC) in January to 90ºF (32ºC) in August. Rainfall is high, averaging 58½ inches (148 cm) per year.

WHAT TO TAKE A light rain jacket and a light sweater or jacket for air-conditioned buildings. Sunscreen and sunglasses.

BEST TIME Winter is warm, and generally dry with less humidity. Most rain falls from mid-May through early October. The hurricane season is from June through November.

NEAREST AIRPORT Miami International Airport is 8 miles (13 km) from the central business district.

ACCOMMODATIONS South Beach's Art Deco hotels are mid-range to expensive. Book well ahead for busy holiday periods and the spring break.

GUIDED TOURS The Miami Design Preservation League offers walking tours from the Art Deco Welcome Center, 1001 Ocean Drive. You can also rent audiotapes for self-guided tours of the Art Deco Historic District.

The hotels on the South Beach strip (**4**) claim to be among the most photographed in the world.

A Retro Revival

As you look at these retro gems today, it is hard to believe they were built for the early budget travelers, rather than for a wealthy clientele. It is even harder to imagine that they were nearly lost to the wrecking ball. By the 1960s, most of the old hotels had became run down. As developers eyed the prime oceanfront real estate, the neglected buildings were threatened with demolition.

Thankfully, Barbara Capitman and five others founded the Miami Design Preservation League to lobby for their protection and restoration. In 1979 an area of South Beach covering 1 square mile (2.6 sq km) and some 800 buildings was listed on the National Register of Historic Places. It was the first twentieth-century district to receive this designation. Investors began renovating the

structures inside and out, and interior designer Leonard Horowitz, a member of the league, introduced the color palette of pastel pink, sherbet yellow, peach, turquoise, and violet that became the area's trademark.

When the television show *Miami Vice* debuted in 1984, it catapulted the city into ultra-hip status. Over its five-year run, numerous scenes were filmed in South Beach, which still had many seedy pockets as well as its sleek new Art Deco façades. Fashion photographers also discovered its fine light and colorful backdrops; models and pop stars moved in; chic nightclubs, bars, and restaurants opened; and South Beach became a vibrant, international hot spot. Today its old Art Deco buildings are stylish once again, and worth a fortune.

NATCHEZ TRACE PARKWAY

Passing ancient Native American burial mounds and unspoiled rural landscape, the Natchez Trace follows America's early frontiersmen on a timeless route through the Deep South.

IMAGINE DRIVING ALL THE WAY across a U.S. state and seeing no billboards, no fast-food chains, no motel strips or convenience stores, only fields and forests that seem little changed from a century ago. Driving or cycling the Natchez Trace Parkway is a rare opportunity to do just that.

The parkway cuts diagonally across Mississippi on its 444-mile (715-km) route from Natchez to Nashville, Tennessee. It was "traced out" by wild animals over 8,000 years ago, and the native Natchez, Choctaw, and Chickasaw Indians used their trails as a hunting and trading path through the dense, primeval forest. They were followed by trappers and frontiersmen such as Davy Crockett and Jim Bowie.

At the end of the eighteenth century, as agriculture expanded in the Ohio River Valley, farmers floated their goods and produce down the rivers on large flatboats to markets in New Orleans. They sold their boats for lumber and returned home on foot or horseback. The Trace was the quickest route, though not necessarily the safest, as travelers faced bandits, disease-carrying mosquitoes, floods, swamps, and other hazards. But they tramped the wilderness trail into a well-worn path.

From 1800 to 1820, the Trace was the busiest road in what was then the Southwest. The first U.S. mail service was started here. General Andrew Jackson led his sharpshooters down the Trace on their way to the Battle of New Orleans in 1815. By the 1820s, however, steamboats offered a faster and more comfortable journey back upriver and the Trace reverted to a quiet forest trail. It might have disappeared altogether but for the Mississippi Chapter of the Daughters of the American Revolution, who began a campaign in 1909 to mark the old Trace.

Today the Natchez Trace Parkway is a federal scenic byway that closely follows the original trail.

The Natchez Trace Parkway passes through timeless rural views near the historic town of Port Gibson (1).

CLIMATE Summers are hot and humid with high temperatures in the 90s°F (32+°C). Winter conditions vary by location; temperatures are mild and generally above freezing near Natchez, with snow and ice a possibility in Tennessee.

WHAT TO TAKE Hiking boots or sturdy walking shoes, insect repellent, rain jacket.

BEST TIME Spring and fall have the most pleasant temperatures, with blossoming trees and shrubs in spring and colorful fall foliage from September to November, along with snowy white cotton bolls in the fields before the October harvest.

NEAREST AIRPORTS The closest commercial airports to the start of the parkway at Natchez are at Jackson, Mississippi, 105 miles (169 km) away or Baton Rouge, Louisiana, 90 miles (145 km) away. Nashville International Airport serves the northern terminus.

ACCOMMODATIONS There are no accommodations on the parkway itself, but towns and cities just off the route have a range of hotels and motels. Many of the old mansions and historic homes in Natchez, Port Gibson, and other towns have been turned into gracious bed and breakfast establishments. There are three campgrounds along the parkway with basic facilities.

TRAVEL TIPS There are no gas stations or food stores on the parkway.

Semi-transparent way markers add to the ethereal feel of the Natchez Trace Parkway (2), dating from the early 1800s.

Mileposts are located along the east side of the road, and historic markers bear witness to important places and people who passed this way. Billboards are prohibited and the speed limit is a leisurely 50 miles (80 km) per hour. There are numerous picnic areas and hiking trails, and regular exits lead to nearby towns for food, gas, and lodging.

From Natchez to Tupelo

The parkway winds through pastures, swamps, cotton fields, and woodland of tall pines and moss-draped oaks. Kudzu, a fast-growing Oriental vine that has invaded the region, covers untended hillsides. Small houses, barns, mission churches, and country stores provide glimpses of rural life. White-tailed deer are numerous along the parkway. Many sites have ancient Indian burial mounds or remnants of early settlers. Keep an eye out for signs directing you to the Old Trace, where you can walk the original forest trail and get a sense of what it was like 200 years ago.

The route begins a few miles north of Natchez off US 61. Soon after entering the parkway, you can see a stretch of the original trail at the Old Trace Exhibit Shelter, milepost 8.7. Just beyond, Emerald Mound is the second-largest Indian ceremonial mound in the nation, built by Natchez ancestors between A.D. 1250-1600. It covers nearly 8 acres (3 ha) and you can climb to the top.

While there are no accommodations on the Trace today, early travelers found food and lodging at basic inns, called "stands," along the way. Several have been restored, such as the one at Mount Locust. Sunken Trace is a short but atmospheric trail through an eroded section of the old path. Rocky Springs has a longer trail on the Old Trace and a path leading to an old townsite.

On the north side of the state capital, Jackson, a popular stop is the Mississippi Crafts Center, with demonstrations and sales of traditional crafts. From the Reservoir Overlook, the parkway parallels the Ross Barnett Reservoir on the Pearl River for 8 miles (13 km), passing Indian burial mounds at Boyd Site. Beyond is a boardwalk trail through the Cypress Swamp.

Other places of interest along the way include the stand at French Camp, which has been a school since 1822; the overlook at Jeff Busby Site, one of the highest spots in Mississippi; and Bynum Mounds, with exhibits on the prehistoric people who built them some 2,000 years ago. A Chickasaw Village, Council House, and Civil War battlefield are highlights on the Trace surrounding the city of Tupelo, birthplace of Elvis Presley.

From Tupelo to Nashville

Twentymile Bottom Overlook shows the typical landscape of the Old Trace. Pharr Mounds is a large complex of eight burial mounds. At milepost

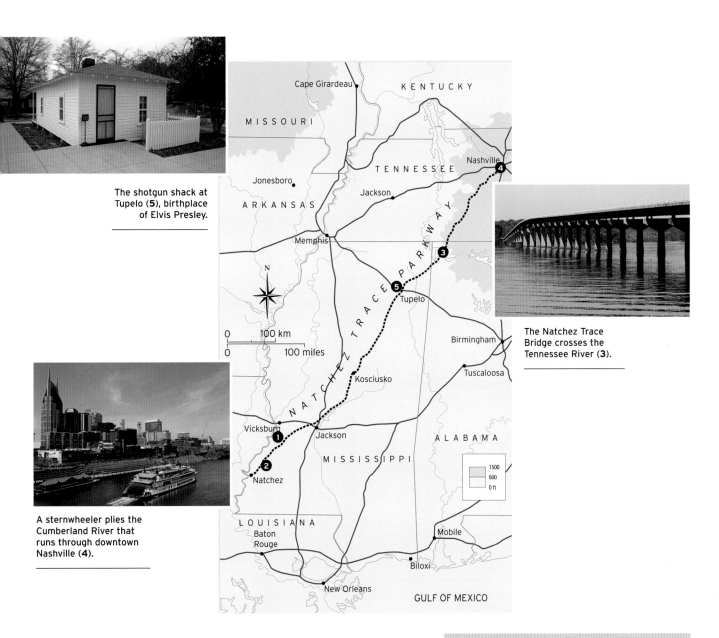

The shotgun shack at Tupelo (**5**), birthplace of Elvis Presley.

The Natchez Trace Bridge crosses the Tennessee River (**3**).

A sternwheeler plies the Cumberland River that runs through downtown Nashville (**4**).

Bald Cypress trees thrive in pockets of swamp habitat (opposite) along the Natchez Trace Parkway, northeast of Jackson, Mississippi.

308.9, the parkway crosses the state line into Alabama. Colbert Ferry is a famous crossing on the Tennessee River.

At milepost 341.8 the parkway enters Tennessee. A detour on the Old Trace Drive follows the original path for a couple of miles with scenic overlooks. A monument at the Meriwether Lewis site marks the grave of the famous explorer from the Lewis and Clark Expedition, who died of gunshot wounds on the Trace at Grinder's Stand in 1809.

The Tobacco Farm has exhibits on one of the major crops of the Old South, with another short drive and walk on the Old Trace nearby. Beyond are Jackson Falls. The parkway terminates on the outskirts of Nashville, country music capital of the United States.

-> Natchez, Belle of the South

Natchez is the oldest town on the Mississippi, set high on a bluff overlooking the river. It grew rich on the nineteenth-century cotton trade, and before the Civil War the city boasted 500 millionaires—more than anywhere in the country except New York. When war broke out, Natchez surrendered without a fight, ensuring the survival of its beautiful antebellum buildings, of which it has the largest number in the nation. Several of these grand mansions are open for tours year-round, including Stanton Hall, Magnolia Hall, and Rosalie.

SOUTHERN UTAH'S NATIONAL PARKS

"This is a landscape that has to be seen to be believed, and even then, confronted directly by the senses, it strains credulity." Edward Abbey, author and essayist.

SOUTHERN UTAH IS AMERICA'S great natural theme park. Not even Disney could imagine, let alone match, the fantastical creations placed here by nature, the master sculptor: soaring rock pinnacles, chiseled buttes, whimsical rock formations, striated cliffs and hoodoos, looping river canyons, and graceful rock arches and bridges that seem to defy gravity.

It lies on the Colorado Plateau, which covers 130,000 square miles (337,000 sq km) of the Four Corners region, where Utah, Arizona, Colorado, and New Mexico meet. This vast province was uplifted by the collision of continental plates around 75 million years ago. Apart from the canyon bottoms, these high tablelands are no lower than 5,000 feet (1,524 m) in elevation and range up to 11,000 feet (3,353 m). Its remarkable features were then carved out over the millennia by the Colorado River and its main tributaries, the Green, Little Colorado, Virgin, and San Juan rivers, and polished off by erosion, primarily from water but also from ice, wind, dust, and rockfall. The palette of hues that changes from soft pink and beige to golden to fiery orange and red throughout the day comes from the varying types of sandstone, limestone, and other rock minerals that reveal ancient geological periods.

The Colorado Plateau contains the highest concentration of parklands in North America: 10 national parks, 17 national monuments, 32 wilderness areas, and dozens of national forests, state parks, tribal parks, and national recreation areas, enough to keep you hiking, biking, or simply gazing in wonder for years. Five of the most spectacular are in southern Utah.

Arches National Park

On the outskirts of Moab, Arches is one of Utah's most accessible parks. It contains over 2,000 natural sandstone arches, the greatest concentration in the world. The stunning red-rock formations include single and double arches, windows, fins, spires, and enormous boulders precariously balanced at the tip of a jagged arm. They range in size from 3 feet (1 m), the minimum to qualify as an arch, to the 306-foot (93-m) span of Landscape Arch, the world's longest natural sandstone arch.

-> FACT FILE

CLIMATE Temperatures vary with elevation. Summer highs can top 100ºF (37ºC) in desert areas. Winter brings snow and ice at higher elevations. Day and night temperatures can vary up to 30ºF (17ºC) at any time of year.

WHAT TO TAKE Bring layers of clothing for changing conditions; sunscreen, sunglasses, sun hat, plenty of water.

BEST TIME Spring and fall have the most comfortable temperatures in the desert regions.

NEAREST AIRPORTS Salt Lake City International Airport is about 240 miles (386 km) from Moab. Domestic flights serve Walker Field in Grand Junction, Colorado, about 120 miles (193 km) from Moab. Las Vegas International Airport is 150 miles (241 km) from Zion, and domestic flights serve the airport at nearby St. George.

ACCOMMODATIONS There are campgrounds in all the parks. Zion Lodge has motel rooms and cabins. There is a range of accommodations in towns near the parks including Moab, St. George, and Kanab.

PARK ENTRANCE An entrance fee per vehicle is valid for seven days. Annual passes good at all national parks are also available.

The hoodoo spires of Bryce Canyon National Park (1) seem to march across the canyon like a vast sandstone army.

141

It's worth the day-long hike to see the swirling colors of The Wave, a sandstone formation east of Kanab (**2**).

All these are found in a park of just 120 square miles (311 sq km). Many striking formations, such as Tower of Babel and Three Gossips, can be seen along the scenic drive, with viewpoints overlooking the Petrified Dunes and Fiery Furnace. Others can be reached on hiking trails. Delicate Arch, with its dramatic position on the edge of a slickrock cliff, is a famous symbol of Utah's parks.

Canyonlands National Park
Utah's largest park sprawls over 527 square miles (1,365 sq km), much of it backcountry wilderness. Its rugged landscape of canyons, buttes, and mesas was carved by the Colorado and Green Rivers. The park has three main sections, which are not directly linked by road. Most accessible is the northern Island in the Sky district, close to Moab. This high, sheer-walled mesa between the rivers stands 1,000 feet (305 m) above the surrounding canyon terrain, with stunning views from overlooks on the scenic rim drive.

The southeastern Needles district was named for its colorful sandstone spires. A scenic drive, hiking routes, and jeep trails lead to striking rock formations, Ancestral Pueblo ruins and rock art, and a magnificent viewpoint overlooking the

confluence of the rivers. The remote, rugged backcountry of the Maze district requires several days to explore. The rivers themselves are a distinct feature of the canyonlands, with boat trips and white-water rafting.

Capitol Reef National Park
This 378-square mile (979-sq km) park protects three-quarters of the 100-mile (161-km) long Waterpocket Fold, a magnificent geological warp characterized by colorful cliffs and ridges. Its name comes from the distinctive white domes of Navajo sandstone that look like those on capitol buildings, and the rocky cliffs that form a barrier, similar to an underwater reef, running north to south. There is a historic district and a highly scenic portion of the fold near the visitor center at Fruita. Cathedral Valley features freestanding reddish monoliths. Deep canyons and gorges, hogback ridges, buttes, arches, and spires are other features in the park.

Bryce Canyon National Park
Bryce Canyon is not really a canyon at all, but a huge natural amphitheater, filled with an army of

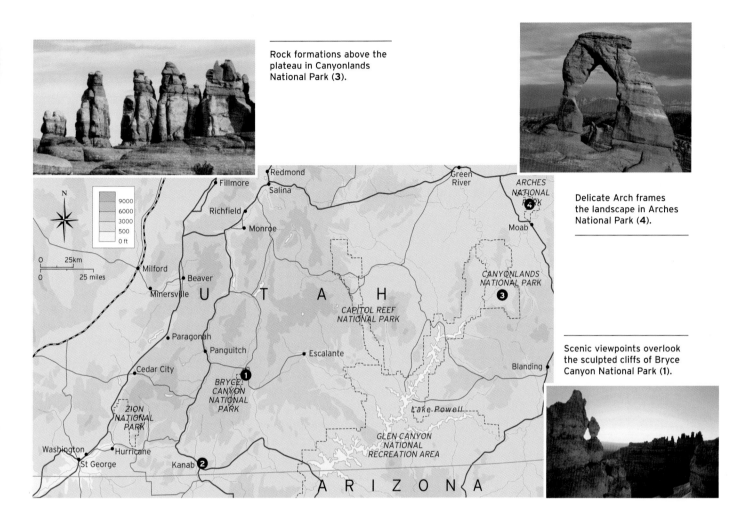

Rock formations above the plateau in Canyonlands National Park (**3**).

Delicate Arch frames the landscape in Arches National Park (**4**).

Scenic viewpoints overlook the sculpted cliffs of Bryce Canyon National Park (**1**).

the unusual, pink-hued totem-pole spires known as "hoodoos." An early homesteader, Ebenezer Bryce, wisely observed that this was "a hell of a place to lose a cow." The park that bears his name covers 56 square miles (145 sq km) and sits at a high elevation, its rim rising from 8,000 to more than 9,000 feet (2,438-2,743 m).

A scenic drive along the plateau's edge takes you to 15 romantically named overlooks such as Fairyland Point and Inspiration Point. From here you can take in the pink cliffs and colorful rock formations, or walk among the eerie, alien world of the hoodoos on several hiking trails.

Zion National Park

Founded in 1909, Zion is Utah's oldest national park. Its name attests to the region's Mormon settlers, to whom its soaring monoliths and massive sandstone cliffs—among the highest in the world—seemed a heavenly sanctuary. At the heart of the 229-square mile (593-sq km) park is Zion Canyon, carved by the north fork of the Virgin River. In summer shuttle buses run along a scenic drive to the top of the canyon.

From here, hiking trails lead into the high country and amazing viewpoints such as Angels

Landing. Zion is famous for its canyons, particularly the awesome riverbed hiking route through The Narrows. The variety of rock strata, minerals, and terrain give the park its rainbow colors. Wildlife thrives in its many habitats, from desert to wooded riverbanks to pine forests. For nature lovers, it is indeed a promised land.

-> Dead Horse Point

Set on a mesa between Arches and Canyonlands is Dead Horse Point State Park. From its overlook there is a magnificent view of the looping "gooseneck" bends of the Colorado River far below. Wild mustangs once ran free on these mesas, and cowboys used the promontory as a natural corral. It was named for an unfortunate herd that was unable to return to the range and died of thirst on the point. It has been used as a film location for *Thelma and Louise* and other movies.

CALIFORNIA'S GIANT REDWOODS

The north coast of California is the land of the giants, where the groves of magnificent redwood trees are the tallest living things on earth.

JOHN STEINBECK CALLED THEM "ambassadors from another time." When you walk among the giant redwoods in a silent, misty forest, your senses ring with the aura of an ancient land. Their sheer size is awesome. They regularly grow to over 300 feet (91 m) and see their 600th birthday, though some are more than three times that age and live for 2,000 years. When the dinosaurs roamed North America, the redwoods were here. Over the centuries they have seen countless species come and go, civilizations rise and fall, and still they remain. They are a rare link with the primeval.

The giant coast redwood, *Sequoia sempervirens*, grows only on the northern coast of California. Here the soil is continually enriched by decaying ferns, mosses, and other forest vegetation. The climate is temperate, with mild, relatively stable temperatures year-round. The region receives 90-100 inches (229-254 cm) of rainfall a year, mostly in the winter. Redwoods rely on the fog that shrouds the Pacific coast to provide moisture during the dry summer months. They receive up to 40 percent of their annual water needs by soaking up its droplets through their leaves and from the forest floor.

Sequoia sempervirens is closely related to the giant sequoias of central California, but while their cousins are more massive in volume, the coast redwoods are taller. In 2006 the tallest tree yet measured was discovered in a remote area of Redwood National Park. Named Hyperion, it is 379 feet (116 m) tall, topping the previous record holder by 9 feet (3 m). Two more giants, Helios and Icarus, were discovered nearby, taking second and third place at over 376 feet (115 m) and 371 feet (113 m) respectively.

The redwoods' amazing ability to live so long and grow so high is a mystery. Their thick, reddish bark has a high tannin content, which makes them resistant to insects and disease. Their high foliage and massive trunks, through which hundreds of gallons of water move upward each day from roots to crown, also help protect them against fire. Their biggest weakness is their shallow root system, which puts them in danger of toppling in high winds. They have only one natural enemy—humans.

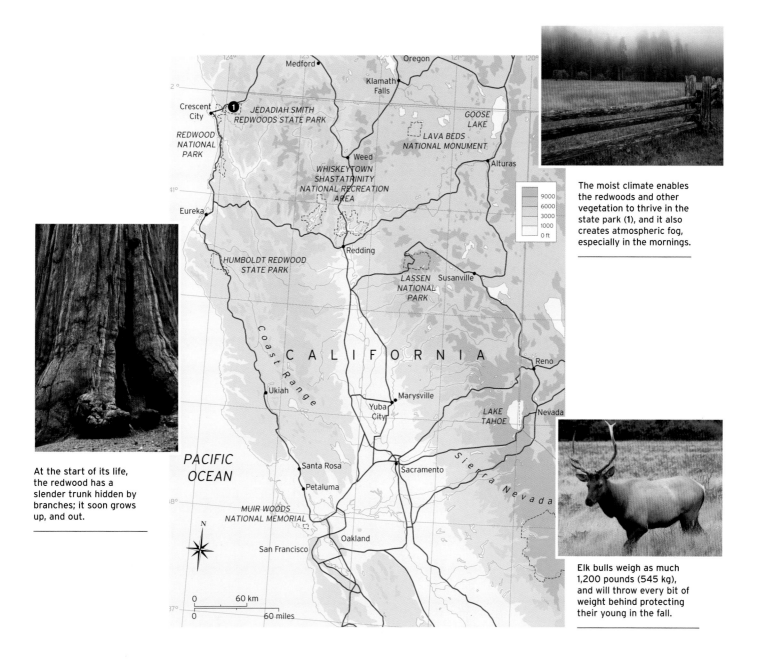

The moist climate enables the redwoods and other vegetation to thrive in the state park (1), and it also creates atmospheric fog, especially in the mornings.

At the start of its life, the redwood has a slender trunk hidden by branches; it soon grows up, and out.

Elk bulls weigh as much 1,200 pounds (545 kg), and will throw every bit of weight behind protecting their young in the fall.

Peering into the heart of a giant redwood, which has survived fire and other perils to live for hundreds of years.

Redwoods' Last Stand

The coast redwoods once covered 2 million acres (809,360 ha) of northern California and southern Oregon. But after the gold rush of the 1850s, white settlers poured in, eyeing the giant trees not for their beauty but for their lumber. In less than a century, extensive logging nearly wiped out these ancient monarchs. Only 4 percent of the old-growth redwood forests exist today.

In 1918 conservationists founded the Save-the-Redwoods League, which began to purchase areas for preservation. These later became state parks. It was not until 1968, however, that Redwood National Park was created. It is now joined with Prairie Creek Redwoods, Del Norte Coast Redwoods, and Jedediah Smith Redwoods under a single management system that protects 45 percent of California's remaining old-growth forests. In the 1980s the importance of these magnificent trees to the world was recognized when Redwood National and State Parks became a World Heritage Site and an International Biosphere Reserve.

The redwoods may be the stars of the park, but they have plenty of company. These forests are dense and diverse, supporting Douglas fir and western hemlock—giants in their own right—Sitka spruce, tanoaks, and madrones, among others, as well as an understory of ferns, azalea, and California rhododendron. Huckleberry, salmonberry, and other berry bushes provide food for black bears. Over 40 other mammal species include Roosevelt elks, deer, mountain lions, bobcats, river

145

-> FACT FILE

CLIMATE The region has a temperate climate with 90-100 inches (229-254 cm) of annual rainfall. Temperatures range from 40-60ºF (4-15ºC) year-round, and are cooler on the coastal lowlands.

WHAT TO TAKE Rain gear, good walking shoes for slippery forest floors, sweater or jacket for cooler weather conditions.

BEST TIME Summer is the dry season, but the parks are busiest from mid-June to September. Just before or after this time is quieter. Winter is the rainy season.

NEAREST AIRPORTS San Francisco has the closest international airport to the redwood coast.

ACCOMMODATIONS There is a range in towns all along the coast, and campgrounds in the parks.

PARK ENTRANCE Redwood National Park is free to visit. There are day-use fees for the state parks.

A glimpse of the sun through these forest skyscrapers can be rare: the trees are so tall and dense that some ground areas get virtually no sunlight, allowing for little growth.

Hiking or cycling is a great way to immerse yourself in the forest; take your pick from 56 miles (90 km) of trails in the national park, 16 miles (26 km) of which are accessible by bike (1).

otters, and beavers. Sea lions, harbor seals, and other marine species can be seen along the shore, and birdlife is plentiful.

Visiting the Redwoods

The components of Redwood National and State Parks are quite spread out along the coast. The Redwood Information Center is just before the town of Orick. Lady Bird Johnson Grove is a good introductory walk along a loop trail. Tall Trees Grove is home to a previous "world's highest" title holder and its companions.

Along with splendid redwoods, herds of Roosevelt elks in the adjoining meadows are a highlight of Prairie Creek Redwoods State Park. Take the Newton B. Drury Scenic Parkway through the park. A great bit of American kitsch awaits at Klamath, where huge statues of Paul Bunyan and his blue ox Babe stand beside the Trees of Mystery. At Del Norte Coast Redwoods State Park, follow

trails from the forest to the sea. Some of the most beautiful areas of old-growth forest are in Jedediah Smith Redwoods State Park, reached by the scenic Howland Hill Road.

The largest contiguous old-growth redwood forest is at Humboldt Redwoods State Park, south of Eureka. North of San Francisco, the redwood grove at Muir Woods National Monument is one of the last remaining stands of old-growth forest in the Bay Area, a fitting tribute to John Muir, the father of the national parks. The southernmost grove of coastal redwood trees is south of the city near Santa Cruz, at Big Basin Redwood State Park.

THE BEACHES OF GULF SHORES

With white sand beaches that sigh beneath your feet, blue skies, tasty seafood, and a friendly welcome, you could be in the Caribbean–but you are in the Deep South of Alabama.

The whispering sands of Alabama's Gulf Shores (1) take on an idyllic glow at sunset, the perfect time and place for a romantic stroll.

THEY CALL IT PLEASURE ISLAND, the stretch of coast at Alabama's southernmost tip along the Gulf of Mexico. For 32 miles (51 km) the white sand beaches run, separated from the rest of the state by the Intracoastal Waterway. When you look out to sea on a hot day, you are well aware that you have your back to the United States and are gazing across the warm Gulf waters toward Mexico or Cuba. Walk along those beaches and the sand is so soft in places that it creates a kind of sighing or whispering sound beneath your feet. For many visitors there is also a sighing in their hearts, knowing they have discovered one of the hidden gems of America–Gulf Shores.

The beaches here have been called some of the best in the world. Certainly when you stroll along

listening to the sand, feeling it soft as powder beneath your feet, and your eyes are dazzled by the miles of brilliant white sparkling diamonds in front of you, it would be hard to argue. The sands blow into sugar-white dunes covered in wispy sea oats, lending a windswept, rural feel. The sea ranges from turquoise blue to deep emerald in color. Backing the beaches are the resort cities of Gulf Shores and Orange Beach, with golf courses, marinas, shopping, and many fine restaurants.

Head east along the beaches and you will eventually reach Florida. Though comparisons are inevitable, Gulf Shores lacks the amusement park development of the Sunshine State, and the crowds and high prices that go with it. It does feel more down-home in Alabama.

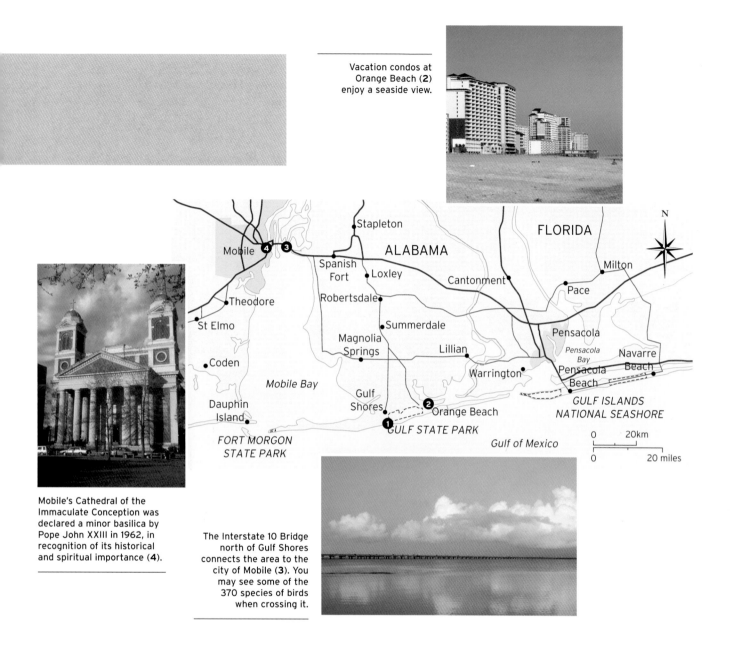

Vacation condos at Orange Beach (**2**) enjoy a seaside view.

Mobile's Cathedral of the Immaculate Conception was declared a minor basilica by Pope John XXIII in 1962, in recognition of its historical and spiritual importance (**4**).

The Interstate 10 Bridge north of Gulf Shores connects the area to the city of Mobile (**3**). You may see some of the 370 species of birds when crossing it.

Dolphins and Sea Turtles

What Alabama also shares with Florida, as well as beaches, is wildlife. The warm waters offshore attract numerous dolphins, so many that the dolphin-watch cruises that leave from Gulf Shores give a 100 percent promise that you will see bottle-nose dolphins.

The mild Gulf Shores climate makes it an appealing spot for migrating birds as well as humans who flock here in winter to escape the harsh northern weather. Freshwater lakes, rivers, bayous, and coves add nearly 400,000 acres (161,872 ha) of protected waters to the area.

At the Bon Secour National Wildlife Refuge there are more than 7,000 acres (2,833 ha) of unspoiled wildlife habitat, bordering the Gulf Coast and the

Bon Secour Bay, which separates Gulf Shores from Mobile Bay and, beyond that, the city of Mobile. At the refuge, more than 370 species of birds have been seen at the height of the migratory seasons, ranging from osprey and herons, loons and pelicans, to kingfishers and tiny hummingbirds. Just as tiny is the endangered and endearing Alabama beach mouse, which enjoys life in the sand dunes and the sea oats that grow here. The recent series of heavy hurricanes not only hit the people of Gulf Shores, they destroyed the mice and their homes too, which are also threatened by the ever-increasing development of the coastline. Refuges like Bon Secour are vital to their survival.

They are also vital to the three species of sea turtle that nest here—the green, loggerhead, and

The beaches and barrier islands along the Intracoastal Waterway are an important refuge for local shorebirds and migratory species.

Sultry breezes from the Gulf of Mexico blow across the tranquil, sugar-white sands of Alabama's Gulf Shores (1).

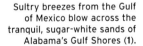

Mobile

Just as these Alabama beaches often get overlooked in favor of the more famous Florida beaches to the east, so the region's major city, Mobile, 50 miles (80 km) from Gulf Shores, is over-shadowed by New Orleans to the west. Yet Mobile has several historic districts boasting the antebellum mansions and wrought-iron architecture for which New Orleans is famous. Mobile also has the oldest Mardi Gras celebrations in the country. They began in 1703, 15 years before New Orleans was established as a settlement. Mobile became the first capital of French Louisiana in 1702; it was later renamed Mobile after the Native American Mobilian tribe who were here when the French arrived.

Kemp's Ridley. They love the soft sand of Alabama every bit as much as human visitors, and come ashore to build nests and bury their eggs on the warm nights from May to August. For the Kemp's Ridley sea turtle, the smallest sea turtle that exists, Bon Secour is indeed a "safe harbor," which is roughly what the name means in French. This turtle is critically endangered, with only a few thousand nesting females left.

Tossing the Mullet

Fortunately the seas here are abundant with creatures that are not endangered, and many of them end up fresh every day on the menus of the many fine eating places, which are another of the area's great pleasures. From fine-dining restaurants

-> FACT FILE

POPULATION 14,500

CLIMATE Gulf Shores has a mild, subtropical climate, and winters average 65ºF (18ºC), though it can drop into the mid-40sºF (about 7ºC) in December-February. Summer highs in the 90sºF (low 30sºC) are tempered by Gulf breezes. Rainfall is not high, though it can come at any time of year. Hurricane season is officially June 1-November 30, September being the worst month in recent years.

WHAT TO TAKE Beach gear, casual clothing, a healthy appetite.

BEST TIME May for the climate, October for the Shrimp Festival, though fall is the hurricane season.

NEAREST AIRPORT Mobile Regional Airport is about 60 miles (96 km) northwest.

ACCOMMODATIONS Lots of choice in all price ranges. Renting condos by the week is popular, and there are plenty of rental agencies in Gulf Shores and Orange Beach.

and oyster bars to boisterous local seafood shacks, Gulf Shores has everything. What it has in particular are royal red shrimp. As one female shrimp can lay up to a million eggs that can hatch within 24 hours, the waters here are thick with these sweet-tasting creatures. By the time they are ready for the table, they are halfway to being a lobster, and each October the Annual National Shrimp Festival celebrates this local delicacy.

Treated with less reverence than most local seafood, the humble mullet is the star of a famous local party cum fundraiser. It takes place on the last weekend of April on the beach at the Florabama, a rocking roadhouse that marks the Florida-Alabama state line. People compete to see who can throw a dead mullet the furthest from Alabama into Florida. The record stands at 189 feet 8 inches (57.8 m). Everyone has a good time, local youth charities benefit financially, and the local seagull population gets a feast of dead mullet.

This sense of fun, unashamed enjoyment of the good things in life, and the natural beauty of its beaches and wildlife trails all combine to make this one small part of the southern United States very special. It is indeed a pleasure island.

ARIZONA'S OLD WEST

From frontier legends to forests of towering saguaros, southern Arizona's Sonoran Desert presents a fun and fascinating look at the Old West.

WITH ITS MASSIVE, CURVED ARMS silhouetted against a flaming sunset, the tall saguaro cactus is a striking symbol of the American West. In fact, these desert giants are specific to just one region—the Sonoran Desert. Covering around 120,000 square miles (310,800 sq km), it stretches from the Baja peninsula across northwestern Mexico, covering most of central Arizona and the southeast corner of California.

The Sonoran is one of the hottest deserts on the continent, but because of winter storms and the summer rains, or "monsoons," it is also the greenest. Of all the North American deserts, it is the most biologically diverse, with more than 2,000 native plant species, 60 mammal species, 350 bird species, and more than 100 reptile species. To help preserve this unique ecosystem, 478,000 acres (193,446 ha) southwest of Phoenix near Gila Bend have been designated as the Sonoran Desert National Monument.

The saguaro is the monarch of the Sonoran, the only place in the world where it grows in the wild.

This tree-size cactus can reach heights of 50 feet (15 m) and weigh more than 8 tons. But it grows very slowly, barely an inch each year. It takes 75 years before it even begins to grow its distinctive arms. The largest ones with many arms may be 150 to 200 years old. Gila woodpeckers and other desert creatures make their homes in its spiny, fluted trunk. In April and May, white night-blooming flowers appear at the top of the stem and arms, producing sweet, ruby-red fruit by the end of June.

In spring the Sonoran is ablaze with color as delicate wildflowers carpet the desert floor. Golden blossoms trail from green-trunked palo verde trees. Deep pink flowers bloom on the pads of prickly pear cacti, while barrel cacti and chollas have bright yellow topknots. House finches and orioles cling to the tops of spindly ocotillos, feeding on nectar from the orange flowers. This floral banquet attracts an amazing variety of birds, making southern Arizona one of the best birdwatching locations in the country.

Forests of giant cacti sprawl across the desert and reach for the sky in Saguaro National Park (**2**).

Wooden boardwalks covered by arcades give Tombstone's (**1**) storefronts a timeless character.

POPULATION 6 million in Arizona.

CLIMATE Summers are extremely hot, and daytime temperatures can exceed 105ºF (40ºC) in the shade from June onward. Monsoon rains July to early September bring intense afternoon downpours. Winters are mild with daytime temperatures averaging 65ºF (18ºC), though it can drop to freezing at night in late December and early January.

WHAT TO TAKE Sunscreen, hat, sunglasses, hiking boots or sturdy shoes for desert trails.

BEST TIME Late February-April is the best time to see wildflowers, with cacti blooming from late April into June. Winter, spring, and late fall are the best times for hiking and outdoor activities, when it is not too hot.

NEAREST AIRPORTS Tucson Airport handles mostly domestic flights. Some international carriers have direct flights to Phoenix Sky Harbor International Airport, 110 miles (177 km) north.

ACCOMMODATIONS Plentiful, ranging from chain motels to luxury golf and spa resorts, to beautiful historic properties with guest rooms in adobe buildings and casitas. There are guest ranches with horseback riding and other activities on the outskirts of Tucson or elsewhere in the region.

TRAVEL TIPS Always carry plenty of drinking water when traveling in southern Arizona, especially when hiking in the desert or undertaking outdoor activities. At least 1 gallon (4.5 L) of water per person per day is recommended. Wear a hat and use sunscreen while hiking, to avoid heatstroke, sunburn, and dehydration.

The Old West mining camp of Bisbee (**3**) was known in its heyday to be the "liveliest spot between El Paso and San Francisco." When the mines shut in the 1970s, the museums opened, telling many a tale of this small town's history.

–> Art and Missions

A few miles south of Tucson, on the Tohono O'odham reservation, is the oldest and best-preserved mission church in the Southwest, San Xavier del Bac. Founded by Father Eusebio Kino in 1700, it is a masterpiece of Spanish Colonial architecture, filled with splendid Mexican Baroque art. Further south is the delightful artists' colony of Tubac, where you will also find the Presidio State Historic Park. Beyond is the old mission of Tumacacori, with the evocative ruins of its enormous adobe church, and a fine museum portraying mission life.

Around Tucson

Most desert wildlife is elusive, and the best place for an up-close look at both plants and animals is the Arizona-Sonora Desert Museum, on the outskirts of Tucson. At this outdoor natural history park, you follow a 2-mile (3-km) path through desert landscapes displaying more than 1,200 kinds of plants. These provide habitat for a fascinating array of wildlife, including coyotes, bobcats, and the curious piglike javelinas, also known as collared peccaries.

Near the museum is the western half of Saguaro National Park. Together with its counterpart on the eastern side of Tucson, it preserves thousands of saguaros and other species in virtual forests spreading across the desert plain and up the hillsides. The oldest saguaros can be seen in the eastern park along Cactus Forest Drive. Both sides have many miles of hiking trails, with some in the western park leading to ancient petroglyphs carved by the Hohokam people. Also near here is Old Tucson Studios, where many Hollywood Westerns were filmed; it is now a theme park and entertainment venue.

Tucson is a good base for exploring southern Arizona, and for getting a sense of the real Old West culture. Downtown's El Presidio Historic District stands on the site of the original eighteenth-century Spanish fort. The Tucson

Organ Pipe rock
formation at the
Chiricahua National
Monument (**4**).

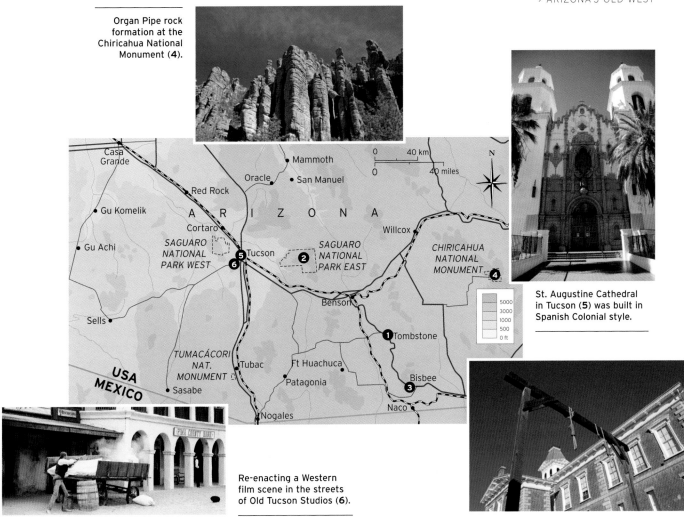

St. Augustine Cathedral
in Tucson (**5**) was built in
Spanish Colonial style.

Re-enacting a Western
film scene in the streets
of Old Tucson Studios (**6**).

The County Courthouse,
a National Historic
Landmark in Tombstone (**1**).

Museum of Art here has examples of Native American and Spanish Colonial art, while the surrounding Historic Block contains the area's oldest buildings dating back to 1850. The city's Mexican heritage is colorfully displayed in the painted adobe houses of the Barrio Historic District.

Tombstone

Tombstone's very name evokes the lawless legends of the Wild West; its founder, Ed Schieffelin, named it for the warning he had received in 1877 when he went prospecting on Apache land and was told "all you'll find out there is your tombstone." He found a mountain of silver instead, and at its height his boom town was larger than San Francisco. It also counted, on average, 20 violent deaths per week as gunmen, gamblers, prospectors, and cowboys flocked in to find their own rich pickings. The famous gunfight at the OK Corral took place here, a scene that is recreated daily by actors in the roles of the Earp brothers, Doc Holliday, and the Clanton gang.

When its fortunes waned, the town itself proved "too tough to die." Today its arcaded wooden boardwalks and historic, false-fronted buildings form one of the region's most popular attractions. Tombstone Courthouse contains artifacts and photographs of the town's notorious characters.

The Bird Cage Theater is a former bordello with original furnishings from its bawdy dancehall days. You can still see the bullet holes in the coffered ceiling of the Crystal Palace Saloon. At the end of town, Boot Hill cemetery is covered with graves and their often amusing epitaphs.

Tombstone is 70 miles (113 km) southeast of Tucson. En route, stop off at the Amerind Foundation, beautifully situated in Texas Canyon, near Benson. Its name is a contraction of "American Indian," and this private anthropological and archeological museum houses one of the finest collections of Native American art and artifacts in the country. The displays contain thousands of objects showing all aspects of native life, representing cultures from central America to Alaska. An adjoining art gallery presents works on Western themes by artists ranging from contemporary Native Americans to leading figures such as Frederic Remington and William Leigh.

NATIONAL MALL IN WASHINGTON, D.C.

From the U.S. Capitol to the Lincoln Memorial, the National Mall contains the greatest collection of monuments and memorials in America, and many fine museums.

Daniel Chester French's famous statue in the Lincoln Memorial (1) depicts the strength and compassion of the sixteenth president.

–> Washington's Cherry Trees

The 3,000 Japanese flowering cherry trees around the Tidal Basin were planted as a gift of friendship from Japan in 1912. The ceremony in which First Lady Taft and the wife of the Japanese ambassador planted the first two trees gave birth to the city's famous Cherry Blossom Festival. In 1965, Japan donated more trees for planting around the Washington Monument.

IT IS THE MOST IMPRESSIVE PUBLIC SPACE in the United States. From the lofty heights of Capitol Hill, the view stretches down the green expanse of the National Mall to the Lincoln Memorial 2 miles (3 km) away. Here, visiting families make pilgrimages to see patriotic landmarks; locals turn out for summer concerts, fireworks, and festivals; and crowds converge from across the land for political rallies, protests, speeches, and commemorations.

Before it was built as the nation's capital in 1791, Washington, D.C. did not exist. The marshy site along the Potomac River was chosen by George Washington as a neutral ground between the Northern and Southern states, with Maryland and Virginia each donating land to create the District of Columbia, a federal city dedicated to the business of government. The city was largely designed by Pierre Charles L'Enfant, a French architect and engineer who gave it the grand avenues and open spaces that enabled it to become such a beautiful symbol of the nation.

For visitors, the many federal offices that surround the National Mall are secondary to the wealth of monuments, memorials, and museums. There are more than 80 historic structures, 170 flower gardens, 35 ornamental pools and fountains, and 150 named parks, squares, circles, and triangles. The Mall is lined with 2,000 American elms, while Washington's famous Japanese cherry trees—some 3,000 of them—surround the Tidal Basin. They are all looked after by the National Park Service.

One of the best things about the Mall is that most of its museums and monuments are free, though you may have to reserve a ticket in advance. Some are also beautifully illuminated at night, particularly the Lincoln and Roosevelt Memorials.

Monuments and Memorials

When laying out the city, L'Enfant famously described Capitol Hill as "a pedestal waiting for a monument." That pedestal was filled with the United States Capitol. Congressional laws are passed in this majestic building with its central dome and rotunda. The north and south wings house the Senate and House of Representatives.

Sunset at the Arlington Bridge, over the Potomac River at the Lincoln Memorial (**1**).

John Adams was the first president to live in the White House (**2**), also known as the Executive Mansion.

Statue of Andrew Jackson, the seventh president, in Lafayette Park (**3**).

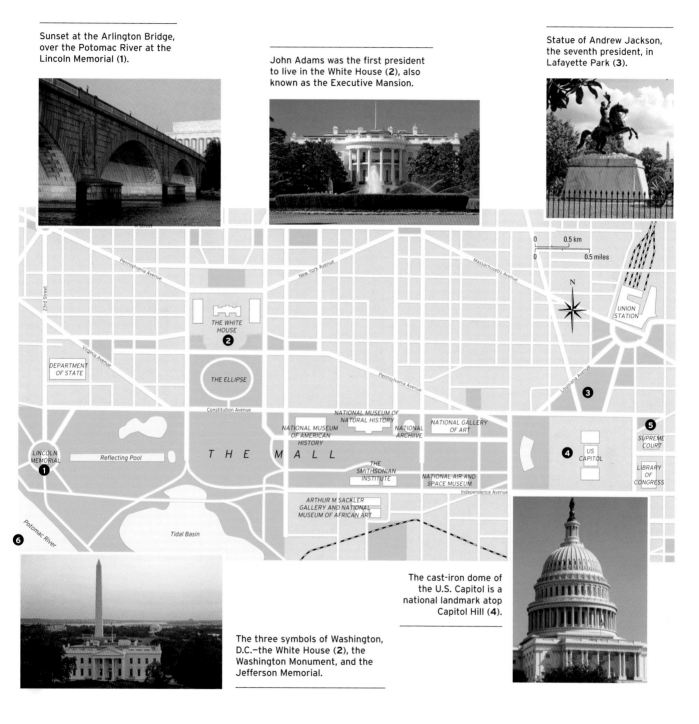

The three symbols of Washington, D.C.–the White House (**2**), the Washington Monument, and the Jefferson Memorial.

The cast-iron dome of the U.S. Capitol is a national landmark atop Capitol Hill (**4**).

You can take a free guided tour or explore its splendid architecture and artwork on your own.

Behind the Capitol are the Supreme Court, the highest court in the land, and the Library of Congress. The world's largest library is ornately decorated with busts, carvings, mosaics, artwork, and a grand fountain at the entrance.

To the west, beside the Capitol Reflecting Pool, the Ulysses S. Grant Memorial is the city's largest sculpture group, depicting the president and general leading the Union Army during the Civil War.

The Mall proper runs between Third and Fourteenth Streets. Beyond is the Washington Monument. The slender granite obelisk is the city's highest structure at 555 1/2 feet (169 m). Ride the elevator to the top for stupendous views.

The monument acts as a crossroads for other highlights, which honor presidents and veterans of America's wars. Straight ahead is the World War II Memorial. A long, slender Reflecting Pool connects it with the Lincoln Memorial. Daniel Chester French's monumental sculpture of the president,

157

-> FACT FILE

POPULATION 588,000

CLIMATE Summers are hot and humid, with averages of 86-92ºF (30-33ºC) and frequent thunder-storms. Winters are cold with daytime highs averaging 43-47ºF (6-8ºC) and snow. Annual rainfall is 39 inches (99 cm).

WHAT TO TAKE Rain jacket or umbrella, good walking shoes, water bottle (there are few places for refreshments on the Mall). Dress up for fine restaurants.

BEST TIME Spring is the most beautiful season, with warm, pleasant weather and blossoming cherry trees. The Cherry Blossom Festival is held late March-early April. Fall is also pleasant with low humidity.

NEAREST AIRPORTS Dulles International Airport is 25 miles (40 km) west of the city. Reagan National Airport is 22 miles (35 km) south. Baltimore-Washington International Airport, 30 miles (48 km) northeast, is also convenient.

ACCOMMODATIONS Hotels near the National Mall are mostly in the middle-high price range. Look for package deals and book ahead.

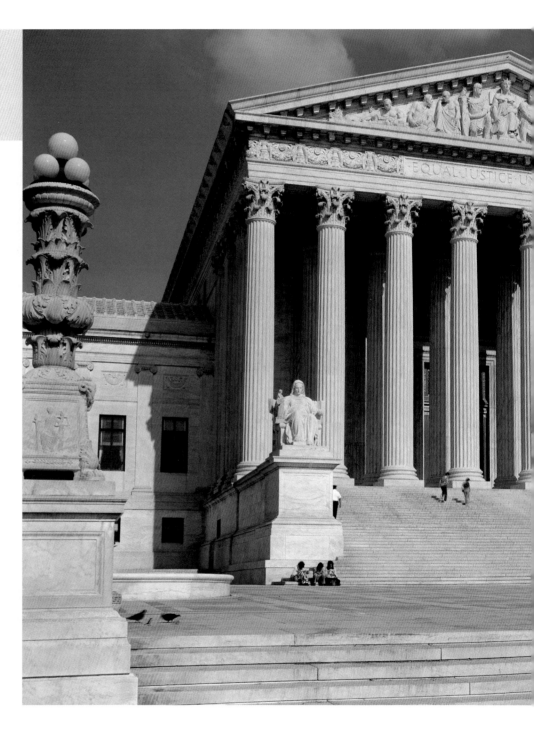

19 feet (5.8 m) high, sitting inside a Greek temple is one of the nation's best-loved memorials.

On the north side of the pool is the Vietnam Veterans Memorial, a tribute with the names of the dead etched on black granite panels. In Constitution Gardens is a memorial to the 56 signatories of the Declaration of Independence. On the south side of the pool is the Korean War Veterans Memorial.

North of the Washington Monument, the broad circle of grass known as the Ellipse affords a grand view of the White House, home to presidents since 1800. Pennsylvania Avenue is a direct route back to the Capitol. Along here, the Old Post Office Tower offers fantastic views from its observation deck. The Declaration of Independence, the Constitution, and the Bill of Rights are on display in the classical-style National Archives building.

South of the Washington Monument, the Thomas Jefferson Memorial stands beside the Tidal Basin. It is modeled after the Pantheon in Rome, which the

Marble Corinthian columns lend weight and dignity to the entrance of the United States Supreme Court Building (**5**).

Arlington National Cemetery (**6**) lies across the river from West Potomac Park.

learned president had always admired. The Franklin Delano Roosevelt Memorial is laid out on a peaceful path with waterfalls, rocks, and pools. On the Basin's west shore is the Mall's first monument to an African-American, the Martin Luther King Jr. National Memorial.

Museums

Lining the Mall on the north and south sides are the diverse museums of the Smithsonian Institution.

Among the country's most prestigious foundations, it was established in 1846 with a gift from British scientist James Smithson.

The red sandstone Smithsonian Castle serves as the visitor center for all the museums. It is flanked by several art museums, including the Freer Gallery of Art, Arthur M. Sackler Gallery, the National Museum of African Art, and the Hirshhorn Museum, and the Arts and Industries Building. The U.S. Holocaust Memorial Museum is nearby.

The most popular is the National Air and Space Museum, with exhibits ranging from the Wright Brothers' first airplane to Apollo 11 space capsules. Next door is the National Museum of the American Indian.

The National Gallery of Art occupies two buildings on the north side of the Mall. Completing the group are two national museums devoted to Natural History and American History. More excellent museums and galleries can be found in the downtown area just north of the Mall, including the excellent Corcoran Gallery of Art.

MARK TWAIN'S MISSISSIPPI RIVER

The mighty Mississippi, which forms the natural dividing line between the eastern and western United States, was a muse to the father of American literature.

THE MISSISSIPPI RIVER is the most prominent natural feature of the American Midwest. The nation's second-longest river, it flows more than 2,500 miles (4,023 km) from northern Minnesota to the Gulf of Mexico, forming the borders between ten states: Minnesota, Wisconsin, Iowa, Illinois, Missouri, Kentucky, Tennessee, Arkansas, Mississippi, and Louisiana.

The Mississippi and the rivers that flow into it form the third-largest watershed in the world. The Mississippi River Basin drains 41 percent of the continental United States and two Canadian provinces, an area of 1.2–1.8 million square miles (3.1–4.7 million sq km).

In the late eighteenth century, farmers in the Ohio Valley began shipping grain and pork down the Mississippi by flatboat to the port of New Orleans. They hazarded its snags, sandbars, and shifting channels on the treacherous three-month journey. At the end of the line they sold their boats and made their way home overland. Efforts at poling or pulling the boats back upstream against the powerful current were fruitless.

But in 1817 a steamboat reached Cincinnati from New Orleans, and within two years there were 60 stern-wheelers plying a two-way route between Louisville and the great Gulf port. Agriculture remains the biggest industry in the region today, and the Mississippi River is the main navigable water route in the country. Sixty percent of all the grain exported from the U.S., as well as raw materials and industrial products, are shipped to ports in New Orleans and South Louisiana.

Mark Twain

The great steamboat age began in about 1845 and lasted for 25 years, etching into history a romantic chapter of riverboat gamblers, sharp-eyed river pilots, well-heeled gentlemen in white suits, and steam-driven paddlewheelers splashing along the wharves. From New Orleans to St. Louis, there was a gaiety about the river life. Townsfolk gathered at the docks to watch the great bustle of activity as workers loaded and unloaded cargo and passengers embarked on exciting journeys.

Mark Twain captured it all with his celebrated wit in his tale of *Life on the Mississippi*. The author even took his pen name from riverboat slang. Born Samuel Langhorne Clemens in 1835, he grew up in Hannibal, Missouri, a river town that became the backdrop for his two most famous novels, *The Adventures of Tom Sawyer* and *Adventures of Huckleberry Finn*. The latter, which is considered one of the finest works of American literature, depicts the humor and cruelty of frontier life on the river he loved.

When he was 21, Twain signed on as a cub steamboat pilot and spent two years learning to navigate the river before becoming a full-fledged pilot in 1859. More than 20 years later, in *Life on the Mississippi*, he wrote, "I loved the profession far better than any I have followed since, and I took a measureless pride in it. The reason is plain: a pilot, in those days, was the only unfettered and entirely independent human being that lived in the earth."

Twain might have remained a riverboat pilot all his life but for the outbreak of the Civil War in 1861, which restricted traffic on the Mississippi. He then headed west with his brother and began his career as a journalist. But the river stayed with him throughout his life, inspiring the popular works that made him one of America's greatest writers.

The boyhood home of Mark Twain (1), with its legendary white picket fence, is now a popular museum dedicated to the author's life and works.

The Mark Twain riverboat plies the waters of the Mississippi near Hannibal (1), Missouri, giving sightseers a taste of life in the mid-nineteenth century.

->FACT FILE

CLIMATE The climate varies widely from north to south. Summer temperatures can reach into the 80s-90s°F (26-32°C) in Minnesota, with similar temperatures but much more humid conditions in the south. Southern winters are mild, but northern winters bring temperatures well below freezing with ice and snow.

WHAT TO TAKE Sunscreen, sun hat, sunglasses, insect repellent, casual clothes.

BEST TIME Spring and fall have generally pleasant temperatures.

NEAREST AIRPORTS There are major international airports at Minneapolis-St. Paul, St. Louis, New Orleans, and many cities in between.

ACCOMMODATIONS Cities and towns all along the river have a good range of accommodations in all price categories.

The Old Mississippi River Bridge and its newer counterpart at Vicksburg (**2**).

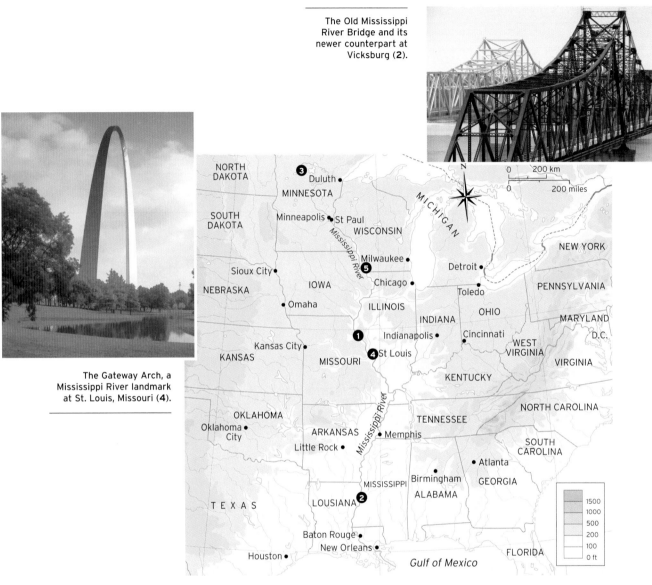

The Gateway Arch, a Mississippi River landmark at St. Louis, Missouri (**4**).

-> Mississippi Wildlife

The Mississippi River and its floodplain are crucial to the continent's wildlife. Sixty percent of North America's 326 bird species use it as their migratory flyway. The river contains 25 percent of all the continent's fish species, as well as dozens of mussel species, amphibians, and reptiles. More than 50 species of mammal live in the Upper Mississippi region alone.

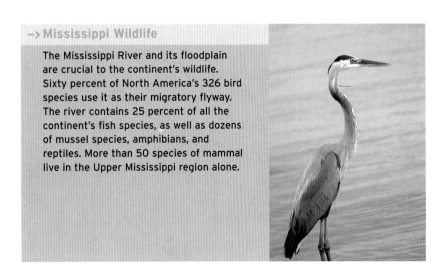

Lake Itasca (**3**) in northern Minnesota, a peaceful birthplace for a mighty river.

Along the Great River

Small-town Hannibal is still bustling today, with tourists who come to see Twain's boyhood home with its white picket fence. Showboats are a thriving business in post-industrial towns such as Dubuque, Iowa, where visitors flock to the waterfront to ride the old paddle wheelers or gamble on the floating casinos.

Most travelers still feel a sense of excitement when they cross the Mississippi, whether they are gazing down from an airplane or driving across one of its historic bridges. The Great River Road, established in 1938, is one of the oldest and longest scenic byways in America, running alongside it for nearly 3,000 miles (4,828 km).

The headwaters of the Mississippi are at Lake Itasca, in Itasca State Park in northern Minnesota. Here the river is so shallow you can wade across. From here, a drop of water takes about three months to reach the Gulf of Mexico.

At Minneapolis the river plunges over St. Anthony Falls, the only natural waterfalls on the entire course. A series of locks were built from this point to help navigate the river, and the surrounding area is a national historic district. Near La Crosse, Wisconsin, the river reaches its widest point at Lake Onalaska, over 4 miles (6.4 km) across.

At St. Louis, the Mississippi meets the Missouri River, the nation's longest. Along the riverfront the Gateway Arch, officially named the Jefferson National Expansion Memorial, is the tallest monument in the country, more than twice the height of the Statue of Liberty. Beyond the city, the river is free-flowing once again, continuing on its course through Memphis (see pages 164-167) and Vicksburg, set on a high bluff along the banks with splendid views. The capture of Vicksburg by the Union Army after a 47-day siege was a turning point in the Civil War.

Mark Twain visited New Orleans often during his riverboat days, and he was of the opinion that "an American has not seen the United States until he has seen Mardi-Gras in New Orleans." It is a fitting place to end a journey, and send the river on its way south of the city to the Gulf of Mexico.

The Upper Mississippi River National Wildlife and Fish Refuge (**5**) lies within four states—Iowa, Wisconsin, Minnesota, and Illinois—and is the longest river refuge in the continental United States.

MEMPHIS: MUSIC CITY

Walking in Memphis is walking in the footsteps of music legends, from the father of the blues to the king of rock 'n' roll.

With the giant guitar outside, there's no missing Sun Studio (1), which is still a working recording studio as well as being a visitor attraction.

THE BLUES WERE BORN deep in the Mississippi Delta, evolving from the field songs and spirituals of poor, black farm laborers as they sang away the poverty and hardships of the rural South. Dozens of blues musicians came out of the Delta, from B. B. King to Muddy Waters to Robert Johnson, who was said to have sold his soul to the devil down at the crossroads. For these musicians there was only one promised land, and it lay north across the border in Tennessee.

The blues came to Memphis on Highway 61— the legendary Blues Highway—that ran along the Mississippi River, through the cotton fields of the Delta and on to the great music city. Here, in the earthy bars of Beale Street, the Delta bluesmen played the tunes that would influence popular music throughout the twentieth century.

A century ago, Beale Street was a rough place known for drinking, gambling, voodoo, and the

occasional murder. During its heyday in the 1920s, nightclubs, theaters, bars, and restaurants boomed. Crowds thronged the street after dark, listening to traveling bluesmen who played in the park for passing change.

For several years Memphis was home to W. C. Handy, who is often called the "father of the blues." He had first heard Delta blues while waiting for a train in Clarksdale, and took it from its gritty roots to an urban audience. His composition, "The Memphis Blues," was the first published song with "blues" in the title. Handy's former home is now a museum on Beale Street.

Today the spirit of old Beale Street thrives along a three-block historic district. Famous music names are embedded on musical notes in the sidewalk along the Walk of Fame. The only survivor of the early days is the A. Schwab general store dating from 1876, but you can hear live blues every night in the street's many music clubs and restaurants.

A Rock 'n' Roll Stroll

Memphis was a musical crossroads where country, blues, gospel, and jazz all came together. Despite its place in the deeply segregated South, Memphis broke down racial barriers in the 1950s and '60s, when black and white artists worked side by side and cultures merged to produce explosive new styles of American popular music.

At the Memphis Rock 'n' Soul Museum off Beale Street you can follow the people and stories that shaped the Memphis Sound, from its rural roots to its social impact across the world. As you explore the collection of instruments, costumes, and music memorabilia, you can listen to more than 100 songs on the audio guide.

Across the way, take a tour of the Gibson Guitar Factory, makers of B. B. King's famous guitar, Lucille. These intricately handcrafted guitars are among the finest in the world, and you can watch skilled luthiers creating beautiful acoustic instruments, each of which takes three and a half weeks to finish.

At Sun Studios, blues and country music collided with a huge bang that was heard around the world. Its founder, Sam Phillips, wanted to record unknown working-class artists and take their music to a larger audience. Almost by accident, he found what

POPULATION City 670,000, metro area 1.1 million.

CLIMATE The average summer temperature is 81ºF (27ºC) with high humidity. The average winter temperature is 43ºF (6ºC). Annual precipitation averages 54 inches (137 cm).

WHAT TO TAKE Casual clothes; take a rain jacket and umbrella as the city averages nine-ten days of rain every month.

BEST TIME Weather is most pleasant in spring and fall and there are fewer crowds. Summer is sweltering, with temperatures in the 90s (32ºC and above). Winters are mild.

NEAREST AIRPORT Memphis International Airport, 12 miles (20 km) southeast of downtown.

ACCOMMODATIONS Memphis is also a business center, so book ahead. The grande dame is the downtown Peabody Hotel with the famous Peabody ducks. Inexpensive chain motels are further away from the center off I-40.

EVENTS January–Elvis Presley's Birthday Tribute at Graceland; May–Beale Street Music Festival; July–Memphis Music and Heritage Festival.

WHAT TO EAT Memphis is famous for its barbecue, particularly pulled pork and dry-rubbed ribs.

Beale Street (**2**) may be a lot safer and more glitzy these days, but it's still the place to go walking in Memphis if you want to hear blues and rock.

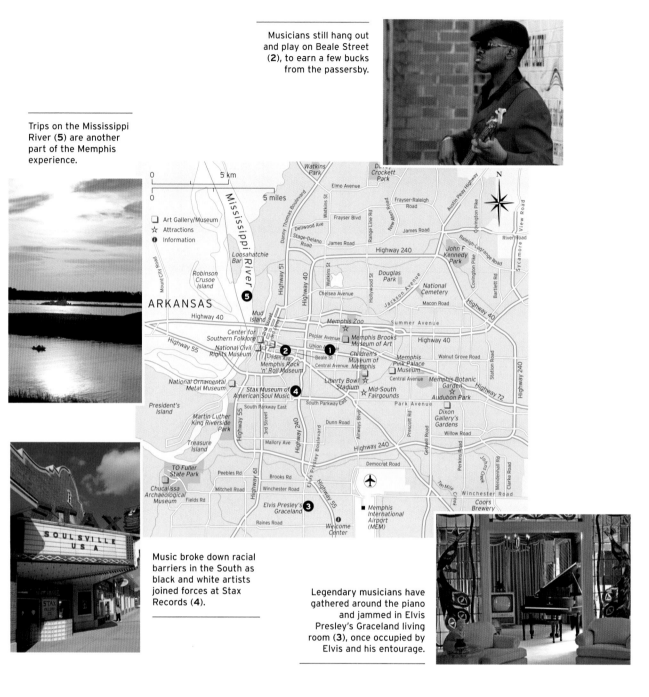

Musicians still hang out and play on Beale Street (**2**), to earn a few bucks from the passersby.

Trips on the Mississippi River (**5**) are another part of the Memphis experience.

Music broke down racial barriers in the South as black and white artists joined forces at Stax Records (**4**).

Legendary musicians have gathered around the piano and jammed in Elvis Presley's Graceland living room (**3**), once occupied by Elvis and his entourage.

he was looking for—a white boy who could sing black music. In July of 1954, he invited 19-year-old Elvis Presley to record some country tracks with two hillbilly artists. During a break, Elvis started fooling around with a rocking version of the old blues song "That's All Right." Sam kept the tape running and realized he had something special. Elvis's first single became a smash hit, and a new sound, rockabilly, was born.

Sun Studios' small brick building on Union Avenue is now a landmark. You can almost hear the music as you stand in the spot that launched the king of rock 'n' roll, and hear tales of the many

other great artists who recorded here: Jerry Lee Lewis, Carl Perkins, Johnny Cash, and Roy Orbison among them.

Few visitors leave Memphis without a visit to Graceland. Elvis bought the mansion when he was 22 and lived here until his tragic death 20 years later. It is now designated a National Historic Landmark. On a self-guided tour you can see parts of the house, including the kitschy Jungle Room, a museum of Elvis artifacts from his gold records to his sparkling jumpsuits, his automobile collection, private jet, and the meditation garden where he is buried.

America's White House is the only residence to get more visitors each year than Elvis's Graceland home (3).

Soulful Sites

In the 1960s and '70s, the primary sound emanating from Memphis was soul. Like Sun Studios, Stax Records was an independent label that propelled neighborhood artists into the international spotlight. Booker T. Jones, Aretha Franklin, Johnny Ace, and others all lived within a few blocks of the studios, an incredible concentration of talent in a poor part of South Memphis. The Stax Museum of American Soul Music, located on the site of the original studios, tells the story through a fascinating collection of exhibits and artifacts, including Isaac Hayes's gold-plated Cadillac.

Sadly, the assassination of Martin Luther King Jr. in Memphis in 1968 contributed to the demise of Stax, as racial tensions put further pressure on the company's financial troubles. The Lorraine Hotel where he was shot is now home to the National Civil Rights Museum, where unforgettable displays create a moving portrayal of the struggle for human rights in the American South.

King's tragic death was a dark chapter in a city that had done so much to bring people of all races and backgrounds together. As Sam Phillips once said, "Nothing has the strength, the power of music."

NEW ENGLAND IN THE FALL

"No pen can describe the turning of the leaves—the insurrection of the tree people against the waning year."
Rudyard Kipling

WRITERS OF KIPLING'S STATURE are seldom lost for words, but such is the splendor of New England in the fall. Day by day, singularly and in patches, vivid yellows, bright golds, fiery reds, and deep crimsons are splashed at random across the landscape; yet, as on an Impressionist's canvas, they come together in a magnificent masterpiece. Like a painting, it has to be absorbed through all the senses, along with the crisp scent of chilled air, the sound of dry leaves crunching underfoot, the feel of a fat orange leaf, as big as your palm and curling at the edges, going down in a blaze of glory before winter covers it in a white blanket of snow.

The great spectacle of fall color happens year upon year. It begins in mid- to late September and by the end of October it is mostly gone. And while leaves change color in the Southeast, the Midwest, and right across the Rocky Mountains too, fall foliage is particularly associated with the six states of New England: Maine, Vermont, New Hampshire, Massachusetts, Connecticut, and Rhode Island. Here, it is coupled with a timeless rural landscape of red barns and covered bridges, pointed white steeples and village greens, rolling hills and quaint towns that date back to the early days of the country.

The sheer variety of hardwood trees and shrubs in New England's woodlands makes fall color so spectacular here: the yellows and golds of birch, elm, and poplar; the orange shades of hickory and mountain ash; sumac's deep maroon and the scarlet hues of sugar maple, red oak, and dogwood; the rich brown tannins of oak leaves. The region's fall climate of mild daytime temperatures and cool nights that stay above freezing also produce ideal foliage conditions.

A Regional Sport

In New England, leaf-peeping—the term for driving scenic routes to see fall color—is an annual ritual. It occupies a place on the fall calendar as important as Halloween and Thanksgiving. Visitors come by the busload from all over the nation and the world to join the parade along New England's most picturesque roads.

Leaf-peeping is approached with the intensity of a sport. There are web sites and newspaper columns devoted to it. Each state has a toll-free

-> FACT FILE

CLIMATE Temperatures vary around the region, and in September–October range between 53–64ºF (12–18ºC). It is much cooler at higher elevations. Rainfall during these months averages 3 ⅓ inches (8.5 cm).

WHAT TO TAKE Warm sweater and jacket; camera.

BEST TIME Late September to mid-October, but it will be busy and you must book everything, from car rental to restaurants, well ahead.

NEAREST AIRPORTS Logan International Airport in Boston is the major international airport. Domestic flights serve larger cities all around the region.

ACCOMMODATIONS There is a variety of lodging from charming bed and breakfast inns to historic hotels, but you must book well ahead for fall foliage season.

The fall foliage colors along the Mount Washington Road (1) meet you around every turn, and cruising above the treeline is the best way to appreciate them.

The White Mountains (**2**) are the perfect place to stop and take it all in.

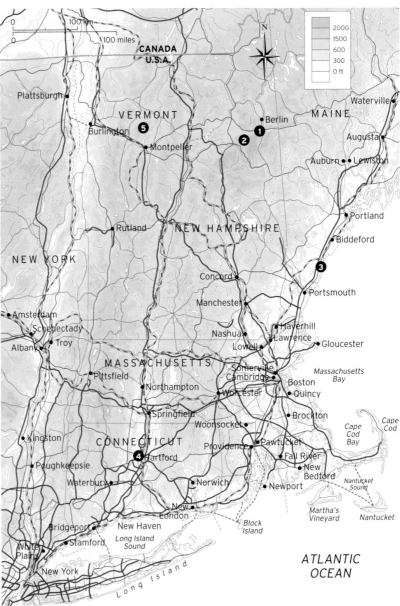

Fishing boats rest on the water at sunset in Perkins Cove (**3**), Maine.

The Connecticut State Capitol (**4**) symbolizes the wealth and power of the state and its ties to its European cultural past.

–> Why Leaves Change Color

Leaves change color when diminishing sunlight and cooler temperatures signal the end of the growing season. The production of chlorophyll, the green pigment that allows trees to convert sunlight into energy through their leaves, gradually ceases. As the chlorophyll breaks down, it allows other pigments in the leaves to shine through. These include yellow and orange-colored carotenoids, and anthocyanins, which produce reds, blues, and purples. These other pigments have been there all along, and are present to varying degrees in different tree and shrub species. Other factors also determine the vividness of their hue. So, in fact, leaves do not really change color—the color is simply unmasked.

hotline detailing the locations where color is emerging or peaking. Armies of dedicated foliage spotters call in reports and analyze data. Timing is everything, as the fall foliage season varies from year to year depending on weather conditions from spring on, while factors such as temperature, precipitation, frost, and wind can shorten or prolong the season.

That said, you cannot really go wrong if you visit New England in the fall. The first two weeks of October traditionally see the greatest peaks of color, but as each tree has its own cycle you are bound to see brilliant color somewhere during the September-October season.

Happy, Shiny Trails

Everyone has their favorite fall foliage route. You do not have to seek out the back roads, either. Magnificent stretches of fall foliage can be seen right along the interstate highways in many places. Better yet, when you have had enough of bumper-to-bumper traffic, get out and enjoy it on New England's many footpaths and hiking trails.

The densely forested, northern state of Maine sees some of the first fall foliage. Route I-95 between Augusta and Bangor is a superb ribbon of color. In the far north Routes 1 and 11 make a scenic loop along the border. The ocean is backed by vibrant hues all along the beautiful Maine coastline. Scenic Route 26 from Portland to the ski town of Bethel is a popular trail; from here you can carry on into the White Mountains.

The mountains of New Hampshire and Vermont are among the most stunning leaf-peeping routes, with grand vistas across the valleys between the peaks. New Hampshire's Kancamagus Highway between Lincoln and Conway is spectacular at any time of year. It cuts through the White Mountains and joins with roads through Franconia Notch and the Mount Washington Valley. Route 124 from Jaffrey to Marlborough around Mount Monadnock is a pretty route in the southwestern part of the state; then join Route 9 at Keene and continue into Vermont for a beautiful drive west across the Green Mountains on the Molly Stark Trail Scenic Byway.

In Vermont, Routes 7 and 100 run up the west and east sides of the Green Mountains. Veer off on side roads to see the state's covered bridges and quaint towns. Another beautiful drive in the north is between the ski resort of Stowe over Smugglers' Notch on Route 108.

The Mohawk Trail, Route 2 from Greenfield to Williamstown, is one of Massachusetts' best foliage drives. From here, follow Route 7 south through the Berkshires; Routes 8, 9, and 116 offer colorful drives in the west. In Connecticut, Route 169 is a national scenic byway. The Blackstone River Valley is one of the best places in Rhode Island for fall foliage.

In the winter, Stowe (5) becomes a skiing and snowboarding mecca; in the fall, it's got a different but equally strong pull for the tourist.

NEW ORLEANS' FRENCH QUARTER

The music is back on Bourbon Street, in the heart of New Orleans' historic French Quarter. Let the good times roll!

_____

Hurricanes may batter New Orleans but General Andrew Jackson still rides in front of the St. Louis Cathedral in Jackson Square (1).

THE DESTRUCTION OF NEW ORLEANS and parts of the Gulf Coast by Hurricane Katrina on August 29, 2005, was the worst natural disaster in the history of the United States. Nearly half of greater New Orleans lies below sea level. The ferocity of the storm caused 53 levee breaches, leaving 80 percent of the city underwater. But the historic French

Quarter, which was built on higher, dry ground 5 feet (1.5 m) above sea level, was spared the worst.

Also called the Vieux Carré, or Old Square, this is the oldest part of the city, laid out in a grid street plan in 1721, three years after the founding of New Orleans by the French. It covers an area of 1 square mile (2.6 sq km), bounded by Canal Street,

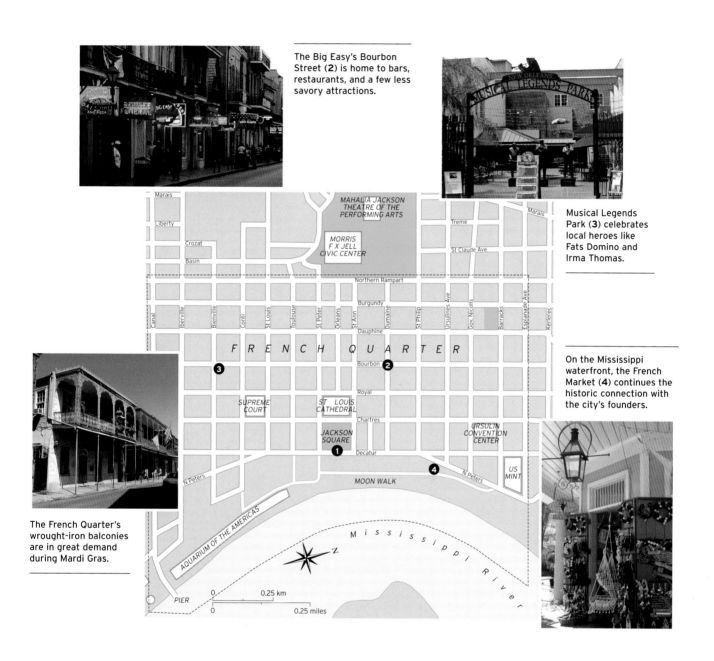

The Big Easy's Bourbon Street (2) is home to bars, restaurants, and a few less savory attractions.

Musical Legends Park (3) celebrates local heroes like Fats Domino and Irma Thomas.

On the Mississippi waterfront, the French Market (4) continues the historic connection with the city's founders.

The French Quarter's wrought-iron balconies are in great demand during Mardi Gras.

Esplanade Avenue, North Rampart Street, and the Mississippi River. Within lies some of America's most beautiful historic architecture and vibrant culture.

In 1762 the French king, Louis XV, gave the Louisiana colony to his cousin, Charles III of Spain. For the next 40 years New Orleans was under Spanish rule. The intermingling of European cultures left a legacy unique among American cities. The term "Creole," often used to describe all things New Orleans, originally meant a native-born person with family links to France or Spain. Over time, it also came to describe light-skinned African-Americans who were descended from liaisons between slave women and French gentlemen. "Cajuns" are descendants of French immigrants from the Acadia region of Nova Scotia. They brought Louisiana its spicy cooking and spirited music and dance.

The old French colonial city was wiped out by two devastating fires in 1788 and 1794. The Spanish governor imposed new fire-resistant building codes, such as stucco walls and flat, ceramic-tiled roofs. The addition of inner courtyards and patios, and elaborate wrought-iron balconies and galleries gave the city a beautiful, grand, and decidedly Spanish appearance. French, however, remained the dominant language and was spoken here well into the twentieth century.

-> FACT FILE

POPULATION 273,000

CLIMATE Summers are hot and very humid, with highs averaging 91ºF (33ºC) in July and August and almost daily rain showers. Winters are mild with highs in the 60sºF (16+ºC). Average annual precipitation is 64¹/₄ inches (163 cm).

WHAT TO TAKE Bring a rain jacket and good walking shoes, and a warm sweater in winter in case of cold spells.

BEST TIME Spring and fall have the best weather with sunshine and pleasantly warm temperatures. October is the driest month. The hurricane season is June–November.

NEAREST AIRPORT Louis Armstrong New Orleans International Airport is about 11 miles (17.5 km) from the French Quarter.

ACCOMMODATIONS Hotels are heavily booked in spring, fall, and during Mardi Gras. There are often good deals in the hotter months of July and August.

WHAT TO EAT Some of the best Cajun cooking can be found in the French Quarter. Dishes to try include *étouffée*–a chunky crawfish bisque–seafood gumbo, and the spicy rice dish jambalaya.

New Orleans has the most famous–and most raucous–Mardi Gras celebrations in the United States, when the French Quarter becomes one big party.

With the Louisiana Purchase in 1803, New Orleans became part of the U.S. It continued to prosper as a rich port city. Over the next century Irish, German, and Italian immigrants, as well as "foreign French" and Haitians poured in. In the early 1900s, the French Quarter became the haunt of writers, artists, bohemians, and above all, musicians as Dixieland jazz wafted from the bars and strip joints on Bourbon Street. In 1965 an 85-block area of the Vieux Carré—corresponding almost exactly to the original city plan—was designated a National Historic Landmark.

Landmarks of the French Quarter

The best way to enjoy the French Quarter is to wander through it at leisure, soaking up its charms. Entire blocks are lined on their upper stories with balconies and galleries (the latter are supported by columns) made of gorgeous ironwork, some of it as intricate as lace. In between are grand Creole town houses, quaint Caribbean cottages, and slim "shotgun houses"—so-called because a bullet fired through the front door would pass through every room and exit out the back.

Narrow cobbled streets and alleyways lead to quiet courtyards with fountains and lush foliage, glimpsed through iron gates. Flower baskets brighten shuttered windows. At night, faded orange and ocher buildings glow softly behind the streetlamps. The sweet scent of night-blooming jasmine drifting from the courtyards is punctuated by spicy, mouthwatering smells emanating from restaurant kitchens.

This is, however, no chocolate box city, painted and tidied up for tourists. Parts of the French Quarter are undoubtedly shabby, and at times it is hot, dirty, and teeming with people. The city has not lost its edge, or its soul.

To take in a few landmarks, start in Jackson Square, the centerpiece of the quarter, bustling with sidewalk artists and street performers. Its surrounding buildings lend it great elegance. The redbrick Pontalba Buildings on either side were built as apartments in 1849-1850. The spires of St. Louis Cathedral rise above the top end of the square. This third cathedral on the site dates from 1851.

Flanking the cathedral on one side is the Cabildo, former home of the Spanish governing council, dating from 1795. The documents for the Louisiana Purchase were signed here. It now houses the Louisiana State Museum. On the other side is the Presbytère, designed as a rectory in 1791, and now housing exhibits on New Orleans' most famous festival, Mardi Gras.

The atmospheric Pirate's Alley is a flagstone passage leading from Jackson Square to Royal Street. William Faulkner wrote his first novel at number 624, now the site of Faulkner House Bookstore. The Voodoo Museum at 724 Dumaine Street provides an insight into the eerie religious

cult brought to New Orleans from Haiti. The only remaining building from the French colonial period is the Ursuline Convent, completed in 1752, at the corner of Chartres and Ursuline Streets.

Visit the French Market, a riverfront trading post since the early days of New Orleans. Be sure and stop at Café du Monde for coffee and *beignets*—square donuts covered in powdered sugar that are a New Orleans specialty.

After dark, take in some of the French Quarter's famous nightlife. Preservation Hall, a former stable, is the venue for some of the best traditional jazz. Have a drink in the atmospheric Lafitte's Blacksmith Shop, named for the pirate and dating back to 1772, and enjoy a Hurricane, the city's famous rum drink, in the lovely courtyard at Pat O'Brien's. In the French Quarter you can have your drink in a plastic "go-cup" and stroll along Bourbon Street, listening to jazz, blues, Cajun, zydeco, and more, pouring through the wide-open doors of the music clubs lining the street.

The French Quarter is back in action and its famous motto prevails, "*Laissez les bon temps roulez*"–"Let the good times roll!"

The lace-like iron balconies date back to the 1850s, when this type of decoration became incredibly popular.

GLACIER NATIONAL PARK

With jewel-like alpine lakes, stunning peaks, and abundant wildlife, this glacier-carved paradise on the U.S.-Canadian border lives up to its title as "Crown of the Continent."

Global warming is evident in the rapidly vanishing Grinnell Glacier (1, opposite) which has been photographed at various stages over several decades.

Smoke from a forest fire wafts though the valleys of Glacier National Park.

GLACIER NATIONAL PARK IS THE GEM of northwestern Montana's Big Sky Country. Established in 1910, this 1,562 square mile (4,046 sq km) park in the northern Rockies is bordered on the west by the north fork of the Flathead River and on the east by the Blackfeet Indian Reservation. Meandering through the middle is the Continental Divide. The entire region is cleaner and clearer than most other parts of the U.S., with dense pine forests and rugged wilderness ranges to the west and the wide open spaces of Montana's grasslands to the east. But what gives the park its sparkle are its snowcapped peaks and ridges and its glistening glaciers. The Native Americans called them the Shining Mountains.

The park's impressive natural features were sculpted by colossal glaciers during the last ice age, which ended some 10,000 years ago. The pointed peaks, razor-sharp ridges, cirques (bowl-shaped hollows), and broad, rounded valleys are all signs of glacier-carved terrain. Many of the park's 130 pristine lakes are contained within massive mounds of glacial debris, known as moraines. While the icy artists who created them have since melted away, there are remnants of later glaciers high up on the mountain slopes.

At the end of the 1850s, 150 glaciers were known to exist in the park. A century later, it was clear that many had retreated or even disappeared. The U.S. Geological Survey began studying the glaciers in the 1980s, and it has become one of the country's leading research programs in Global Climate Change. Only 27 glaciers remained in 2005, and if global warming continues, they are predicted to disappear by 2030.

A Timeless Landscape

Glaciers are not the only endangered things in the park. It provides one of the last habitats in the "Lower 48" states for threatened large mammals. Glacier has one of the largest grizzly bear populations outside Alaska, estimated at nearly 350 individuals. Canadian lynx and wolverines are other rare animals living here. Gray wolves are also thriving. Unlike in other parks, snow-white mountain goats are often seen here on the slopes of the Continental Divide. Moose, elks, black bears, mountain lions, and bighorn sheep and many smaller mammal species are among the park-dwellers. More than 260 bird species have also been spotted, from bald eagles, osprey, and great horned owls to brightly colored harlequin ducks.

Visiting Glacier is like stepping back in time. All of the plants and animals that were here when the first white men arrived in the region can be found in the park today. Its 1,132 plant species range from ancient cedar and hemlock forests to rainbow wildflower meadows to delicate alpine plants over a century old. The park has 30 endemic species found only in this region.

More than 750 miles (1,207 km) of hiking trails bring you up close to the park's flora, fauna, lakes, wetlands, mountains, meadows, and waterfalls.

—> International Peace Park

Glacier National Park is the hub of a much larger area of protected wilderness land known as the Crown of the Continent Ecosystem. Its spectacular scenery continues over the border in the adjoining Waterton Lakes National Park in Canada. In 1932 the two were designated as the Waterton-Glacier International Peace Park, the first such park of its kind. Both parks were named UNESCO Biosphere Reserves in 1976, and each became a World Heritage Site in 1995.

McDonald Creek (**2**) empties into Lake McDonald.

A moose walks through the marsh in Waterton National Park (**3**), Alberta.

Glacier-carved peaks are reflected in the clear waters of St. Mary Lake (**4**).

Black bears as well as grizzly bears make their homes in Glacier National Park.

There is a striking difference, too, traveling from the lusher, wetter, mountainous western side of the Continental Divide, and dropping down to the flat, windswept prairie beyond the eastern entrance.

Going-to-the-Sun Road

Only one paved road cuts directly through the park, and it is a stunner. The 50-mile (80-km) Going-to-the-Sun Road is one of the most scenic roads on the continent, winding steeply up the mountainsides and over Logan Pass, connecting two beautiful valleys at either end. Prior to its construction, visitors had to spend several days on horseback to see these views. The road, a feat of civil engineering, took 11 years to build and was completed in 1932. It is now a listed national historic landmark. To help control traffic, the park now operates a free shuttle system on the road between Apgar and St. Mary.

Lake McDonald, the largest lake in the park, is just beyond the west entrance. The road starts at its western end and runs along its 10-mile (16-km) length. It is estimated that the glacier that carved the surrounding valley was around 2,200 feet (671 m) thick. The Lake McDonald Valley contains some of the oldest and deepest temperate rain forest in the park. It has several popular hiking trails, such as the Trail of the Cedars through a primeval atmosphere of mossy paths, ferns, and soaring cedar and hemlock trees. Also here is the park's oldest hotel, Lake McDonald Lodge.

The road climbs along the steep, sharp ridge known as the Garden Wall, its slopes covered in wildflowers, shrubs, and berry bushes, which make it a good place to spot bears in the fall. It crosses the Continental Divide at Logan Pass, 6,646 feet (2,026 m) high. The surrounding scenery is simply breathtaking. Trails lead to the Hidden Lake Overlook and other backcountry routes.

The glacier-carved valley surrounding St. Mary Lake (4) gives awesome views of the surrounding mountains.

On the eastern side of the pass, watch for the Jackson Glacier Overlook, where you can see the park's fifth-largest glacier, one of the few visible from the road. Beyond, the road descends through the broad, glacial valley surrounding St. Mary Lake. There are fantastic views from Sun Point at the head of the lake.

To the north, the Many Glacier valley is a magnificent high basin, encircled by mountains, meadows, and small lakes. Hiking trails lead to some of the park's most accessible glaciers, such as the Grinnell Glacier discovered by the early conservationist George Bird Grinnell in 1885, and now rapidly receding. The valley is a good area for spotting elusive large animals such as bighorn sheep, mountain goats, and bears. Another beautiful glacial basin lies to the south at Two Medicine Lakes.

-> FACT FILE

CLIMATE The climate is variable year-round, with the possibility of going from sunshine to snow showers in a single day. It can be a few degrees cooler at higher elevations. Average highs in July are 79ºF (26ºC). Maximum temperatures in winter are below freezing. Average annual rainfall is 29 inches (74 cm), average annual snowfall is 157 inches (398 cm).

WHAT TO TAKE Pack layers for all weather conditions, including rain gear and warm clothing.

BEST TIME Summer is the busiest season. The weather is more variable in spring and late fall, but with fewer crowds there is a better chance of seeing wildlife. The park is open year-round, but roads may be closed due to snow.

NEAREST AIRPORTS Some domestic airlines serve Glacier Park International Airport between Whitefish and Kalispell, a short drive from the west entrance. Larger airports are Great Falls International Airport, 155 miles (249 km) from the park and Missoula International Airport, 150 miles (241 km) away.

ACCOMMODATIONS Historic lodges and hotels within the park, along with a few backcountry chalets and campgrounds.

PARK ENTRANCE An entrance fee per vehicle is valid for seven days. Annual passes good at all national parks are also available.

BLACK HILLS AND BADLANDS

South Dakota's Black Hills and Badlands harbor some remarkable sculptures—natural and man-made—carved into the high plains and rugged rock.

IN WESTERN SOUTH DAKOTA the rolling grasslands of the central prairie give way to high, dry plains as they rise toward the front range of the Rockies. Here the Black Hills and the Badlands contain some of the most fascinating features in the Midwest. At first sight the landscape is deceiving. Its grassy expanse can seem dull and lonely, the parched Badlands desolate and forbidding. But look closer and you will find its meadows teeming with wildlife, its hills "blackened" by rich pine forests, and beneath it all a labyrinth of limestone caves studded with crystals.

For more than 10,000 years this land was the domain of Native Americans, most recently the Lakota Sioux, who claimed the land in the eighteenth century. The Treaty of Laramie in 1868 established the Black Hills as part of the Great Sioux reservation. But in 1874 gold was discovered and white prospectors rushed to the Black Hills in violation of the treaty. After a series of battles, the government took control of the region and forced the tribes to move to other reservations. By 1880 the camps around Deadwood, Lead, and Central City were booming, the gold and silver mines producing around $7 million a year.

Ownership of the Black Hills is still disputed, and the story of the Plains Indians' last stand remains a tangible part of the region. Today, the gold in the hills comes from tourism rather than mining.

Six Grandfathers, Four Presidents

To the Lakota, the granite outcrop was known as the Six Grandfathers. It was renamed Mount Rushmore by prospectors after an expedition in 1885. Today it is the most famous attraction in the Black Hills. The 60-foot (18-m) high faces of four presidents—George Washington, Thomas Jefferson, Abraham Lincoln, and Theodore Roosevelt—are carved along the ridge, a colossal portrait gazing out from 5,725 feet (1,745 m).

Now a national memorial, Mount Rushmore was built solely to attract tourists. It was the brainchild of Doane Robinson, South Dakota's state historian, who originally envisioned carving heroes of the Old West. But sculptor Gutzon Borglum wanted to depict these four presidents because of their roles in founding, preserving, and expanding the nation. When he saw Mount Rushmore he declared, "America will march along that skyline." He chose it for its grandeur, sunny position, and solid granite, which could withstand sculpting and erodes only 1 inch (2.5 cm) every 10,000 years.

When work began in 1927, Borglum was 60 years old. It took 14 years and 400 workers to build the memorial. Using dynamite and jackhammers, they blasted away around 450,000 tons of granite, then used smaller tools to carve and polish the surface. The project had its problems. Jefferson was originally meant to be on Washington's right, but

–> The Devil's Tower

The Black Hills National Forest extends into eastern Wyoming. Near Sundance, a volcanic monolith rises straight up from the surrounding woodland and prairie. Devil's Tower National Monument stands 1,267 feet (386 m) high and its corrugated, near vertical sides attract rock climbers from around the world. The rock was made famous in the 1977 film *Close Encounters of the Third Kind.*

The four presidents sculpted on Mount Rushmore **(1)** were chosen because they represent the ideals of the nation's heritage: life, liberty, and the pursuit of happiness.

–> FACT FILE

CLIMATE Summers are hot with low humidity, with July-August temperatures reaching the 90sºF (32+ºC). Winters are cold, with highs in January-February in the 30sºF (-1ºC). March is the snowiest month. Spring and fall are mild with highs in the 60s-70sºF (15-21ºC). High winds are frequent year-round in the Badlands.

WHAT TO TAKE Sunscreen, sun hat, sunglasses, hiking boots or good walking shoes; take plenty of water when hiking, especially in the Badlands.

BEST TIME May-June and September-October are mild and pleasant, with some afternoon thunderstorms in spring.

NEAREST AIRPORTS Rapid City Regional Airport, on the eastern edge of the Black Hills, has domestic flights from U.S. cities.

ACCOMMODATIONS Stay in Rapid City, Deadwood, Sturgis, Keystone, and many other towns throughout the region. Prices are higher during the summer season and it is essential to book ahead.

PARK ENTRANCE It is free to visit Mount Rushmore National Memorial, but there is a parking fee. There is an entry fee for Badlands National Park, and fees for cave tours at Wind Cave and Jewel Cave, though you can drive or hike through the parks for free.

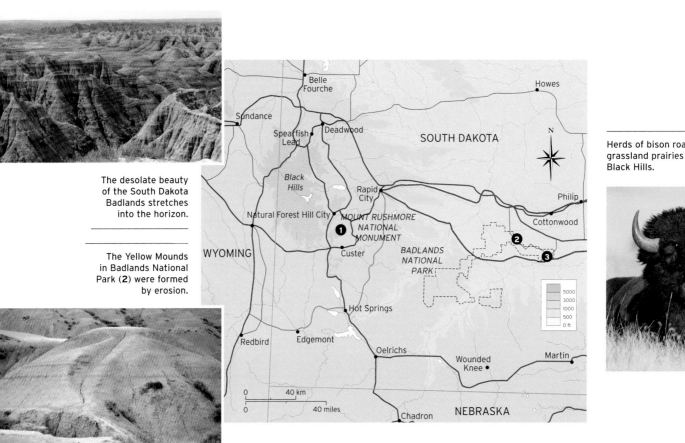

The desolate beauty of the South Dakota Badlands stretches into the horizon.

The Yellow Mounds in Badlands National Park (**2**) were formed by erosion.

Herds of bison roam the grassland prairies of the Black Hills.

when cracks were found in the stone he had to be dynamited off and repositioned. The original model called for the figures to be carved to the waist, but due to lack of funding only the faces were sculpted. Borglum died in 1941, and his son Lincoln completed the work.

As impressive as these figures are, an even bigger sculpture is being carved out of Thunderhead Mountain a few miles away. The Crazy Horse Memorial, which honors the Lakota warrior who defeated Custer at the Battle of Little Bighorn, will measure 563 feet (172 m) high and 641 feet (195 m) long when finished, making it the world's largest sculpture.

Around the Black Hills

The Black Hills, a small, isolated range, have been called the "Island in the Prairie," their dark, forested slopes rising above the Great Plains. Most of the land is national forest, crisscrossed with wonderful hiking and biking trails, streams, and scenic byways. The highest point is Harney Peak at 7,242 feet (2,207 m). It lies in Custer State Park, whose magnificent landscape contains a large herd of free-roaming bison and a host of other wildlife.

Below the grasslands of Wind Cave National Park, more than 127 miles (204 km) of passages have been explored, making it the third-longest cave in the country and fourth-longest in the world. It contains rare and beautiful "boxwork" calcite formations. The surrounding park preserves one of the last remaining mixed-grass prairies, which once covered the Great Plains. Nearby is the Jewel Cave

National Monument. At 143 miles (230 km) it is the world's second-longest cave and gets its name from the sparkling calcite crystals that line its walls. Both caves can be toured.

The Badlands

East of the Black Hills lies the rugged, tortured landscape of The Badlands. Its twisted ridges, eroded buttes and pinnacles, fissured banks, and deep, snaking ravines are hauntingly beautiful. This desolate terrain is best seen in the pink glow of sunrise, or in the evening when the setting sun brings out the warm red and amber tones of its multistrata rock, and shadows dramatize the cliffs and crevices. The road through Badlands National Park leads to scenic overlooks, and there are hiking trails into the backcountry.

South of the park is Wounded Knee, site of the 1890 massacre of more than 250 Lakota men, women, and children, most unarmed, who were rounded up by U.S. soldiers while returning to the Pine Ridge reservation. It left a tragic scar on a beautiful land, deeper than any other in the Badlands.

A landscape of pinnacle rock formations and tall grass prairie in Badlands (3) are easily observed at Cedar Pass.

BOSTON'S FREEDOM TRAIL

Follow the red line through the heart of this historic city to see rare colonial architecture and famous sites from the days of the American Revolution.

An equestrian statue of George Washington graces Boston Public Garden (1).

THE BOSTON TEA PARTY. The Boston Massacre. The Midnight Ride of Paul Revere. These bold tales from the American Revolution capture the imagination of schoolchildren and students of American history, and what is more, they are true. Apart from Philadelphia, no other city has as many extant buildings from colonial times as Boston. Sixteen of the most important historic sites are linked together on the Freedom Trail, a 3-mile (5-km) painted walking path that takes you through some of the most interesting parts of the city center.

The Freedom Trail was the brainchild of William Schofield, a newspaperman who was concerned about the difficulty of finding Boston's historic gems amid its compact but winding central streets. He took up the cause in his daily columns in 1951, and the trail was established by June that year. It is now operated by the National Park Service as Boston National Historical Park.

The Freedom Trail runs from Boston Common to the Bunker Hill Monument, across the river in Charlestown. It is signposted and marked by either a painted red line or a double row of red bricks in the pavement. Free Freedom Trail maps are available from the visitor centers. You can walk the trail in a day, though two days will allow for more leisurely browsing in the fascinating sites and museums.

Beacon Hill and Downtown

The 44 acres (18 ha) of Boston Common form the country's oldest public park. In the seventeenth century it was grazing land for livestock and was later used as a military training ground and hanging ground for witches and pirates. At the northeast corner, the golden-domed "new" State House of 1798 is a masterpiece by Charles Bullfinch, the leading architect of his day. The Massachusetts legislature meets in its chambers.

A lofty Georgian steeple rises above Park Street Church. William Lloyd Garrison gave his first speech against slavery from its pulpit in 1829, launching the abolitionist movement. Paul Revere, John Hancock, and other famous patriots, as well as the nursery-rhyme writer Mother Goose, were laid to

The gleaming dome of the Massachusetts State House (2) was originally made of wood shingles, replaced with copper in 1802 and gilded in 1861.

POPULATION City 596,000; metro area 3.4 million.

CLIMATE Pleasantly hot summers with temperatures averaging 77-82ºF (25-28ºC). Winters are cold and often snowy, with January temperatures averaging 36ºF (2ºC), though it can drop much lower.

WHAT TO TAKE Good walking shoes. Dress up for fine restaurants, otherwise casual attire.

BEST TIME Temperatures are pleasant spring through fall. Fall brings gorgeous color to the outskirts of the city and beyond.

NEAREST AIRPORTS Logan International Airport is just 3 miles (5 km) from downtown Boston.

ACCOMMODATIONS Book ahead; although there are many city center hotels, they fill up for conventions. Good subway connections make it easy to stay outside the center.

GUIDED TOURS Freedom Trail Foundation guides dressed in eighteenth-century costumes give daily tours from the Boston Common Visitor Information Center and the Bostix Booth at Faneuil Hall. There are also guided tours from the National Park Visitor Center at 15 State Street, next to the Old State House.

The red brick Old State House (**3**), a key political meeting place in colonial times, holds its own in the modern city center.

rest in the Old Granary Burying Ground. Two years before his death in 1818, Revere crafted the massive bell in the tower of King's Chapel. Step inside to see its Georgian interior, considered the finest of its kind in the country. The adjoining King's Chapel Burying Ground is the city's oldest, dating from 1630. Look for Joseph Tapping's striking headstone depicting a skeleton battling with Father Time.

A statue of former pupil Benjamin Franklin stands near the site of the Boston Latin School, America's first public school built in 1635. Further

along School Street is the Old Corner Bookstore, where the works of Longfellow, Hawthorne, Emerson, and other nineteenth-century literary greats were published and sold.

As the largest building in Boston in the 1770s, the Old South Meeting House played an important role in the growing call for independence. Colonists held angry protests here against British troops and taxes, one of which led to the dumping of 342 chests of tea into Boston Harbor—the infamous Boston Tea Party. It now houses a museum.

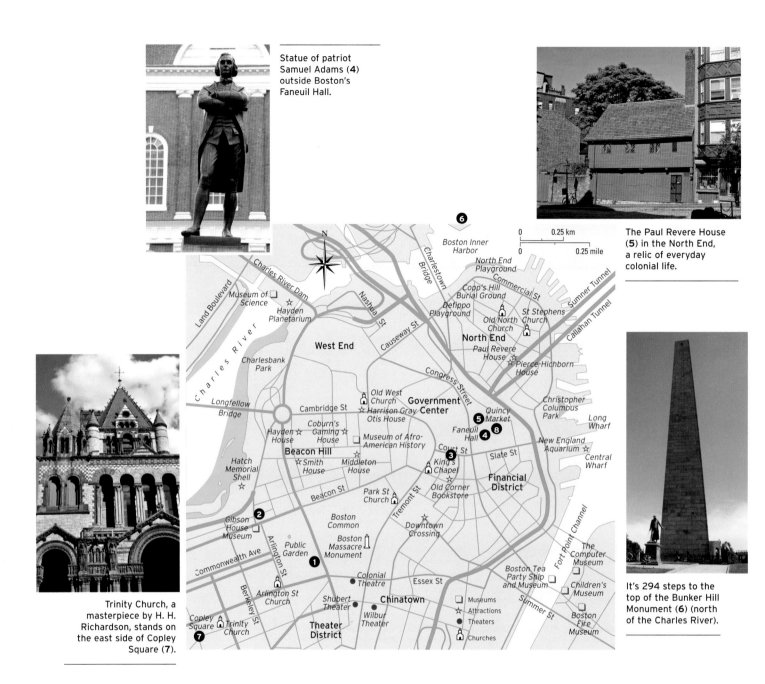

Statue of patriot Samuel Adams (**4**) outside Boston's Faneuil Hall.

The Paul Revere House (**5**) in the North End, a relic of everyday colonial life.

Trinity Church, a masterpiece by H. H. Richardson, stands on the east side of Copley Square (**7**).

It's 294 steps to the top of the Bunker Hill Monument (**6**) (north of the Charles River).

The Old State House is Boston's oldest public building, and still sports the golden lion and silver unicorn statues that symbolized British rule. The Boston Massacre erupted outside in 1770, killing five colonists; a ring of cobblestones marks the spot where they fell. In 1776 the Declaration of Independence was read out from the balcony. Inside is a museum of historic artifacts, including a vial of tea that survived the Boston Tea Party.

A statue of patriot Samuel Adams stands outside Faneuil Hall. It was built for Boston's merchants in 1741, with a marketplace on the ground floor. The meeting hall above soon came to be called the "Cradle of Liberty" as rebels railed against Crown

–> Paul Revere

Paul Revere (1735-1818) became the most colorful of Boston's patriots with his midnight ride on April 18, 1775. A talented silversmith by trade, he was also the best bell-maker of his day, an expert on explosives, a skilled horseman, artillery colonel, merchant, printer, and maker of the copper sheathing for the USS *Constitution*. He had 16 children by his two wives, and pursued his many interests and talents to the ripe old age of 83.

oppression, and later abolitionists took the stage. Now part of the vibrant Quincy Market district, it remains a forum for contemporary debate.

North End and Charlestown

The Freedom Trail continues into the North End, Boston's Italian quarter. At 19 North Square, the Paul Revere House, built in 1676, is the oldest building in downtown Boston and a rare example of colonial domestic architecture. It has been restored to the way it was when the patriot bought it in 1770, and contains some of his furniture and silver items that he made. The house gives a fascinating glimpse of daily life in the eighteenth century.

Revere lived here when he made his famous midnight ride in 1775 to warn fellow patriots that British troops were marching on Lexington and Concord. He had been alerted by signal lanterns hung in the belfry of the Old North Church. Built in 1723, it is Boston's oldest church and boasts its tallest steeple, 191 feet (58 m) high.

Step inside to see the tall pew boxes that kept families warm on wintry Sundays. Nearby is another colonial graveyard, Copp's Hill Burying Ground.

Cross the bridge over the Charles River to Charlestown for the last two sights on the Freedom Trail. The USS *Constitution*, nicknamed "Old Ironsides," is docked in the Charlestown Navy Yard. Built in Boston in 1778, it is the world's oldest commissioned warship. The USS *Constitution* Museum is nearby.

The Bunker Hill Monument, a granite obelisk 221 feet (67 m) high, rises above the green of Monument Square. It marks the site of the first major battle of the American Revolution. The poorly armed colonists held their own against the British Army. And the rest, as they say, is history.

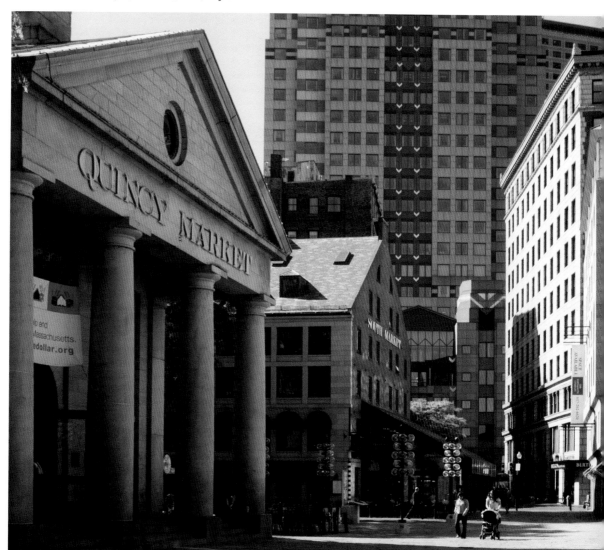

Now filled with popular restaurants, pubs, and shops, Quincy Market (**8**) was Boston's main produce market in the 1800s.

THE MODERN BUILDINGS OF CHICAGO

The greatest names in modern architecture have made Chicago a fascinating city to explore from the ground up... and up... and up.

Chicago's Railway Exchange Building (in the center) (1) is also known as the Santa Fe Building because it was originally built for the Santa Fe Railway in 1904. Today its 17 stories seem very modest.

WE CAN THANK MRS. O'LEARY'S COW. When, according to the popular legend, the cow kicked over the lantern that started the Great Chicago Fire in 1871, she also kick-started the rise of modern architecture. A city's loss was an architect's gain. The burned landscape was a blank canvas on which to try out new ideas, designs, and technologies. The phoenix that rose out of Chicago's ashes would influence architecture around the world for the next century.

After the fire, top architects and engineers from America and Europe came to Chicago to make their mark. Here they were free from the strict styles of the past, and worked together to create new forms of architecture that reflected American ideals. Among them were William Le Baron Jenney, Daniel Burnham, William Holabird, Martin Roche, John Root, Louis H. Sullivan, and his protégé, Frank Lloyd Wright. Collectively their work became known as the Chicago School of Architecture.

In the latter nineteenth century, Chicago was a thriving business and industrial city, with the need for big buildings and the money to finance them. It was a city on the edge of the frontier, reaching for the stars. No wonder it was the birthplace of the skyscraper. It is amazing to think that the man who created the skyscraper had served in the Civil War only 20 years earlier, but it was a sign of how fast America was moving.

Jenney, who had studied engineering in Paris, is called "the father of the skyscraper." He invented the metal-frame construction that enabled high-rise buildings to stand. Previously, buildings were limited in height by their outer load-bearing walls; the higher the building, the more massive its base had to be to support it. Skyscrapers, with their sturdy interior frames and light, outer "curtain" walls, could be higher and more slender. The first was Jenney's ten-story Home Insurance Building, built in 1883-1884.

In the Loop

Jenney's first skyscraper is long gone, but many more early Chicago landmarks still stand within the Loop, the historical center of downtown Chicago. Seeking out these architectural gems is a good way to explore this area, which lies beneath the elevated train system, "the El." For an excellent introduction,

stop by the ArchiCenter, run by the Chicago Architecture Foundation, in the Santa Fe Building, 224 S. Michigan Avenue. It was designed by Daniel Burnham in 1904 as the Railway Exchange Building.

One of the oldest buildings is Burnham and Root's 1885 Rookery. Eleven stories high, it was one of the first in the country to have a sunlit central court; this was renovated by Frank Lloyd Wright in 1905. The Monadnock Building, built 1889–1892, marked the transition between architectural styles with its part masonry, part steel-frame construction.

The Reliance Building of 1895, which now houses the Hotel Burnham named after the architect, is considered a masterpiece of the Chicago School with its elegant glass and white terra-cotta façade. The Marquette Building (Holabird & Roche, 1895), another fine example, is covered in decorative terra-cotta, a material used for fireproofing metal-frame structures. Both buildings have the

The Chicago skyline rivals New York's; ever-growing, ever-changing, defining the city as it looks to the future.

–> FACT FILE

POPULATION City 2.87 million; metro area 9.2 million.

CLIMATE Summer is hot and humid, with temperatures in July–August averaging 85ºF (29ºC). Winters are cold and snowy; January highs average 32ºF (0ºC) but are often well below this. Chicago is called the Windy City, and winter gusts coming off Lake Michigan can be frigid. Annual precipitation averages 34 inches (86 cm).

WHAT TO TAKE Rain jacket and umbrella. In summer, a light sweater is handy for air-conditioned buildings. Casual clothes.

BEST TIME Late spring and fall have the best temperatures and little humidity. Although summer is hot, it is the best time to enjoy the outdoors, with concerts and festivals at Navy Pier.

NEAREST AIRPORTS O'Hare International Airport is 17 miles (27 km) northwest of the Loop. Chicago Midway International Airport is 8 miles (13 km) southwest.

ACCOMMODATIONS Generally expensive in the city center, so look for package deals or discount hotel booking agencies online. Book ahead on weekends and check when conventions are in town.

ARCHITECTURAL TOURS The Chicago Architecture Foundation offers a variety of tours. Walking tours start from the ArchiCenter at 224 S. Michigan. See *www.architecture.org* for information.

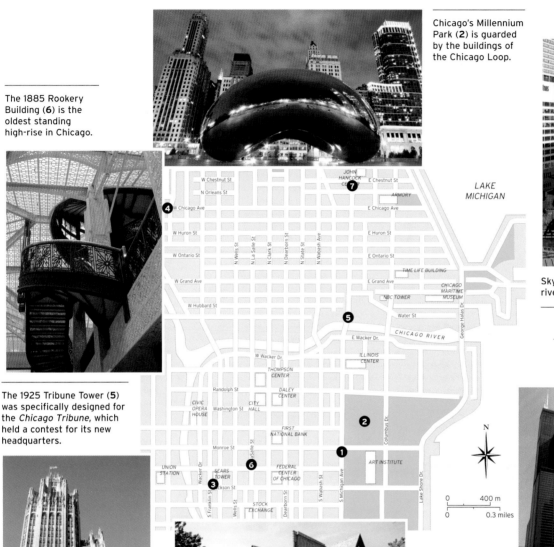

Chicago's Millennium Park (**2**) is guarded by the buildings of the Chicago Loop.

The 1885 Rookery Building (**6**) is the oldest standing high-rise in Chicago.

Skyscrapers crowd the riverbank in the city center.

The 1925 Tribune Tower (**5**) was specifically designed for the *Chicago Tribune*, which held a contest for its new headquarters.

Sears Tower (**3**) is still the highest building in North America.

Architect Frank Lloyd Wright's house on Chicago Avenue (**4**) in Oak Park.

–> Frank Lloyd Wright

Born in Wisconsin, Frank Lloyd Wright has been lauded as America's greatest architect. He began his career in Chicago in 1887, working under his mentor Louis H. Sullivan. He became famous for his prairie-style houses, many of which can be seen in Chicago's Oak Park neighborhood, including Wright's own home. The Robie House in Hyde Park is another outstanding example of his work.

trademark "Chicago windows," invented by Jenney, with a large central glass panel bordered by narrow windows that can be opened for the breeze.

Though the department store itself is now closed, the Carson Pirie Scott building is an early work of one of Chicago's most famous architects, Louis H. Sullivan. Dating from 1899, it sports the striking ornamentation he so favored in his buildings. With Dankmar Adler, Sullivan designed the Auditorium Building in 1889, whose decorative Auditorium Theater is still one of the finest performance spaces in the city. Another highly ornate interior can be seen in the Chicago Cultural

Center, built in 1897 in the Beaux Arts style.
It boasts the world's largest Tiffany glass dome.

Onward and Upward

The form established by these early buildings
enabled skyscraper designers to fully exploit later
architectural styles. Holabird & Root's Chicago
Board of Trade is one of the city's finest Art Deco
skyscrapers. Built in 1930, at 45 stories high it was
the tallest in Chicago for the next 25 years. Another
Art Deco beauty, the Carbide and Carbon Building,
was supposedly inspired by a bottle of champagne.
Designed by Burnham's sons, it stands just north of
the Loop and now makes a jazzy home for the
Hardrock Hotel.

What it lacks in height, the Inland Steel Building
makes up for in beauty. This fine example of 1950s
Modernism from Skidmore, Owings & Merrill was
the first Chicago building with open interior floor
space, full air-conditioning, and underground
parking. The black Federal Center buildings,
completed in 1974, represent the "glass box"
international style of Ludwig Mies van der Rohe.
They are set around the Federal Plaza, with its
bright red Calder sculpture, the first of downtown's
outdoor public plazas featuring large works of art.
Postmodern architecture is colorfully displayed in
Helmut Jahn's 1985 James R. Thompson Center,
with its 17-story atrium.

Skidmore, Owings & Merrill literally reached
their heights in 1974 with the Sears Tower, Chicago's
most famous skyscraper. Standing 1,450 feet
(442 m) high, it was the world's tallest building for
22 years. On a clear day you can see four states
from its 103rd-floor Skydeck observatory.

The city's second-highest building is the
1,136-foot (346-m) AON Center. It overlooks
Millennium Park, where the curved metal shapes of
Frank Gehry's Jay Pritzker Pavilion form the city's
latest landmark. The John Hancock Center with its
94th-floor observatory is further north on Michigan
Avenue. They will all soon be dwarfed by Santiago
Calatrava's twisting Chicago Spire, now under
construction northeast of the Loop, on the shore
of Lake Michigan near Navy Pier. At 2,000 feet
(610 m), this graceful, residential tower will become
North America's tallest skyscraper.

The historic Water Tower
(7) was built in 1869 and
is the only building still
standing in the city that
survived the disastrous
1871 Great Chicago Fire.

THE GREAT LAKES

North America's great inland seas form a natural waterway that stretches from the middle of the continent to the Atlantic, providing recreation, transport, and beauty.

THE FIVE GREAT LAKES of North America are the largest expanse of freshwater in the world. Together, the surfaces of Lakes Superior, Michigan, Huron, Erie, and Ontario cover about 94,250 square miles (244,100 sq km), an area almost as large as the United Kingdom. They form much of the border between Canada and the eastern United States; in fact, the boundary line runs right through the middle of all of them except Lake Michigan, which lies entirely within the United States. In addition to the five main lakes, the system contains numerous rivers, channels, small lakes, and some 35,000 islands.

On the Canadian side, the entire northern shoreline of the Great Lakes is in the province of Ontario. On the U.S. side, the Great Lakes region includes eight states: Minnesota, Wisconsin, Michigan, Illinois, Indiana, Ohio, Pennsylvania, and New York. Some of the continent's largest cities—Toronto, Chicago, Detroit, among them—rose to prominence because of their location on the lakes.

Ground water from this vast surrounding region is the main source of water for the lakes, which drain an area more than twice the size of the lakes themselves. The Great Lakes contain around one-fifth of the world's surface freshwater. If they were to empty out across the contiguous United States, the flood would cover all 48 states to a depth of 9 ½ feet (2.9 m).

Deepest, Smallest, Steepest

Water flows from west to east along the Great Lakes system. Westernmost in the chain is Lake Superior. The largest and deepest of the lakes, it plunges to 1,332 feet (406 m) at its deepest point. Swimming here is cold! Covering 31,820 square miles (82,411 sq km), Lake Superior is the world's largest freshwater lake by surface area. During storms, waves on the lake swell to heights of 20-30 feet (6-9 m). No wonder the Great Lakes are sometimes called North America's inland seas.

A rock formation stands sentry on the shore of remote Flowerpot Island, which lies in the Fathom Five National Marine Park in Lake Huron (1).

Sinclair Cove is a good spot for boating in Lake Superior Provincial Park (**4**).

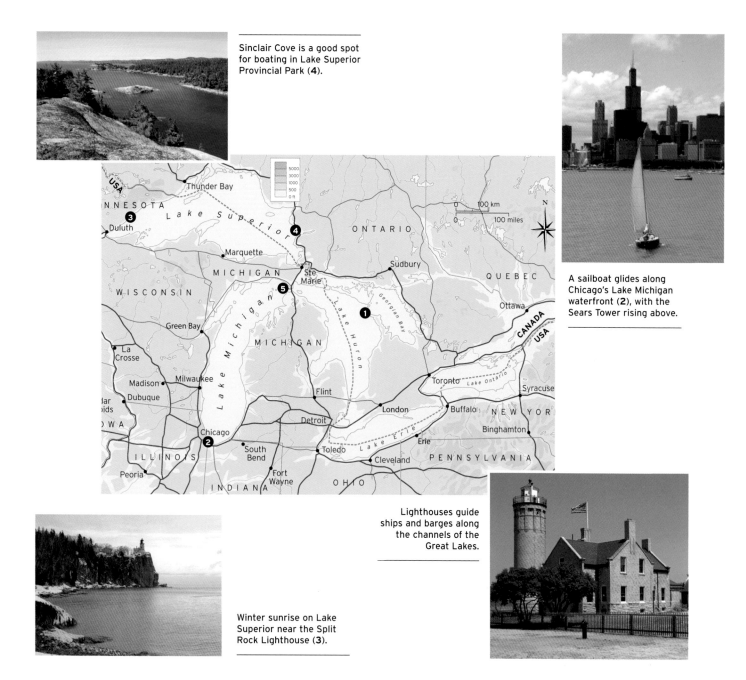

A sailboat glides along Chicago's Lake Michigan waterfront (**2**), with the Sears Tower rising above.

Lighthouses guide ships and barges along the channels of the Great Lakes.

Winter sunrise on Lake Superior near the Split Rock Lighthouse (**3**).

Because of its vast size, a drop of water will be retained in this lake for 191 years before flowing out again.

Sausage-shaped Lake Michigan is 307 miles (494 km) long, dropping down to meet Chicago on its southern shore. It is known for its sandy beaches and big dunes. Lake Huron and Lake Michigan are the second and third largest of the chain, and are connected by the Straits of Mackinac. They share the same elevation and are the same body of water from a hydrological standpoint. Lake Huron's Manitoulin Island is the largest island and contains several lakes of its own; Lake Manitou being the biggest lake-within-a-lake anywhere.

Alongside Detroit, Lake Huron drops down through little Lake St. Clair—too small to be considered a Great Lake—and then into Lake Erie. At an average depth of only 62 feet (19 m), this is the shallowest of the lakes, more than three times shallower than Huron, the next deepest. Bordering the U.S. industrial belt, it suffered from pollution in the 1960s and '70s. At its east end, it flows into the Niagara River and over Niagara Falls into Lake Ontario. The 326-foot (99-m) drop is the steepest change in water level between any of the lakes. Lake Ontario, the smallest lake, connects with the St. Lawrence River, which flows on into the Atlantic Ocean.

Channels of Prosperity

The Great Lakes region is rich in natural resources. For a start, millions of people get their drinking water from the lakes. The fertile farmland is particularly suited to growing corn and cereals, as well as dairy farming. In the eighteenth and nineteenth centuries, farmers used barges to transport their goods along the lakes and through the Erie Canal to markets in the East.

The region is rich in minerals, too. Large deposits of iron ore were found in Minnesota and the Upper Michigan peninsula, while the western Pennsylvania coal fields yielded huge quantities of anthracite.

They provided the raw materials for the steelworks, automobile plants, and other factories that made the region an industrial powerhouse in the latter nineteenth and twentieth centuries. All of these were shipped along the lakes by barge or freighter, and transport became a key economic activity. The Great Lakes developed their own maritime customs and lingo as more and more lakers–boats that trade mainly on the lakes–plied the waters.

The lakes were the best means of moving people, too. Passenger lines carried millions of immigrants westward along the lakes to new lives in the factories and farms of the Midwest, where

The Mackinac Bridge across Lake Huron's Straits of Mackinac (5) connects the Upper and Lower Michigan peninsulas.

communities in every state still proudly honor their Old-World heritage.

Ocean-going ships can sail from the Atlantic all the way to Duluth, Minnesota, the world's most inland port, thanks to the system of channels, locks, and canals along the St. Lawrence Seaway and the Great Lakes Waterway. These include the Welland Canal that bypasses Niagara Falls, and the Soo Locks that bypass rapids on the St. Mary's River between Lakes Superior and Huron. The lakes can freeze over in winter and icebreakers are used to keep the channels open. Canada and the United States share the operation of this dual waterway.

Recreational boating is a big part of Great Lakes tourism, from personal pleasure craft to small cruise ships and sailing ships. Sport fishing takes place year-round. The lakes are hugely popular summer vacation spots, with a wealth of options for sightseeing, scenic drives, and outdoor activities such as swimming, biking, fishing, and boating surrounding their shores.

–> FACT FILE

CLIMATE Weather varies around the lakes but the region has four distinct seasons. Summers are hot and sunny with temperatures ranging in the 70s–90s°F (21–32°C). Winters can be bitterly cold with much snowfall. Daytime temperatures average in the 20s and 30s°F (-7–1°C) but sometimes much colder, dropping below 0°F (-18°C). Spring and early summer get the most rain. There can be strong winds off the lakes year-round.

WHAT TO TAKE Sunscreen, rain jacket, sweater or jacket for cool nights in summer.

BEST TIME Fall is a beautiful season with colorful foliage. Summer is the best time for outdoor recreation apart from winter sports. Spring weather can be lovely but unpredictable.

NEAREST AIRPORTS Toronto, Chicago, and Detroit have the largest international airports. Other cities all around the region are served by scheduled domestic flights.

ACCOMMODATIONS There are a variety of accommodations in towns and cities all around the region. Book well ahead for lakeside resorts June–August, as they fill up with vacationing families from around the region.

CAPE COD NATIONAL SEASHORE

The Pilgrims were the first Europeans to see this jewel of the Atlantic coast, and it looks much the same today with its pristine beaches, dunes, and wildlife.

Provincetown Heritage Museum towers over the picturesque waterfront of Cape Cod's main fishing port and tourist resort (1).

WITH BEACHFRONT PROPERTY at a premium and most of the U.S. coastline devoured by cities, hotels, beach resorts, and vacation homes, finding an undeveloped stretch of virgin coast is like finding a goldmine. Cape Cod National Seashore is the treasure of New England, one of only ten national seashores in the National Park System. It preserves nearly 40 miles (64 km) of idyllic Atlantic coastline, encompassing white-sand beaches, high dunes, heathlands, pinewoods, freshwater ponds, and marshes. A number of historic sites survive here too, some marking one of the first European settlements in the New World.

Henry David Thoreau gave the best description of the peninsula, which curves around Cape Cod Bay: "Cape Cod is the bared and bended arm of Massachusetts: the shoulder is at Buzzard's Bay; the elbow, or crazy-bone, at Cape Mallebarre; the wrist at Truro; and the sandy fist at Provincetown." Locals refer to it in three sections: the Upper Cape, closest to the mainland; Mid-Cape, from around Barnstable to Chatham and the elbow's bend; and Lower Cape, from Orleans along the forearm to the tip of the fist.

Cape Cod National Seashore stretches along the Atlantic coast of the Lower Cape, all the way from

Made of granite, the Pilgrim Monument (1) rises 252 feet (77 m) high.

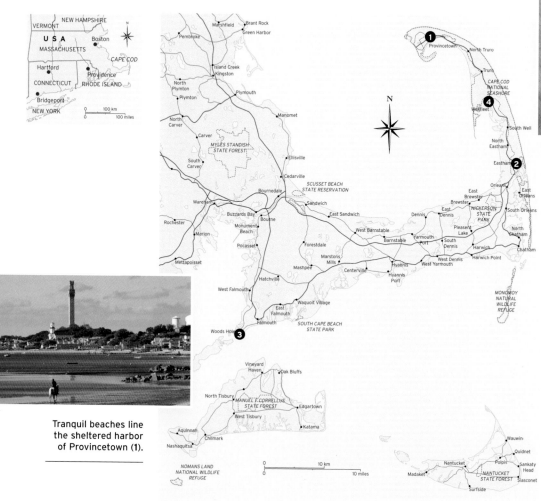

Tranquil beaches line the sheltered harbor of Provincetown (1).

Built in 1680, the Eastham Windmill (2) is still used occasionally to grind corn.

Chatham to Provincetown. Established in 1961 by President John F. Kennedy, whose family home at Hyannisport stands on the Mid-Cape overlooking Nantucket Sound, the parkland covers 44,600 acres (18,049 ha). While Bostonians and other vacationers flock here for the beaches in summer, the seashore has many other attractions.

Sea Birds and Kettle Ponds

The Salt Pond Visitor Center near Eastham is a good introduction to the seashore. Exhibits here tell the story of the dunes and heathlands that stretch all along the coast behind the beaches. The Cape contains both freshwater and saltwater marshes, with white cedar and red maple forests growing among the swamps. Near the "wrist" the Cape gives way to a wilder, windswept landscape of scrub oak and sandplain grasses.

One of the most interesting features of the seashore is the freshwater kettle ponds, created by glaciers during the last ice age. There are over 300 of them, and 20 are permanently flooded,

ranging in size from 2 ½-100 acres (1-40 ha). Although they are close to the ocean, the sea salts are flushed out by groundwater, leaving freshwater ponds 6-65 feet (2-20 m) deep.

Along with the marshes, the kettle ponds provide habitat for numerous species of waterfowl and shore birds, including many migratory species; the adorable piping plover is one example. This sparrow-like shore bird is among 25 threatened species that can be found along the seashore. The many habitats of the Cape Cod National Seashore support an amazing number of creatures—some 450 species of birds, mammals, reptiles, amphibians, fish, and invertebrate animals. The Wellfleet Bay Wildlife Sanctuary is a good place to see some of them.

A delightful feature of the Cape landscape is its cranberry bogs, a reminder of old rural pleasures. In fact, the Pamet Cranberry Bog at Truro was once a thriving business, maintained and picked for commercial produce from the 1880s until 1961. The company harvested around

Lobster trap buoys hanging on a wall are a colorful symbol of the peninsula's fishing heritage.

Nobska Point Lighthouse at Woods Hole (**3**) is one of many gracing the shoreline of Cape Cod.

166 barrels of cranberries every fall during its heyday. Today you can hike the Cranberry Bog Trail east of Truro, where the old Bog House still stands.

Pilgrim's Landing

In 1620, after a two-month Atlantic crossing on the *Mayflower*, the Pilgrims first set eyes on the New World at Cape Cod. They were meant to settle further south in Virginia, but after hitting troubled waters they turned back to the Cape, landing at what is now Provincetown. They spent six weeks here before moving on to Plymouth. The Pilgrim Memorial commemorates this historic event with a graceful Italianate tower, which you can climb for splendid views. There is an excellent museum in its base.

Bustling, commercial Provincetown—a fishing port, art colony, and gay resort—is a jarring contrast to the peaceful scenery of the national seashore. Recapture the natural serenity at the tip of the Cape, at Race Point and Herring Cove beaches, with lovely Race Point Lighthouse nestled in the dunes. The oldest lighthouse on the seashore is Highland Light, also called Cape Cod Light, erected in 1857. Another picturesque lighthouse stands at Nauset Light Beach. Nearby Marconi Beach was the site of the first wireless station in the country. In 1903, Guglielmo Marconi transmitted the first public

transatlantic wireless message from here, between the president, Theodore Roosevelt, and the British king, Edward VII.

The Lower Cape is very narrow in places, so you can easily go from the pounding surf of the windy Atlantic side to the calm, shallow waters of the westside bay. Biking trails wind through the woodlands, dunes, lakes, and marshes in between. A highlight is the Cape Cod Rail Trail, a paved path that runs for 25 miles (40 km) along a former train track, used by cyclists, skaters, and pedestrians. Scenic spur trails run from Eastham and Wellfleet through the national seashore to the Atlantic shore.

When the Pilgrims arrived on Cape Cod National Seashore they had all of America before them. Today, this tranquil place has a different allure for those seeking the pristine beauty of nature. Thoreau, once again, said it best: "A man may stand there and put all America behind him."

Idyllic beaches line the shore at Wellfleet (4), a harbor town famous for its many art galleries and the Wellfleet oyster.

–> FACT FILE

CLIMATE Summer daytime temperatures range from 70-80°F (21-26°C) with cool nights. Winter highs range between 30-40°F (-1-4°C) but can drop below 0°F (-18°C). Springtime conditions can remain cool and damp with temperatures in the mid-40s°F (7°C).

WHAT TO TAKE Sunscreen, hat, insect repellent, windbreaker.

BEST TIME Midsummer has the best temperatures but is also the busiest season. Late spring/early summer and early fall are quieter and pleasant.

NEAREST AIRPORTS Boston's Logan International Airport is the closest major airport. From Boston there are scheduled domestic flights into Hyannis and Provincetown.

ACCOMMODATIONS There are a variety of accommodations in towns along Cape Cod and the National Seashore, from quaint bed and breakfasts to small hotels. Book well ahead for July and August, when lodgings are filled to capacity.

PARK ENTRANCE There is a beach entrance fee per vehicle or per pedestrian, from late June through early September when lifeguards are on duty. Seasonal and annual passes are available.

PUEBLOS OF THE FOUR CORNERS

The real beginnings of American history lie in the elaborate cliff dwellings built by the Ancestral Pueblo people of the Four Corners region.

The Pueblo dwelling known as "the White House" (opposite) is built into a cliff at Canyon de Chelly National Monument (1).

THEY HAD COME AND GONE long before America was ever discovered by Europeans. They left no written texts or tablets, no testimony to tell us who they were or where they went. But a mysterious, ancient race left thousands of pithouses, pueblos, and cliff dwellings scattered throughout the Southwest in the Four Corners region where Colorado, New Mexico, Arizona, and Utah meet.

These early Native Americans are often called the Anasazi, a term adopted by archeologists in the 1930s to describe the people who lived and farmed here between the first century and A.D. 1300, and whose culture possibly dates back as far as 1500 B.C. But despite its colorful ring to Western ears, there was no such tribe as the Anasazi. It is actually a Navajo word meaning "ancient enemy or stranger." Modern Pueblo Indians are descended from this prehistoric civilization, and they prefer the terms Ancestral Puebloans or Ancient Pueblo People.

The Ancestral Puebloans hunted and cultivated corn, squash, beans, and other crops. They wove beautiful coiled baskets from plant fibers, and began making pottery around A.D. 500. Their earliest dwellings were pithouses, made by excavating a shallow area and covering it with mud and sticks. These evolved into the ceremonial kivas used by later communities. Next came single-story pueblos made of stones and clay. Around A.D. 900-1000, multilevel, multiroomed complexes began to appear. Most fascinating of all are the cliff dwellings, built between 1200 and 1300. These large pueblo complexes were built into a cave or overhanging cliffs, providing a defensive position as well as shelter.

Then, at the end of the thirteenth century, the Ancestral Puebloans suddenly disappeared from the Four Corners. No one knows why they abandoned their homes. No one knows for certain where they went. Some theories indicate that crop failures due to drought and changing climate conditions caused them to seek a more fertile location. Others suggest that they were threatened by hostile tribes moving north from Mexico. Most people believe they migrated south to Arizona and New Mexico, their descendants now occupying Hopi lands, the Rio Grande pueblos, and other Native American communities. They left behind a fascinating legacy of ruins, artifacts, and unsolved mystery.

Mesa Verde

The most impressive and accessible ruins are in southwest Colorado's Mesa Verde National Park. It sprawls over 54,000 acres (21,853 ha), protecting more than 4,000 archeological sites, including 600 cliff dwellings. Rangers give tours of the magnificent Cliff Palace, the largest cliff dwelling with 150 rooms, and the nearby Balcony House, where you get a feel for pueblo life by climbing ladders and squeezing through tunnels. Long House, the second-largest dwelling on the distant Wetherill Mesa, can also be toured. You can explore Spruce Tree House—behind the informative Chapin Archeological Museum—on your own during summer months. There are scenic loop roads and hiking trails throughout the park that give access to stunning views and close-up looks at kivas, towers, and other structures.

As one of the country's top national parks, Mesa Verde can get very busy. Hovenweep National Monument, 50 miles (80 km) west on the Utah border, offers a quieter look at the Ancient Pueblo people. Here, six towers rise above the canyon rim,

Navajo rock paintings depict a nineteenth-century Spanish expedition.

FACT FILE <—

CLIMATE Temperatures vary with elevation and will be much hotter on the canyon floors. Summers are usually hot, with daytime temperatures ranging from around 85ºF (29ºC) to over 100ºF (37ºC), with cool nights and afternoon thunderstorms in July–August. Winters range from mild to cold at different sites; snow can fall at Mesa Verde as late as May and as early as October.

WHAT TO TAKE Sunscreen, sun hat, sunglasses, good hiking boots, high-energy food, plenty of water. Dress in layers for changing weather.

BEST TIME Late spring and early summer, or fall have the most pleasant temperatures for hiking. Midsummer is very busy at popular sites; tour numbers are limited and tickets are snapped up early. Tours of some sites may not operate in winter.

NEAREST AIRPORTS The nearest international airports are at Phoenix, Arizona; Albuquerque, New Mexico; and Denver, Colorado. There are closer regional airports at Cortez and Durango, Colorado; and Farmington, New Mexico.

ACCOMMODATIONS There are hotels and motels at Farmington, Cortez, Durango, and other towns in the region; camp-grounds at Mesa Verde and other sites.

PARK ENTRANCE Fees apply at most national parks and monuments. Some have free entrance but charge for driving or hiking on the canyon floors.

Hundreds of rooms and circular kivas were found in the ruins of Pueblo Bonito in Chaco Culture National Historic Park (**2**).

which may have been storage towers or lookout posts. In between the parks is the Canyon of the Ancients National Monument, created in 2000, which preserves over 6,000 archeological sites, the largest concentration in the country.

Chaco Canyon

The reconstructed kiva at Aztec Ruins National Monument in northern New Mexico is an insight into ceremonial life, and has large pueblo ruins. Further south, reached by a remote dirt road, are the impressive remains of a major center of Ancestral Puebloan life at Chaco Culture National Historical Park. Its nine Great Houses, kivas, and other structures were built between 900 and 1150.

The 9-mile (14-km) Canyon Loop Drive leads to six major sites, including the highlight, Pueblo Bonito (Beautiful Village). The semicircular site, which rose over four stories high on one side, covered some 2 acres (1 ha), had 650 rooms and dozens of kivas. Chaco appears to have been a place of trade, ritual, and power. Exquisite pottery, precious stones, and ceremonial objects have been excavated. Turquoise was brought here from mines near Santa Fe for processing and trading. Priest-

astronomers studied the heavens. It was Pueblo civilization in full flower. But, like Mesa Verde, its fortunes waned and its people moved on.

Canyon de Chelly

Navajo farmers still live on their ancestral lands at Canyon de Chelly National Monument, located on tribal lands in northeastern Arizona. Here, cliff dwellings, pithouses, and other ancient sites are nestled into the sandstone walls of three long, deep canyons. You can see some sites from above on the two rim drives, such as Spider Rock, an incredible sandstone spire rising from the canyon floor, but to go down into the canyon for a close-up look at the ruins, rock art, and petroglyphs, you must have a Navajo guide. The only self-guided trail leads to the White House cliff dwelling.

Navajo National Monument lies northwest across the reservation, near Kayenta. Three of the most intact Ancestral Puebloan cliff dwellings are sheltered in the alcoves of the canyon. Rangers lead the 5-mile (8-km) hikes to see Betatakin up close. Keet Seel, a larger pueblo, requires a longer hike into the backcountry.

Cliff Palace in Mesa Verde National Park (**5**) is one of the best preserved ancient cliff dwellings.

Ruins inside the Long House cliff dwelling (**3**) in Mesa Verde National Park.

Hovenweep Castle is a distinctive ruin found in Hovenweep National Monument (**4**).

OLYMPIC NATIONAL PARK

From glacier-topped mountains to unspoiled Pacific shoreline to ancient stands of temperate rainforest, you can visit three parks in one in this great northwestern wilderness.

MOUNT OLYMPUS was the home of Zeus and the gods and goddesses of ancient Greece. While the American Mount Olympus is the territory of mere mortals and a host of wildlife, it too is a heavenly domain. This 7,965-foot (2,428-m) mountain king is draped in shining robes of glacial ice. Thanks to heavy winter snowfalls of up to 50 feet (15 m) a year, Mount Olympus sustains no less than six large glaciers even though it is relatively modest in height, from Blue Glacier, the most massive, to Hoh Glacier, the longest at more than 3 miles (5 km). It is surrounded by a pearly court of other glacier-clad peaks.

Mount Olympus crowns the 922,561 acres (373,342 ha) of wilderness that comprise Olympic National Park, which covers most of the tip of the Olympic Peninsula. Bordered by the Pacific Ocean on the west, the Puget Sound to the east, and Juan de Fuca Strait to the north, it forms the thumb of northwest Washington State. The same glaciers that sculpted the park's mountains, lakes, and valleys also carved these watery channels that isolated the peninsula from most of the mainland. Thus it developed a unique range of flora and fauna species found nowhere else in the world, such as the Olympic marmot and Olympic snow mole.

The peninsula became a refuge for other plants and animals native to the Pacific Northwest, such as Roosevelt elk, the largest elk species in North America. Partly to protect these elks, the land was preserved as the Mount Olympus National Monument in 1909, and became a national park in 1938. Because of its unique natural history, it was designated an International Biosphere Reserve in 1976 and a World Heritage Site five years later.

Three Parks in One

Olympic National Park contains three distinct environments—the Olympic Mountains, wilderness Pacific beaches, and rare temperate rain forest. Bordering the park on the east and west is the Olympic National Forest. Over a dozen major rivers flow down from the central mountains across the valleys and floodplains in their natural state, some providing an important link to the sea.

There is a great contrast in climate across the peninsula. The valleys on the western side of the park are the wettest places in the continental United States. The northeastern side lies in a dry rainshadow. The Hoh Rain Forest receives over 140 inches (356 cm) of rain each year. Compared with this, the town of Sequim on the northeast edge of the park gets only 16 inches (41 cm) of rain a year. Here farmers have to irrigate their fields less than 35 miles (56 km) from the rainforest.

Ninety-five percent of the park is designated wilderness. Highway 101 broadly circles around three-quarters of the park, but none of the access roads go very far into the park's interior and there is no route all the way through the center. There are, however, more than 600 miles (966 km) of hiking trails, ranging from easy strolls to strenuous backcountry treks.

Mountains

The best place to start is on the north side of the park, at the Olympic National Park Visitor Center and Museum in Port Angeles. Then head into the park along a steep, twisting 17-mile (27-km) road to Hurricane Ridge, the highest point accessible by car. You will be rewarded with stupendous views of Mount Olympus and Blue Glacier, rising above Mount Carrie. In summer you can continue on an even steeper dirt road to Obstruction Peak, or set off on foot to explore trails through wildflower meadows.

Deer range from the lowland valleys to the highland meadows in Olympic National Park.

The rocky coast at Rialto Beach (1), west of Forks, is a good place for viewing the sea stacks and islets offshore.

Further west, Lake Crescent is a lovely glacial lake; here an easy trail through old-growth forest leads to pretty Marymere Falls. Alpine tarns and waterfalls feature highly in this watery park. Beyond the lake, the road into the Sol Duc River valley runs through the transitional zone between the western rain forest and the lowland forest to the east. It leads to hot springs and another splendid cataract, Sol Duc Falls.

Rain Forest

There are very few temperate rain forests on the planet. Two are in New Zealand and Patagonia; the largest is here, in Olympic National Park. Although it sits at a higher latitude than tropical environments, the combination of mild

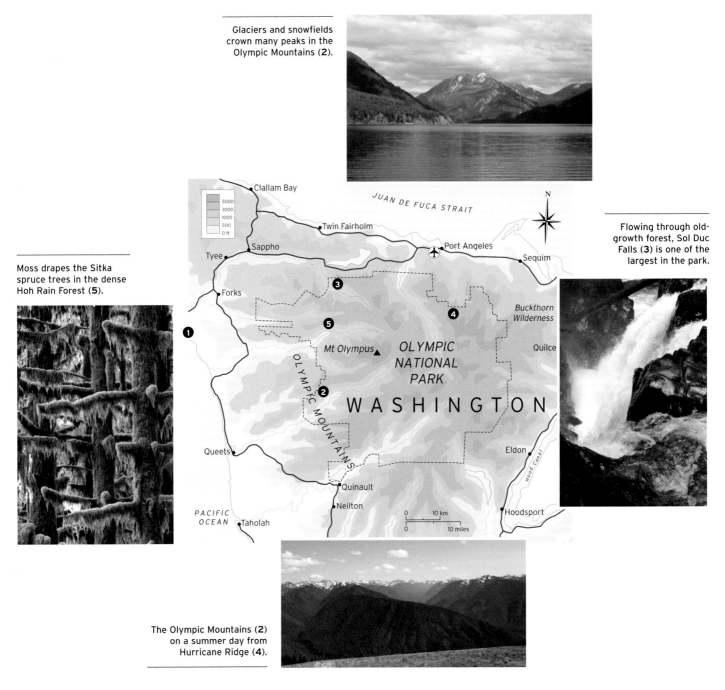

Glaciers and snowfields crown many peaks in the Olympic Mountains (**2**).

Moss drapes the Sitka spruce trees in the dense Hoh Rain Forest (**5**).

Flowing through old-growth forest, Sol Duc Falls (**3**) is one of the largest in the park.

The Olympic Mountains (**2**) on a summer day from Hurricane Ridge (**4**).

temperatures, abundant moisture from rain and fog, and a thick layer of organic matter produce lush, dense forests of enormous trees such as Sitka spruce, maple, and western hemlock. The trees and forest floor are thickly coated with mosses, lichens, ferns, and fungi, giving it a jungle-like appearance.

Hoh Rain Forest is the most visited in the park, with a good visitor center and two easy trails—the Hall of Mosses and Spruce trails. The Queets Rain Forest and the Quinault Rain Forest are more remote in the southwestern section of the park, but both have moderate trails. Queets is home to the world's largest Douglas fir, 220 feet (67 m) high and 45 feet (14 m) in circumference.

Beaches

Running for 73 miles (117 km) along the edge of the peninsula are the last wild ocean beaches in the lower United States. This narrow strip is separated from the main park and borders several Native American reservations. Highway 101 runs along the southern beaches, where Ruby Beach is a highlight. Strong currents and floating logs make them unsuitable for swimming, but the misty, unspoiled landscape, with its pebbly shoreline and dark sea stacks and rock arches offshore, make for excellent hiking. There are fascinating tidal pools brimming with sealife, while the coastline is home to sea lions, seals, and a host of seabirds.

Hurricane Ridge (**4**) provides scenic views for hikers in summer and alpine and Nordic skiing for winter sports enthusiasts.

→ FACT FILE

CLIMATE Most of the peninsula has a moderate marine climate. Summers are mild with average high temperatures ranging 65-75°F (18-24°C). Winters are mild and wet, with averages in the 30s and 40sºF (-1-5ºC) at lower elevations, with heavy snowfall in the mountains. Average annual precipitation is 135 inches (343 cm) on the western side.

WHAT TO TAKE Hiking boots; rain gear and extra pair of dry shoes; layered clothing; insect repellent.

BEST TIME July-September are the driest months, with heavier rainfall during the rest of the year. Be prepared for rain and changing conditions at any time of year.

NEAREST AIRPORTS Seattle-Tacoma International Airport is the closest major airport. There are several routes to the park, with driving time 2 ½-3 hours to Port Angeles.

ACCOMMODATIONS There are four lodges within the park and several campgrounds. Book ahead. There are a variety of accommodations in the small communities bordering the park.

DRIVING Some of the gravel roads in the park are very rough and may not be suitable for ordinary cars, especially in wet weather. Check with park rangers before setting out on backcountry roads.

HIKING Pick up a tide table if you plan to hike the beaches to avoid getting stranded by incoming tides.

PARK ENTRANCE An entrance fee per vehicle is valid for seven days. Annual passes good at all national parks are also available.

MEXICO

"I was taken in by the bravado
and the sounds of Mexico...
not so much the music, but the spirit."

Herb Alpert, American musician, 1935-

SAN MIGUEL DE ALLENDE

This small city with its cobblestone streets is one of the finest and prettiest of Mexico's many colonial settlements, with a thriving artistic community.

SAN MIGUEL DE ALLENDE traces its roots back to 1542, when it was founded by the Franciscan monk Juan de San Miguel. It prospered and grew, and its wealth produced numerous beautiful colonial-style mansions. Many of these still exist today and have been lovingly restored, some of them used as hotels to welcome the visitors–both short term and long term–that come here.

In 1926 San Miguel was declared a protected national monument, and today new buildings must conform to the colonial style, bringing a sense of harmony to the modern city. Despite the numerous foreign visitors it attracts, including a large and thriving American expatriate community, it retains a lively and characterful Mexican flavor and is one of the country's undoubted highlights. In 2008 it was added to UNESCO'S list of World Heritage Sites.

A Silver City

Fra. Juan de San Miguel built his first mission a few miles from the center of the present town, near a river that was prone to running dry. As the story goes, Fra. Juan was a great dog lover, and one day his dogs wandered off in search of water, and settled down at the fresh spring of El Chorro. When Fra. Juan found them he realized this was a much better spot in which to live, and a new mission was built here.

A few years later, in 1555, the Spanish built a garrison here as San Miguel was an ideal stopping point on the Camino Real, the Royal Road used to travel between the far-flung colonial settlements. Here the road was carrying silver; large deposits had been found in Zacatecas in 1546, about 170 miles (274 km) to the northeast, and San Miguel was about halfway between Zacatecas and Mexico City. There were other silver mines too, some close to San Miguel, and today it is often referred to as one of Mexico's colonial Silver Cities.

As it prospered the town became known as San Miguel el Grande, and it was not until 1826 that it became San Miguel de Allende. It was renamed in honor of one of its most prominent local sons, Ignacio Allende. Allende came from a wealthy San Miguel family, and despite his comfortable lifestyle

Traditional ocher colors brighten the houses on the old colonial streets of San Miguel de Allende.

POPULATION 62,000

CURRENCY Mexican peso

CLIMATE San Miguel has a mild, semidesert climate, and there can be long spells without rain from November–May. June–October is the rainy season, when it will rain a few times a week, but some of the rainfall can be very heavy. December is the coldest month when the daily temperature will range from 46-70°F (8-21°C), and the warmest month is May, when the range is 57-83°F (14-28°C).

WHAT TO TAKE Good waterproof clothing in the rainy season, as when it rains it can really rain; sunscreen; something warm for the evenings.

BEST TIME April–May is good, but so too is August, when the rain brings the desert flowers into bloom.

NEAREST AIRPORTS Leon is the closest, about two hours away. Mexico City is further, about three-four hours, but may offer better flight options and prices.

ACCOMMODATIONS The town, though small, has a good choice of accommodations ranging from budget hostels for the many language students it attracts to more expensive old colonial mansions. For longer visits consider renting an apartment, of which there are many.

The entrance to Parroquia San Miguel Arcángel (1), symbol of the city, is strewn with colorful Easter decorations.

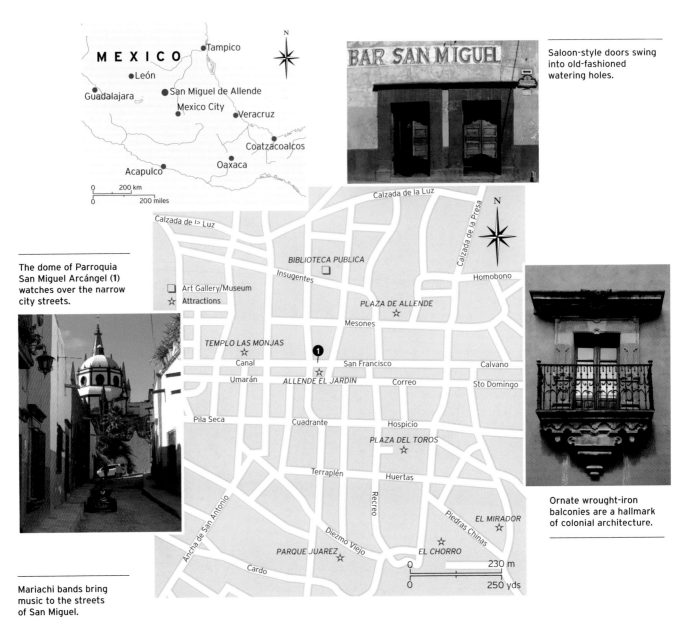

MEXICO

Tampico
León
Guadalajara
San Miguel de Allende
Mexico City
Veracruz
Coatzacoalcos
Acapulco
Oaxaca

0   200 km
0   200 miles

BAR SAN MIGUEL

Saloon-style doors swing into old-fashioned watering holes.

The dome of Parroquia San Miguel Arcángel (1) watches over the narrow city streets.

Calzada de la Luz
Calzada de la Luz
Calzada de la Presa
BIBLIOTECA PUBLICA
Insugentes
Homobono
Art Gallery/Museum
Attractions
PLAZA DE ALLENDE
Mesones
TEMPLO LAS MONJAS
Canal
San Francisco
Calvano
ALLENDE EL JARDIN
Umarán
Correo
Sto Domingo
Pila Seca
Cuadrante
Hospicio
PLAZA DEL TOROS
Terraplén
Huertas
Recreo
Ancha de San Antonio
Piedras Chinas
EL MIRADOR
Diezmo Viejo
EL CHORRO
PARQUE JUAREZ
Cardo

0   230 m
0   250 yds

Ornate wrought-iron balconies are a hallmark of colonial architecture.

Mariachi bands bring music to the streets of San Miguel.

he fought against the Spanish and became a general during the Mexican War of Independence. Eventually he gave his life for the cause. He was captured by the Spanish, put in front of a firing squad in Chihuahua in 1811, and then beheaded. His head was put on public display as an example to the local people, though perhaps with a different effect from what the Spanish intended. Mexico gained its independence in 1821, and Allende remains a national hero.

A Special Nature

This proud history is part of the fabric of life in San Miguel, and the greatest pleasure lies in simply being here, and for as long as possible, rather than seeing particular sights. Not that there are not plenty to visit, with many of them conveniently close to each other in the center of town. But San Miguel also demands that you find time to relax—especially as much of it stands over 6,000 feet

(1,829 m) above sea level, and most visitors need time to acclimatize.

Some visitors acclimatize so well that they never leave, which is why there is a big and busy artistic community here, especially artists and writers from the United States, but also from Mexico City and elsewhere in the country. It gives San Miguel a lively feel, where something is always going on. Couple this with the natural Mexican exuberance and the above-average number of feasts and festivals, and you start to realize why San Miguel captivates–and ultimately captures–many travelers.

There are some things every visitor should see, and indeed it is hard to miss La Parroquia de San Miguel Arcángel. It is a church like no other, anywhere in the world, and has become an icon of the city. The original colonial-style parish church was built in the late seventeenth century, but in 1888 a local architect was hired to enlarge the church and give it a new façade. The authorities wanted a Gothic-style church, perhaps like Nôtre-Dame in Paris. The architect, Zeferino Gutiérrez, had never seen a real Gothic church, but worked from postcards and, in some versions of the story, did drawings in the dirt to show his workmen what he wanted. The result is a pseudo-Gothic-style church drafted onto a colonial original, which some hate but most citizens have great affection for.

The Museo Casa de Allende, at the birthplace of General Ignacio Allende, gives a fascinating insight into his life, the Mexican fight for independence, and this chapter in the history of San Miguel. There are other museums, churches, and some refreshing parks and gardens to visit. In fact, the main square is called El Jardin, The Garden. It is here in the early morning that for many the new day in San Miguel begins, with a coffee, a newspaper, a conversation. It is also the place a visitor should come, to get a sense of this magical town and the pull it has over people.

Twilight falls around the soaring spires and lighted dome of Parroquia San Miguel Arcángel (1), set on the Jardin, the main city square.

MAYAN PYRAMIDS OF YUCATÁN

The temples and pyramids built by the Mayans in Mexico's Yucatán state are among the finest and most fascinating archeological sites in the country.

POPULATION 1,800,000 (Yucatán)

CURRENCY Mexican peso

CLIMATE Yucatán has a hot and humid climate, with temperatures averaging 80-90ºF (26-32ºC) all year. The rainy seasons are roughly April-July and October-January, and the hurricane season June-November. On the coast the rains can really settle in during the rainy seasons, and you might get several days of nonstop rain. Inland will be a little drier but you should still be prepared for some rain most days. Cancún has been hit by several hurricanes in recent years. It is not something that should put you off traveling at this time, but do check ahead and try to get forecasts.

WHAT TO TAKE Good waterproof gear for the rainy season, sunscreen, and a water bottle, as visits to the archeological sites can be long and hot.

BEST TIME September is an ideal month—still warm from the summer and not yet wet. February-March are also good months, when it should be warm and dry.

NEAREST AIRPORTS Cancún for the east of the region, Mérida for the west.

ACCOMMODATIONS Many people use Cancún as a base for visiting the region, where there are plenty of options at all levels. Mérida is also a good base, and here there are some lovely old colonial-style hotels.

Daylight breaks over El Castillo, the formidable pyramid at Chichén Itzá (1) dedicated to the feathered serpent Kukulkan.

YUCATÁN'S MAYAN PYRAMIDS are breathtaking in more ways than one, as anyone who has climbed to the top of the El Castillo pyramid at Chichén Itzá will know. The sheer steep steps up these remarkable structures are a test for the faint-hearted and the unfit, but after you have gazed in wonder at the structure from below for a while, it is a natural instinct to want to get to the top and see the view from there. The rewards make the pain and the panting all worth it, and it is a good excuse to then sit and consider what these curious buildings are all about.

The Mayan People

Like the Incas in South America and the ancient Egyptians, the Mayan civilization that developed in and around Mexico was one of the most advanced cultures in the world. It extended throughout Mexico and into the northern area of Central America, including Guatemala and Belize, but it is Mexico's Yucatán state that was the heart of the Mayan people.

The first Mayan people are known to have been in this area by at least 10,000 B.C., but the civilization was at its height from about the third-tenth centuries A.D. The Mayans developed a very sophisticated culture, and were knowledgeable farmers and architects as well as mathematicians, astronomers, artists, and linguists. They had the only complex written language in all the Americas prior to the arrival of the European explorers.

Some of the Mayan cities were, in their day, every bit as big and as cultured as those of ancient Greece and Rome. Like all civilizations, they developed their own religious rituals, and the extraordinary pyramids that rise out of the jungles were part of that. The Mayans built two types of pyramid: some were short and squat and had temples on top, where ritual sacrifices would be carried out; others were taller and steeper, and were meant to be worshiped, not climbed. The pyramids were built high for two main reasons, one spiritual and one practical. The practical

Ruins at Tulum (**3**), one of the few walled cities ever built by the ancient Mayans.

Cancún's (**2**) idyllic beaches make it one of Mexico's top resorts.

A headless Mayan statue at Chitzén Itzá (**1**) hints at bloody ancient rituals.

The beach at Tulum (**3**) was an important landing place for Mayan trading ships.

Reclining Chac-Mool figures are found in or near ancient Toltec sites in the Yucatán.

reason was so that they could be seen standing above the jungle and act as landmarks for travelers. The spiritual reason was to take the priests closer to the gods when they carried out their holy rites.

Chichén Itzá

One of the greatest of the Mayan remains is at Chichén Itzá, a popular tourist destination as it is easily reached from both the Yucatán capital, Mérida, and from the busy holiday resort of Cancún. It has been drawing tourists for more than a century, since the site was rediscovered in the jungles of Yucatán by European visitors, who marveled at it and wrote vivid accounts that attracted the world's archeologists. Chichén Itzá had apparently declined after a civil war in the early thirteenth century, perhaps even before then, though the full reason for its startling change from thriving city to overgrown jungle ruin is just one of its many mysteries.

The pyramid at Chichén Itzá, El Castillo (The Castle), is both a mysterious and overwhelming structure. It towers 79 feet (24 m) high, and its steep stone steps on all four sides look defiantly down as if daring you to start climbing. There are 91 steps on each side, 364 altogether, and with the

platform at the top it is believed they deliberately represented the 365 days of the Mayan calendar. El Castillo is more correctly known as the Temple of Kukulkan, the feathered serpent, and on the spring and fall equinoxes crowds gather to watch Kukulkan announce his presence. It is on those two days that the corner of the temple casts a serpentine shadow down the northern staircase, a shadow that seems to slither down as the sun moves in the sky.

Uxmal

South of Mérida lies Uxmal, which is probably the most beautiful of all the Mayan ruins. Most of the remains that we see today were built when Mayan architecture was at its finest, from about A.D. 700-1000. Uxmal was flourishing long before that, however, and it is thought that at its height the city would have been home to some 25,000 people. At 115 feet (35 m), the pyramid here is much bigger than El Castillo and was begun in the sixth century A.D., built on top of four previous structures, which was the Mayan style. Its graceful rounded sides, its height, and the staggering steepness of its steps make this, known as the Magician's Pyramid, one of the most remarkable of all Mayan buildings.

Tulum

Uxmal was still a flourishing city when the Spanish arrived in the sixteenth century, as was Tulum, the most accessible and therefore the busiest of the Mayan sites. It was never conquered by the Spanish conquistadores, and although it was later

abandoned it remained a potent symbol for the Mayan people and was still used informally by them for religious purposes until late into the twentieth century. Tulum has a spectacular location on a cliff overlooking the bright turquoise waters of the Caribbean, and this alone sets it apart from other Mayan sites. Together, though, these sites provide a chance to look again and admire one of the world's great civilizations, one whose descendants now make up part of the cultural mix of Mexico.

The Court of the Thousand Columns, which symbolize warriors, flanks the Temple of the Warriors at Chitzén Itzá (1).

Wall carvings at Chitzén Itzá (1) depict a gruesome *tzompantli*, a rack of impaled human skulls.

DIRECTORY OF USEFUL ADDRESSES

Note: Most web sites have a contact form for e-mailing queries to the organization listed.

Adirondack State Park
www.visitadirondacks.com
Adirondack Regional Tourism Council
P.O. Box 2149
Plattsburgh, NY 12901
Tel: 518-846-8016

Alaska
www.travelalaska.com
Alaska Travel Industry Association
2600 Cordova Street, Ste. 201
Anchorage, AK 99503

Banff & Jasper National Parks
www.pc.gc.ca/pn-np/ab/banff/index_E.asp
Banff National Park, Box 900, Banff AB,
Canada T1L 1K2
Email: banff.vrc@pc.qc.ca
Tel: 403-762-1550

www.pc.gc.ca/pn-np/ab/jasper/visit/visit42_e.asp
Jasper National Park, Box 10, Jasper AB,
Canada T0E 1E0
Email: pnj.jnp@pc.qc.ca
Tel: 780-852-6176

Blue Ridge Parkway
www.nps.gov/blri
National Park Service
199 Hemphill Knob Road
Asheville, NC 28803
Tel: Recorded Park Information: 828-298-0398
Park Headquarters: 828-271-4779

Boston
www.bostonusa.com
Greater Boston Convention & Visitors Bureau
Two Copley Place, Suite 105
Boston, MA 02116-6501
Tel: 888-733-2678

California Deserts
www.nps.gov/deva/
Death Valley National Park
P.O. Box 579, Death Valley, California 92328
Tel: 760-786-3200

www.nps.gov/jotr
Joshua Tree National Park
74485 National Park Drive
Twentynine Palms, CA 92277
Tel: 760-367-5500

Cape Cod National Seashore
www.nps.gov/caco
Cape Cod National Seashore
99 Marconi Site Road
Wellfleet, MA 02667
Tel: 508-349-3785

Carlsbad Caverns
www.nps.gov/cave
Carlsbad Caverns National Park
3225 National Parks Highway
Carlsbad, New Mexico 88220
Tel: 505-785-2232

Charleston, South Carolina
www.charlestoncvb.com
CACVB Executive Offices
423 King Street
Charleston, SC 29403
Tel: 843-853-8000

Chicago
www.choosechicago.com
Chicago CTB
2301 S. Lake Shore Drive
Chicago, IL 60616
Tel: 312-567-8500

Churchill, Manitoba
www.travelmanitoba.com
Travel Manitoba
7th Floor, 155 Carlton St., Winnipeg
Manitoba, Canada R3C 3H8
Tel: 800-665-0040; 204-927-7800

www.polarbearalley.com/travel-to-churchill.html

Denali National Park
www.nps.gov/dena
Denali National Park & Preserve
P.O. Box 9
Denali Park, Alaska 99755
Tel: 907-683-2294

Everglades National Park
www.nps.gov/ever
40001 State Road 9336
Homestead, Florida 33034-6733
Tel: 305-242-7700

Four Corners Native American Pueblos
www.nps.gov/meve
Mesa Verde National Park
P.O. Box 8
Mesa Verde, Colorado 81330
Tel: 970-529-4465

www.nps.gov/chcu
Chaco Culture National Historical Park
P. O. Box 220
Nageezi, New Mexico 87037
Tel: 505-786-7014

www.nps.gov/cach
Canyon de Chelly National Monument
P.O. Box 588
Chinle, AZ 86503
Tel: 928-674-5500

Glacier National Park
www.nps.gov/glac
Glacier National Park
Park Headquarters
P.O. Box 128
West Glacier, MT 59936
Tel: 406-888-7800

Grand Canyon
www.nps.gov/grca
Grand Canyon National Park
P.O. Box 129
Grand Canyon, AZ 86023
Tel: 928-638-7888

Great Lakes
www.great-lakes.net
Great Lakes Commission
Eisenhower Corporate Park
2805 S. Industrial Hwy., Suite #100
Ann Arbor, MI 48104-6791

Gulf Shores, Alabama
www.gulfshores.com
Alabama Gulf Coast CVB
P.O. Drawer 457
Gulf Shores, AL 36547
Tel: 251-968-7511

Hawaii Volcanoes National Park
www.nps.gov/havo
Hawaii Volcanoes National Park
P.O. Box 52
Hawaii National Park, HI 96718-0052
Tel: 808-985-6000

Las Vegas
www.visitlasvegas.com
Las Vegas Convention and Visitors Authority
3150 Paradise Road
Las Vegas, NV 89109
Tel: 702-892-0711

Memphis, Tennessee
www.memphistravel.com
Memphis Convention & Visitors Bureau
47 Union Avenue
Memphis, TN 38103
Tel: 901-543-5300

Miami, Florida
www.miamiandbeaches.com
Greater Miami Convention & Visitors Bureau
701 Brickell Avenue, Suite 2700
Miami, FL 33131
Tel: 305-539-3000; 800-933-8448

Mississippi River
www.experiencemississippiriver.com

Monument Valley
www.navajonationparks.org/htm/monumentvalley.htm
Monument Valley Navajo Tribal Park
P.O. Box 360289
Monument Valley, Utah 84536
navajoparks@yahoo.com
Tel: 435-727-5874/5870; 435-727-5875

Mount Rushmore and Badlands
www.nps.gov/moru
Mount Rushmore National Memorial
13000 Hwy 244, Bldg 31, Suite 1
Keystone, SD 57751
Tel: 605-574-2523

www.nps.gov/badl
Badlands National Park
25216 Ben Reifel Road
P.O. Box 6
Interior, South Dakota 57750
Tel: 605-433-5361

Napa Valley
www.napavalley.org
The Napa Valley Conference & Visitors Bureau
1310 Napa Town Center
Napa, CA 94559
Tel: 707-226-7459

Na Pali Coast of Kauai
www.kauai-hawaii.com
Tel: 800-262-1400

Natchez Trace Parkway
www.nps.gov/natr
Natchez Trace Parkway
2680 Natchez Trace Parkway
Tupelo, MS 38804
Tel: 800-305-7417

New England
www.discovernewengland.org/index.html
Discover New England Head Office
P.O. Box 3809
Stowe, Vermont 05672
Tel: 802-253-2500

Newfoundland and Labrador
www.newfoundlandlabrador.com
Department of Tourism, Culture, and Recreation
P.O. Box 8700
St. John's, NL Canada A1B 4J6
Email: contactus@newfoundlandlabrador.com
Tel: 709-729-0862

New Orleans
www.neworleanscvb.com
New Orleans CVB
2020 St. Charles Avenue
New Orleans, LA 7013
Email: internet@neworleanscvb.com
Tel: 800-672-6124

New York City
http://nycvisit.com
NYC & Company
810 Seventh Avenue
New York, NY 10019
Email: visitorinfo@nycvisit.com
Tel: 212-484-1200

Niagara Falls
www.visitbuffaloniagara.com
Buffalo Niagara Convention & Visitors Bureau
617 Main Street, Suite 200
Buffalo, NY 14203
Email: info@buffalocvb.org
Tel: 800-BUFFALO

Olympic National Park
www.nps.gov/olym
Olympic National Park
600 East Park Avenue
Port Angeles, WA 98362
Tel: 360-565-3130

Pacific Coast Highway
www.pacific-coast-highway-travel.com

www.onlyinsanfrancisco.com
San Francisco Visitor Information Center
900 Market Street
San Francisco, CA 94102-2804
Email: vic1@sfcvb.org
Tel: 415-391-2000

www.discoverlosangeles.com
Los Angeles Convention and Visitors Bureau
333 South Hope Street, 18th Floor
Los Angeles, CA 90071
Tel: 213-624-7300; toll free 1- 800-228-2452

Prince Edward Island National Park
www.pc.gc.ca/pn-np/pe/pei-ipe/index_e.asp
Prince Edward Island National Park
2 Palmers Lane
Charlottetown
PE Canada, C1A 5V6
Email: pnipe.peinp@pc.qc.ca
Tel: 902-672-6350

Québec City
www.quebecregion.com/e
Québec City Tourism
399 Saint-Joseph Est, Québec
QC G1K 8E2, Canada
Tel: 418-641-6654; toll free 1-877-783-1608

Redwood National and State Parks
www.nps.gov/redw
Redwood National and State Parks
1111 Second Street
Crescent City, California 95531
Tel: 707-464-6101

Rocky Mountain National Park
www.nps.gov/romo
Rocky Mountain National Park
1000 Highway 36
Estes Park, Colorado 80517
Tel: 970-586-1206

San Miguel de Allende
www.visitmexico.com
Email: contact@visitmexico.com
Tel: 00-800-111-12266

Santa Fe
www.santafe.org
Santa Fe Convention & Visitors Bureau
P.O. Box 909
Santa Fe, NM 87504-0909
Email: scenter@santafe.org
Tel: 1-800-777-2489

Savannah, Georgia
www.savannahvisit.com
Savannah Area Convention & Visitors Bureau
101 E. Bay Street
Savannah, GA 31401
Tel: 912-644-6401; toll free 1-877-SAVANNAH

Tucson Convention and Visitors Bureau
www.visittucson.org
Tucson Visitor Center & Administrative Offices
100 S. Church Ave.
Tucson, Arizona 85701
Tel: 520-624-1817; toll free 1-800-638-8350

Utah's National Parks
Arches
www.nps.gov/arch
Arches National Park
P.O. Box 907
Moab, UT 84532
Tel: 435-719-2299

Bryce Canyon
www.nps.gov/brca
Bryce Canyon National Park
P.O. Box 640201
Bryce, UT 84764-0201
Tel: 435-834-5322

Canyonlands
www.nps.gov/cany
Canyonlands National Park
2282 SW Resource Blvd.
Moab, UT 84532
Tel: 435-719-2313

Zion
www.nps.gov/zion
Zion National Park
Springdale, UT 84767
Tel: 435-772-3256

Vancouver
www.tourismvancouver.com/visitors
Vancouver Tourist Information Center
Plaza Level, 200 Burrard St.
Vancouver
British Columbia, Canada V6C 3L6
Tel: 604-683-2000

Washington, D.C.
www.washington.org
Destination D.C.
901 7th Street NW, 4th Floor
Washington, D.C. 20001-3719
Tel: 202-789-7000

Yellowstone National Park
www.nps.gov/yell
P.O. Box 168
Yellowstone National Park, WY 82190-0168
Tel: 307-344-7381

Yosemite National Park
www.nps.gov/yose
P.O. Box 577
Yosemite National Park, CA 95389
Tel: 209-372-0200

Yucatán
http://cancun.travel
Blvd.Kukulcan km. 9 "Cancún Center 1st. Floor"
Hotel Zone, Cancún
77500, Q.Roo, Mexico
Email: cvb@cancun.travel
Tel: 52-998-8812745

INDEX

INDEX

CREDITS

Quarto would like to thank the following agencies for
supplying images for inclusion in this book:

l = left; r = right; b = bottom; t = top

4Corners www.4cornersimages.com
pages 1, 2-3, 128, 140-141, 198l

Getty www.gettyimages.com
pages 4-5, 64b, 73, 75, 127, 134b, 142, 146, 160-161, 177, 180, 194-195,
198r, 199, 200-201, 213, 214, 216b

Robert Harding www.robertharding.com
pages 12, 15, 21, 24, 33, 34-35, 38, 40-41, 45, 46-47b, 49, 56-57b, 60,
64t, 67, 88, 90-91, 96-97, 99, 112-113, 115, 124, 134, 146, 153, 164-165,
178br, 179, 182-183b, 188-189, 191,196, 202

Alamy www.alamy.com
pages 19, 23, 26-27, 28-29, 31, 50-51, 54, 59, 63br, 68-69, 71, 79, 80,
83, 84-85, 87, 93, 95, 100, 102-103, 116-117, 123, 131, 136-137, 138, 144,
147, 148, 149ml, 150, 152, 158, 162bl, 163, 164-165, 166bl, 171, 174-175,
181, 185, 187, 188, 192, 204, 205, 207, 210-211, 217

Corbis www.corbis.com
pages 42-43, 52, 72-73, 81, 132, 154, 167, 182mr

Lonely Planet Images www.lonelyplanetimages.com
pages 168-169

page 173tr Michael Lynch

We would also like to thank the following:

Shutterstock
iStock
Dreamstime
Flickr
Moira Clinch